Oil and Water

Oil and Water

Being Han in Xinjiang

TOM CLIFF

The University of Chicago Press   Chicago and London

TOM CLIFF is an anthropologist based at the Australian National University.

The University of Chicago Press, Chicago 60637
The University of Chicago Press, Ltd., London
© 2016 by The University of Chicago
All rights reserved. Published 2016.
Printed in the United States of America

25 24 23 22 21 20 19 18 17 16   1 2 3 4 5

ISBN-13: 978-0-226-35993-9 (cloth)
ISBN-13: 978-0-226-36013-3 (paper)
ISBN-13: 978-0-226-36027-0 (e-book)
DOI: 10.7208/chicago/9780226360270.001.0001

Library of Congress Cataloging-in-Publication Data
Names: Cliff, Tom, author.
Title: Oil and water : being Han in Xinjiang / Tom Cliff.
Description: Chicago ; London : The University of Chicago Press, 2016. | Includes bibliographical references and index.
Identifiers: LCCN 2016002295 | ISBN 9780226359939 (cloth : alk. paper) | ISBN 9780226360133 (pbk. : alk. paper) | ISBN 9780226360270 (e-book)
Subjects: LCSH: Chinese—China—Xinjiang Uygur Zizhiqu—Social conditions. | Xinjiang Uygur Zizhiqu (China)—Social conditions.
Classification: LCC DS793.S62 C55 2016 | DDC 305.8951/0516—dc23
LC record available at http://lccn.loc.gov/2016002295

♾ This paper meets the requirements of ANSI/NISO Z39.48–1992 (Permanence of Paper).

For my parents, as ever

And for Lina and Abraham, for ever

Contents

Acknowledgments ix

Introduction 1

1. Constructing the Civilized City 27
2. The Individual and the Era-Defining Institutions of State 50
3. Structured Mobility in a Neo-*Danwei* 73
4. Legends and Aspirations of the Oil Elite 100
5. Lives of *Guanxi* 130
6. Married to the Structure 159
7. The Partnership of Stability in Xinjiang 180

Conclusion 208

Notes 217   *Bibliography* 223   *Index* 247
Photo Essay: Urban development in Korla, 2007–10, following page   44
Photo Essay: Portraits of "Old Xinjiang People," following page   156

Acknowledgments

To understand just one life, you have to swallow the world. THE NARRATOR, SALEEM SINAI, IN SALMAN RUSHDIE'S *MIDNIGHT'S CHILDREN* (1981, 108)

Saleem Sinai's mantra may be equally true the other way around: individual lives provide windows into worlds. This book, which puts life histories at the center of the analysis, implicitly asserts that the closer that you get to that window, the more of that world you see. Better still if you have multiple windows to look through. Hence my greatest debt is to my friends and interlocutors in Korla, who allowed me to look into their worlds. Without their willingness to share their life stories, hopes, and disappointments, I could not have written this book. Some people went a lot further, mobilizing their extensive networks to connect me with important people, transport me to otherwise inaccessible places, and protect me from powerful enemies. They know who they are, and I hope that I have lived up to their trust and done their stories justice.

In the academic world, my closest colleagues at the Australian National University helped me to make sense of the mass of personal and secondary experiences that I brought back from my field trips. Andrew Kipnis has, at various times, been my lecturer, supervisor, and coinvestigator over the 12 years (and counting) that I have known him. Andy is a consummate professional who is making a lasting contribution to anthropology and to China studies, and I have learned much from him. Luigi Tomba has treated me as a close friend since before I met him. My understanding of the institutional structures of life, in China and elsewhere, owes a great deal to Luigi's nuanced and creative thought. Jonathan Unger has always been more than generous with his time, his funds, and his encyclopedic knowledge. I thank Bob Miller for his insistence on the continuing relevance of the Soviet era to global politics and ideology. The counsel of Peter Van Ness has been invaluable. I have also received support and advice from Edward Aspinall, Darrell Dorrington, Greg Fealy, Paul Hutchcroft, Tamara Jacka, Hans-Joerg Kraus, Stephen Milnes, Anthony Reid, and Sally Sargeson. The maps were produced by CartoGIS, the ANU College of Asia and the Pacific.

Many people gave up their time to read pieces of my writing and offer perceptive nudges in fruitful directions. The comments and recommendations of David S. Goodman and Joel Andreas helped me to frame the study. In very different ways, Mark Elliott and Stephanie Hemelryk Donald encouraged me to further explore visual methodologies and inspired me with their insights into the frontier and the cultural politics of contemporary China. Particularly astute readings and generous commentary by Tom Gold and Gardner Bovingdon helped me to view the strengths and weaknesses of the draft manuscript with much greater clarity. Borge Bakken, David Brophy, Sinclair Dinnen, Ayxem Eli, Anthony Garnaut, Piers Kelly, Lewis Mayo, Kevin O'Brien, Catherine Smith, Lina Tan, Beibei Tang, Justin Tighe, Aat Vervoorn, and Qian Ying have also provided feedback and assistance on multiple occasions along the way, as well as their friendship. Priya S. Nelson gently chaperoned the manuscript through the review process, and the team at the University of Chicago Press saw it successfully through production. The two anonymous reviewers clearly both spent a lot of time looking back and forth over my draft manuscript, and their detailed comments piloted me through the final revisions. Errors of navigation are all my own. For all this, I am deeply honored.

I wrote this book while based at the College of Asia and the Pacific, the Australian National University. Funding for my position and ongoing research while I finalized the manuscript was provided by an Australian Research Council Laureate Fellowship (FL 120100155), led by Tessa MorrisSuzuki, and supplemented by an Australian Research Council Discovery Project Award (DP 140101289), led by Andrew Kipnis. I am particularly grateful to Tessa for allowing me time out from my Laureate research project to complete the manuscript.

Three of the chapters in this book are based on or contain parts of work published elsewhere. Chapter 1 builds on "Peripheral Urbanism: Making History on China's Northwest Frontier," which was published in *China Perspectives* in September 2013. Chapter 3 is a slight modification of "Post-Socialist Aspirations in a Neo-*Danwei*," published in the *China*

Journal (no. 73, January 2015). The *China Journal* (no. 68, July 2012) also published an earlier version of chapter 7 as "The Partnership of Stability in Xinjiang: State-Society Interactions following the July 2009 Unrest." I am grateful to the publishers.

The artistic side of this project has been shaped in conversation with visual artists from Amsterdam (a cosmopolitan city in Europe) to Ipswich (a rural town in Queensland, Australia), and many places in between. David MacDougall's advice played an important role in the shooting and categorization of my images; all along, I have aspired to his sense of timing and beauty. I never failed to feel inspired and enlivened by my weekly meetings with Martyn Jolly at the ANU School of Art. Martyn was always enthusiastic about and supportive of my project but did not hesitate to tell me when I was on the wrong track. I must also thank my brother, Nathaniel Simon Cliff, Esq. Nathaniel's uncompromising artistic vision has constantly and quietly challenged the visual cultures of the museum, the archive, and the magazine stand, and I have tried to apply his critical insights to the hypermodern behindness of the Chinese frontier.

The other members of my close family are all, also, in this book. On long treks over the High Atlas (Morocco) and Tianshan (Xinjiang), and through the Australian desert, my youngest brother, Titus, and my father, Rod, eventually instilled in me the joy and necessity of slowing down, or pausing midway. In a book like this, centrally concerned with how people got to where they are, the destination is not more important than the journey. Both of my parents knew that, and acted on it; if they did not, I would not be a second-generation immigrant, and, who knows, may not be interested in studying my mirror in far western China. I managed to learn only some of the lessons that my mother, Mary, strove to teach me, but those lessons continue to inform my ethnographic method, my writing, and my marriage. My resolute and uniquely perceptive wife Lina has been close by since I began to write this book. Our son, Abraham, earlier than expected and critically unwell, entered this world in a maelstrom just as I was finishing it off. Lina remained by his side, day and night, as he fought against all odds to stay alive, and many weeks of bad news upon bad news gradually took a turn for the better. After four and a half months in hospital, Abraham came home for the first time. I am in awe of my wife and son. I dedicate this book to them, and to my own parents, for essentially the same reasons—devotion, generosity, and love that is as unconditional as anything can ever be.

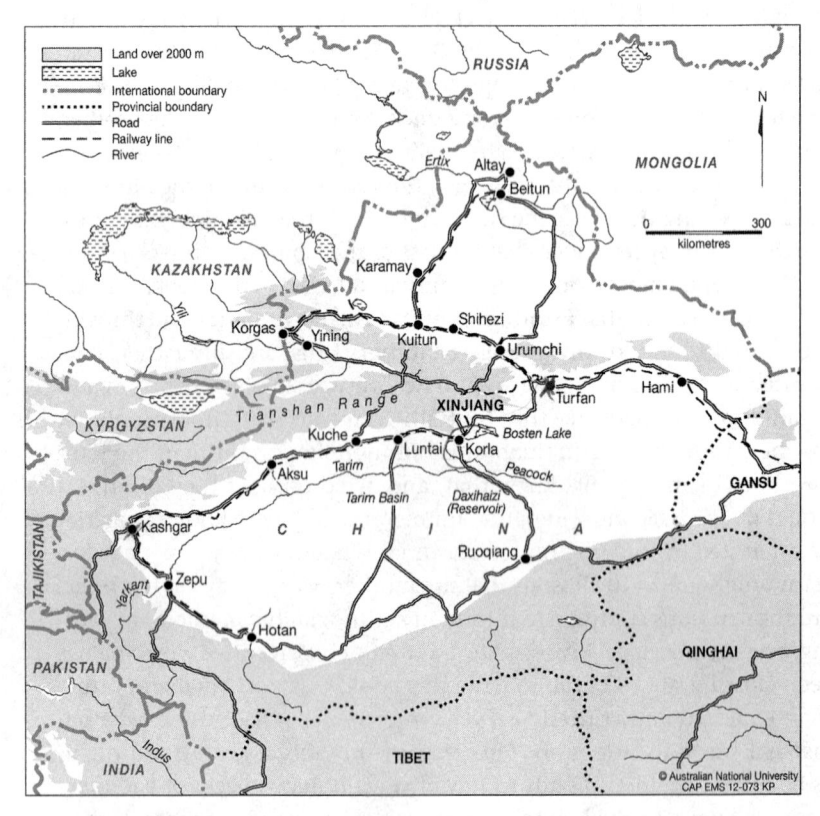

0.1   Map of Xinjiang

Introduction

The railway line from Turfan to Kashgar runs through a county town called Yanqi, a place surrounded by farms of the Xinjiang Production and Construction Corps, or *bingtuan* (兵团).[1] South and west along the line are the urban centers of Korla, Kuche, and Kashgar. North and east is everything else: Urumchi, Lanzhou, Xi'an . . . and on to central and eastern China (*neidi* 内地), the metropole that defines Xinjiang as a periphery.

In 2003 Zhang Yonglei, a 28-year-old traditional Chinese medicine doctor from Gansu province, was passing by Yanqi en route to Korla to make his fortune. He had never been to Xinjiang, knew nobody in Korla, and was a self-sponsored migrant. It was midspring, and the vegetation was still pretty sparse. He told me this story:

When I first came to Xinjiang, I came by train. When we got to Yanqi, I looked out and saw that flat, bare land, small dirt houses, and dusty roads, and I thought, "This is worse than our Gansu. What have I come *here* for?"

Yonglei swept his arm at the imaginary scene passing by and pulled a face of distaste.

I was feeling very bad. My heart felt tight. I felt that I'd made a very bad decision. Then I got to Korla Station and walked out onto the station forecourt, and I suddenly felt relieved and happy. The buses and taxis were all lined up—not jumbled around in a confused and messy way like in *neidi*. There were no touts pulling me this way and that in

INTRODUCTION

0.2 North of Korla. November 2009

an attempt to get my business, and I felt that there was less chance of being pickpocketed because here there was space for everyone and less places to hide in the crowd.

"The buildings were tall and made of modern materials," he said—unlike the dirt shacks that he had been horrified to see when he woke up on the train that morning. This distinction made him feel as if he had come to a place that was not "behind" (*luohou* 落后)—a place where he could develop himself and his career.

What Yonglei saw was urban, multistory, concrete and glass, but it was certainly not the image of advanced modernity that Korla tries to present to the world. Yonglei did not see the present simply as it was, but *how it could be*. He saw the present through the lens of an imagined future.

Some six and a half years later, I passed by the same railway station on a stroll with a retired Han couple who are friends of mine. They were up ahead, and I was meandering, photographing. The man in figure 0.3 picked a watermelon rind out of the bin and brushed some black spots off it. I was still 20 yards or so from him, and walking in his direction when he registered me and turned away to stand still. I suppose he was waiting for me to pass before he went on doing whatever he was doing. As I walked toward him, I thought, "It is summer. Watermelon is 0.8 *yuan*/kg (US$.12/kg) and low in calories. And that rind has virtually nothing on it, anyway. Is he so poor that he needs to eat something so dirty? It will not quench his hunger or his thirst. And if he is used to scavenging in trash bins in broad daylight, then why does he care if I see him doing it?"

The man's need to protect his sense of dignity amid his desperation made a lasting impression on me. Weeks later, I told this story to a class of young professionals at the Tarim Oilfield Company, where I worked as an English teacher. The professionals were all graduates of good universities in *neidi* or the spouses of men who were. Speaking English more fluently could improve their chances of being included in overseas delegations and other career-advancing activities, but equally important was the sense of sophistication that they associated with a European language. Such self-improvement was seen by many of them as the ideal accessory to the brand-name clothing and other material goods of their aspirant lifestyles.

After the class, a financial manager in her early 30s said to me, "That man who was digging in the bin—that was very moving. I didn't know that we had people so poor in our society. It is terrible that our society cannot provide for them." Having lived in the Tarim Oilfield Company compound for almost two years at that time, I knew that it was socially and spatially distinct, even cut off, from the surrounding city. I was nevertheless taken aback by her claim to be unaware of such poverty.

0.3   Korla railway station forecourt. June 2009

Migration, Empire, and Time

Since I first lived in Xinjiang for eight months during 2001–2, I have been asking myself, What is it like to be a Han person living in Xinjiang? The short stories above stake out the key reference points of my response to that question, this book. Three main themes come up: migration, empire, and time. I center this investigation on individuals' life histories, the main historical and institutional structures of their lives, and the urban space of the city that they now live in—Korla, the capital of Bayingguoleng Mongol Autonomous Prefecture[2] (Bazhou 巴州) in South Xinjiang.

Korla is a palimpsest of post-1949 Han settlement in Xinjiang. Of Korla's 500,000-strong population, 70% are Han. Most of the rest are Turkic Uyghurs. The 2008 urban plan aims to double the population and the urban area by 2020. An additional 200,000 people come to work in the city and surrounds each year, and some of them stay behind. Korla is surrounded by *bingtuan* farms and "Third Front" military industry factories (*sanxian gongcheng* 三线工程) in various stages of decay and renewal, and the layout of the city center still echoes the heyday of the *bingtuan* and intermediate generations of dominant state-owned enterprises (SOEs). Newer parts of Korla showcase contemporary PRC fashions in urban design. Today, the economic and ideational heart of Korla is Tazhi (塔指), the Tarim Oilfield Company Headquarters.[3] (Tazhi has both administrative and spatial dimensions and can refer to the Tarim Oilfield Company or to the compound it occupies). Tazhi is a powerful and privileged central government–controlled SOE (*zhongyang qiye* 中央企业) and employs very few non-Han. Outside Korla, South Xinjiang is populated predominantly by Uyghurs, and there is an underlying tension between Uyghur and Han in Xinjiang that occasionally flares up into violence. For these reasons, Korla is an excellent place to observe the Chinese Communist Party's (CCP) nation-building project—the "colonial endeavor"—in Xinjiang.

The experience of being Han in Xinjiang is part of the broader experience of migration and colonial settlement in PRC-era China. Yonglei's narrative foregrounds the lived experience of the colonial endeavor. He talks about the role of the self-developing individual in this project, especially through migration to and settlement of the periphery, and about the role of the city. The city's role is evident here in Yonglei's description of Korla as an outpost of civility that surpasses its own model, the Han metropole: Empire imposes a strange chronology on the frontier.

INTRODUCTION

The theme of *migration* is concerned with how people got to where they are—including social as well as spatial mobility. Both social and spatial mobility are shaped by the institutions of state and society, and by the interplay of such structures with agency and with chance. Comparing life histories provides insight into the social advantages and disadvantages of different cohorts (Zhou 2004, 272–75). Life histories also highlight fateful, but not fate-determining, mutual bonds between individuals and the formal institutions that they belong to. Tazhi is a good example, being one of the primary institutional means through which distinctions in wealth, health, and governance are produced and sustained in urban Korla. Meanwhile, the watermelon story reminds us of hierarchies and inequalities even among the Han of Korla, contrasting life at the bottom with the cloistered security of the elite Tarim Oilfield Company. Individuals of all socioeconomic levels confront a dilemma rooted in their own aspiration: stability is the basis of social reproduction, but uncertainty is the basis of possibility.

Most Han in Korla are migrants within a generation or two. The Han in Korla today have come to the region in a series of waves since 1949, two main ones being the state-sponsored migration to the *bingtuan* through the 1950s and the economically motivated self-sponsored migration that began in the early 1990s. The very act of migration into the "behindness" that is Xinjiang imbues the Han migrant with behindness, although at the very same time the movement often helps to raise their relative social status. Military officers and bureaucratic cadres posted to Xinjiang during the early Mao era were typically promoted one level; incoming non-*bingtuan* settlers are often granted land packages that provide an income far in excess of what they could earn in *neidi*. Han in-migration to Xinjiang has always been closely linked to questions of nation building, the nature of the frontier, and core-periphery relations (cf. Millward 1998; Becquelin 2000; Cliff 2005).

The theme of *empire* is concerned with the core-periphery relationship. Political culture in all its forms and functions is a particularly important aspect of this theme. In listening to and observing people, I consider what their stories and actions reveal about how they see themselves (as Xinjiang people) in relation to the rest of China. I give equal weight to how Xinjiang helps to produce modern China and how Xinjiang is produced by and fits into modern China. The central problematic of this theme is *normalization*. In the Foucauldian sense, normalization is a process of disciplining through the imposition of precise norms (Foucault 1977). I use normalization in this way and, more specifically, to mean the process of making Xinjiang more like *neidi*, and especially people in Xinjiang more like people in *neidi*.

The theme of *time* is concerned with the patterns of the past, present, and future. All stories are told for present purposes, so these personal accounts are revealing of how the narrators see where they are, where they have been, and where they want to go. Implicit in the words of both Yonglei and the oil company employee is a *prospective orientation* on the experienced realities of the present. Both of them in some way choose to ignore the nonideal parts of the picture. The oil company employee clings tightly to an image of Korla as a well-off society, which is something Korla's city government claims to have achieved. Yonglei fixates on a particular aesthetic that, in the state discourse and thus to him, represents progress. He sees himself as a *constructor* (*jianshezhe* 建设者) of this always-unfolding vision of material and spiritual *civilization* (*wenming* 文明). Both of these beliefs—in already-existing prosperity and in the imperative of ongoing ethnoculturally mediated transformation—are related to the governing practices of the colonial endeavor in Xinjiang.

A Colonial Endeavor

The question of whether Xinjiang and other peripheral, minority ethnicity–inhabited regions are Han Chinese colonies is contentious. Uyghur independence groups claim that Xinjiang is a colony of Communist China and that incoming Han are colonists (Clarke 2008, 274; Dāmalā 2011). Many non-Chinese scholars (Cannon 1990; Gladney 1998b; Hansen 2005; Bovingdon 2010), as well as at least one semidissident Chinese intellectual (Wang 2007a), also argue that Xinjiang is a colony or an internal colony. Barry Sautman's (2000) attempt to disprove the existence of internal colonialism in Xinjiang was internally coherent but has largely failed to be taken up by the English-language scholarly community. Chinese scholars employed in the PRC refute suggestions that Xinjiang is a colony or that China is an empire, perhaps because to do so may be seen to undermine the legitimacy of the current form of the PRC nation-state.

Soviet republics of Central Asia and their predecessor, Russian Turkistan, evoke an obvious comparison to the situation in Xinjiang. In the 19th-century "age of empire," both the Russian tsars and the Qing saw their possessions and vassals in Central Asia as confirmations of their own greatness. Comparing themselves to the Europeans, they came to the conclusion that a "real" great power must have colonies that are "behind" the metropole, and in which the metropole carries out civilizing projects (Waley-Cohen 2003, 324; Khalid 2006, 236; Sahadeo 2007, 5). In both Russia and China, revolutions overthrew long-running imperial dynasties, and the new rulers had a profound antipathy to imperialism. Moreover, the ethnic policies of the CCP drew on those developed by Stalin in the Soviet Union (Mullaney 2004b, 226). Adeeb Khalid argues that Russian imperialism in Central Asia did not continue across the 1917 "revolutionary divide," basing his argument on Partha Chatterjee's (1993) criteria for a modern colonial regime of power—"the rule of colonial difference, whereby 'natives' are exempted from the universalist claims of the ruling order." Khalid claims that the Bolsheviks' "universalist project of social revolution" precluded colonial difference (2006, 235–37). Given Sun Yat-sen's ideal of the "Republic of Five Races," and the Communists' claim that all (eventually 56) of the classified nationalities would enjoy equal rights under a unified republic, the same argument could be made for China after 1911 or after 1949. The most obvious flaw in this argument is its conflation of rhetoric with practice. However, even if we accept that the rule of colonial difference does not apply in Xinjiang, there are too many similarities of style and practice between the classic colonial form and the nature of metropolitan domination in Xinjiang today to simply dismiss a claim that Xinjiang represents a colonial situation.

Continuity need not imply stasis: renovating the colonial project is a condition of its continuity. Prasenjit Duara's concept of the "new imperialism" is useful. New imperialism combines developmentalism with exploitation and domination; it seeks to modernize "institutions and identities" in the colony. According to Duara, the first "full-blown instance" of the new imperialism was Japanese rule in northeast China, Manchukuo, in the interwar period (2006). The Japanese incursions into China in the 1930s and '40s are felt in China today as a painful example of foreign subjugation: the culmination of the nation's "century of humiliation" (Gries 2004, 43). With the experience, or the narrative of the experience, of Manchukuo so firmly imprinted on the Chinese national psyche, it should come as no surprise that key elements of Japanese imperial policy find their echo in Xinjiang, nor that a suggestion of such parallels is offensive to the PRC state and to most Chinese people.

To further complicate things for the party theoreticians and leaders in Beijing, it could be argued that, from a Marxist-Leninist standpoint, Chinese imperialism in Xinjiang only became possible with the resurgence of Chinese capitalism in the reform era. John Hobson's *Imperialism: A Study* (1902) and Lenin's *Imperialism: The Highest Stage of Capitalism* (1947 [1916]) both made strong (and strongly contested) cases for the connections between capitalism and imperialism. In their respective books on colonialism and culture, both Nicholas Dirks and Nicholas Thomas point out that capitalism and colonialism are inextricably tied together (1992, viii; 1994, 29). In other words, if the party center felt that it had a fairly solid ideological defense against accusations of imperialism during the Mao era, the circumstances that allowed this defense have now been all but lost. Ania Loomba rejects even this defense, arguing that colonialism was the vector for the export of a particular idea of progress—modernity—that was shared by both capitalist and socialist regimes (1998, 21).

The threat to metropolitan power on the periphery, moreover, does not come only from the "natives" or from the critiques of the international or academic community. Colonialism, in its classic form at least, has passed in most places of the world. Not all postcolonial transitions were peaceful; by definition none of them resulted in the metropole retaining power. Sometimes the natives pushed out the colonizers, but in the most successful postcolonial states, the settlers themselves formed a new nation. In the case of the United States, this new nation was formed against the will of the imperial center—the settlers threw off the shackles of (their own) empire. To think that these processes have escaped notice by the current regime in Beijing would be to seriously underestimate the Chinese and Marxist-Leninist regard for history. The now-immortal first line of *The Romance of the Three Kingdoms*—"The empire, long divided, must unite; long united, must divide" (*fen jiu bi he, he jiu bi fen* 分久必合, 合久必分) (Luo 2000, 3)—apparently makes no distinction as to who is doing the separating. Fitting Xinjiang into the global historical experience of colonialism helps to make sense of the central government anxieties that directly impact the daily lives of each and every person in the region. These anxieties are focused on the Han population of Xinjiang—as the solution, and as themselves a major problem. I argue in the final chapter that retaining the loyalty of the Han in Xinjiang and their commitment to pan-Chinese unity is a consideration that, in this region, is second to none for the party center.

Under the rubric "imperial formations," Stoler and McGranahan put forward a broad comparative framework for approaching the study of empire, imperialism, and colonialism amid these concepts' overlapping and contested definitions. Cutting the Gordian knot, they advise that "we attend less to what empires are than to what they did and do." The "poaching of practices" from elsewhere and the invigoration of "categories of exception and difference" (2007, 5) can be seen in Xinjiang, where feudal, colonial, and developmental modes of governance are spatially and socially differentiated, and also overlap and bleed into one another. "Imperial formations are founded" on the sort of "sliding scales of basic rights" (ibid., 10) that are formalized in institutions like the Tarim Oilfield Company (see chapter 3) and the *bingtuan* (see chapter 1). Essentially, imperial formations are outlined in such broad strokes as to include not only Xinjiang, but arguably the whole of China. Certain attributes, however, are of particular relevance to Xinjiang. These include imperial formations' dependence on "material and discursive postponements," including "the 'civilizing mission,' imperial guardianship, and manifest destiny." Uyghurs, especially, may find bitter familiarity in imperial formations' creation of "new subjects that must be relocated to be productive and exploitable, dispossessed to be modern, disciplined to be independent, converted to be human, stripped of old cultural bearings to be citizens, coerced to be free" (ibid., 8). These "new subjects" include young Uyghurs (especially women) coerced into factory labor in southeast China (Hess 2009), Uyghur farmers who have been moved off their land to make way for development and enable massive profits by Han from elsewhere (Radio Free Asia 2011; 2012), Uyghur migrant workers and schoolchildren in *neidi* institutions (Zhang Zongtang 2009), Uyghur parents and children subject to compulsory Mandarin-medium education, and all those who feel that limitations are placed on their practice of Islam or other markers of Uyghur-ness that Han or the state see as threatening or uncivilized (Amnesty International 2001; 2002; Reuters 2012a). In recognition of the many competing definitions of *colonialism* and *empire*, and that Xinjiang accords to many of the characteristics that constitute these definitions while contradicting certain others, I term the actions and aspirations of the Chinese metropole with regard to Xinjiang a "colonial endeavor." I use this term in a descriptive, not an evaluative, way.

The key to understanding this colonial endeavor is culture. Nicholas Dirks has argued that "in certain important ways, culture was what colonialism was all about" (1992, 3). The ultimate concern of the Englishman Lord Milner, a long-serving colonial administrator who described his life's work as "the integrity and consolidation of the British Empire," was a racially specific culture (Milner 1913, xi–xiii). Parts of Lord Milner's "gospel of creative imperialism" (Thomas 1994, 150) are eerily resonant of present-day Chinese nationalist discourse: "It is a mistake to think of [imperialism] as principally concerned with the extension of territory. . . . It is not a question of a couple of hundred thousand square miles more or less. It is a question of preserving the unity of a great race, of enabling it, by maintaining that unity, to develop freely on its own lines, and to continue to fulfil its distinctive mission in the world" (Milner 1913, xxxii).

INTRODUCTION

This imperative to propagate the advanced culture of the dominant people of the core area is not lost on the minority "other" in Xinjiang. The headmistress of a number of schools in the Uyghur-populated suburbs of Korla, a Uyghur herself, lamented a little peevishly, "When the Chinese get their hands on anything, it goes bad" (*bian weir* 变味儿). Switching from perfect Mandarin into English, she continued, "[To them] China is all shiny and great, and the not-shiny China is suppressed." To this woman, the dismantling of local culture in all its guises was the biggest crime of Chinese occupation in Xinjiang.

The Cultural Frontier

Colonial cultures are formed and re-formed on imperial frontiers. Spatially, the term *frontier* denotes a region, not a line (Lattimore 1962, 469–70; Waldron 1990, 42). Giersch suggests "conceiv[ing] of the frontier as 'middle ground,' the destructively creative formulation of 'something new' in lands where alien cultural and political institutions meet" (2001, 88–89). The concept of *middle ground* explicitly focuses on contact between populations of different ethnic stock (White 1991). But even a single ethnic stock is often made up of culturally or socioeconomically distinct populations, and even if they share a common identity in the present day, it is likely that their predecessors thought of themselves as altogether incomparable at some time in the past. This process is described as *merging*. An alternative or parallel process is *fragmentation*, whereby an ethnic or sociocultural group splits into different, usually competing, subgroups. The frontier provides a strong catalyst for both identity merger and fragmentation among populations that come into contact there (Rice and Rice 2005; Rodseth 2005). More broadly, the frontier can be thought of as a place of particularly dynamic, if not downright fickle, allegiances.

Frontiers are not permanent: they may change their relationship to the core region by becoming integrated into the core (thus closing the frontier), by detaching and becoming either a core polity themselves or the frontier of a different polity, or by becoming a different type of frontier. A simple model can be developed from Gaubatz's description of two types of frontier—"frontiers of control" and "frontiers of settlement." Frontiers of control are characterized by settlers staying close to a fortified urban center, perceiving the surrounding environment as too harsh or too dangerous to sustain them. The role of frontiers of control is to provide a buffer zone and keep trade routes open. Frontiers of settlement arise when "settlers from the core penetrate and increasingly occupy an area, residing not only in the cities but in the rural areas as well"

(1996, 21). Economic development of the frontier zone by the settlers (was and) is a major factor in shifting the emphasis from control to settlement. This gives us four ideal states: unoccupied by the core; frontier of control; frontier of settlement; and integrated into the core. Frontiers are thus formed, conceived of, and exist in relation to (and in distinction to) a core area or culture. Conversely, the core can be thought of as a center of cultural and political power that deems itself such and makes forceful overtures to that effect. The metropole and the periphery define themselves by the existence of the other.

Frontiers are not measurable purely in terms of space or territory, nor are they driven exclusively by political and military power. Social forces also motivate the frontier. Gaubatz reminds us that "the Chinese conception of the heartland was ethnic as well as spatial" (1996, 24). If we take this into the present, it suggests that as long as non-Han people populate a region in large numbers, it will always be seen from the metropole as a frontier of sorts. Conversely, demographic Sinification implies, but does not necessarily clinch, the closing of the frontier. Owen Lattimore concluded, "The changing significance, for changing societies, of an unchanging physical configuration which may at one time be a frontier, at another time a frontier of different significance (as when an old external frontier becomes an internal demarcation within an enlarged community), and at another time no frontier at all (as in the case of the western frontier of expansion of European man across the North American continent), leads to the axiomatic statement that *frontiers are of social, not geographic origin*." (1962, 471, emphasis added). Discussing the frontiers of European colonialism, Lattimore later continues, "the new frontiers were shaped less by geographical and material conditions than by the cultural momentum and impact of those who created them" (ibid., 489). Comprehensive cultural displacement and normalization emerge here as necessary conditions of peripheral integration by the core, and thus the closing of the frontier.

Historians have pointed out that in the dynastic era (up to the early 20th century), China's northwest frontier regions displayed a cyclic quality, expanding and contracting with the power and will of the core regime (Gaubatz 1996, 20; Lary 2007, 9). Unlike Lattimore's description of the American West, they have not had a linear spatial expansion that ends with peripheral integration by the core. The teleological discourses of development, civilization, and integration often ring loud, but rarely ring true, in the Chinese context. That is not to say that such discourses are not important. On the contrary, even as they declare their missions of closure, these discourses help to shape and perpetuate the frontier.

Since, with the constant turmoil of social merging and fragmentation, the culture of the periphery is likely to be always distinct from the core and (thus, and also) characterized as behind by the core, integration becomes a matter of degree. One could argue that, as an ideal model, integration may be approached but never reached.

Inseparable from the discourse of peripheral behindness is the notion of the frontier as a site of innovation. Numerous scholars have recognized what one might (only half-jokingly) call "the perennially perceived potential of the periphery." Parker and Rodseth present that "throughout history, . . . societies have been formed and transformed in relation to their frontiers" (2005, 3). For James Millward, the Qing frontier was at times "a laboratory of sorts" for policies and institutions that were subsequently established in the core (1998, 110). The idea of the northwest as the "only way to solve China's current social and political problems" continued into the Republican era (Ma Hetian [1924, 1] in Tighe 2009, 69–70). Similarly, Northrop (2004, 7) asserts, Soviet Russians envisaged Soviet-era Turkistan as a "kind of civilizational laboratory, a place for thousands of Russian men and women to work out who they were" (Sahadeo 2007, 4). Such experimentation, however, was not always conscious, and rarely was the center able to control it entirely. Alexander Woodside highlights the problems of the Chinese borderlands' capriciousness, writing, "The central realm and the borderlands realm were locked into a psychological symbiosis. In this symbiosis, the borderlands might compel institutional change at the center . . . or raise subversive questions about the political center's own inconsistent bureaucratic culture" (2007, 15). Woodside sketches a picture of the center as flawed and made vulnerable by its own ambitions to "concentrate different types of political capital: military, fiscal, cultural-informational, and moral-symbolic" (ibid., 15)—a vulnerability exaggerated by the impulsive inclusion of the (shifting) borderlands in this schema. It is of course no coincidence that Woodside's language of centers and borderlands could easily be transposed with that of metropoles and colonies.

Oil and Water

Water and oil are the liquid foundations of empires past and empires present. Karl Wittfogel famously coined the term *hydraulic empires* in reference to the feudal formations in which the center commanded the coercive power to mobilize the population, through corvée or slave labor, to build extensive networks of transportation canals and irrigation channels (1957; March 1974, 68–101). Control over water, in a rather different sense, was also the basis of expansionist European colonial empires from the Spanish and Portuguese to the British. These empires relied on their naval prowess—exporting their early modern technologies of power (bureaucracy, culture, and gunpowder-based armaments) into a spatial context where these technologies conferred an insuperable advantage over the "natives." In Xinjiang, the *bingtuan* established the irrigated basis on which extensive Han settlement beyond the oases could be sustained—thus transforming, throughout most of the region, the frontier of control into a frontier of settlement.

Water remains important, but oil now flows through the channels of the imperial landscape. Many wars and invasive maneuvers of the recent past have been motivated by the desire for oil. Oil also fuels and lubricates the global economy and supports and maintains the global status quo. Oil pipelines trace the linkages between political blocs, simultaneously blurring and affirming their boundaries and loyalties. Xinjiang is both an oil- and gas-producing base, and an essential transit point for hydrocarbons extracted in Central Asia and consumed in China's eastern metropolises. Despite being a domestic company, China National Petroleum Corporation (CNPC) is increasingly involved in offshore investment and oil field development, as well as being the majority player within the PRC. CNPC is the Tarim Oilfield Company's parent. The trope of "oil and water" thus references the liquids that motivate and enable Han activities in Xinjiang, the oil company and the *bingtuan* (as the formal institutions most closely associated with these respective liquids), and more generally, the resources that have played and are playing the key roles in the expansion and maintenance of imperial formations. Last but certainly not least, "oil and water" metaphorically expresses the diverse experiences of Han people in Xinjiang.

Diversity of Han Experience

It is important to study the Han in Xinjiang because they are a significant social force in the region and because their origins, self-identities, and relations to the state are many and varied. They cannot justifiably be treated as a homogenous bloc. Moreover, the passing of time since the initial waves of migration, the high proportion of Han now in Xinjiang, urbanization, and fast but uneven economic development make distinctions within the Han community of increasing relevance to their own conduct of everyday life.[4] Official figures state that 87% of the Han population of Xinjiang has arrived since the founding of the PRC and that the proportion of Han in Xinjiang (about 40%) has been only a few percentage points behind that of the Uyghurs (about 45%) since the late 1970s (XJTJNJ 2010, sections 3–1, 3–8). Han and Uyghur population numbers come out almost equal when one takes into account that official figures do not include the military or security forces stationed in Xinjiang or people whose household registration (*hukou* 户口) is elsewhere.⁵

Almost every Han person in Xinjiang is from somewhere else originally, and the vast majority identify with having a place of origin somewhere in *neidi*. Many Han who were born in Xinjiang, however, have an identity which incorporates the migration of their forebears but asserts their own distinctiveness: they may claim to be *from neidi* but to be *of* Xinjiang. For example, it is not uncommon for one individual to claim "I am from Sichuan" or (putting a little more distance between themselves and *neidi*) "my old home (*laojia* 老家) is Sichuan" and, on the same or a different occasion, claim "I am a Xinjiang person" or, yet more definitively, "I am an old Xinjiang person." While "old Xinjiang people" (*lao Xinjiang ren* 老新疆人) are Han who arrived in Xinjiang before the 1970s, or whose parents did, even relatively recent migrants may claim to be *Xinjiang ren* because such a claim is based on how one feels or wants to be seen by others. For their part, Uyghurs may adopt the term *Xinjiang ren* to refer exclusively to their co-ethnics.

Just as Xinjiang helps to constitute the identity of many Han who live there, the Han settlers make an equal contribution to the picture of Xinjiang today. Xinjiang is not simply a place where Uyghurs and other ethnic minorities live, and Han are not merely transient "sojourners, making money so that they can eventually go back to their own homes" (Lary 2007, 8). Rather, many Han in Xinjiang do "regard their settlement as permanent" and consider Xinjiang their own home. By the beginning of the reform era, and certainly by the turn of the 21st century, "the peoples of the [Chinese] borderlands" could no longer exclusively refer to non-Han (ibid., 8, 10). Furthermore, although ethnicity is clearly an important influence on identity (including cultural and political orientation) and life chances in Xinjiang (Rudelson 1997; Gilley 2001; Castets 2003; Bovingdon 2010; Zang 2011), it should not be assumed that ethnicity is the only marker of social distinction in the region. Nor can it be assumed that Han settlers in Xinjiang are of the same mind as the Han-led authorities in Beijing and Urumchi.

The Uyghur presence is an essential aspect of this ethnography of the Han in Xinjiang. This is not because the Han in Korla have a lot to do with Uyghurs—on the contrary, Uyghurs barely figure in the daily interactions of most Han in Korla, and Han tend to be far more concerned

0.4 Looking to the future: Han on the outskirts of the city. July 2009

0.5 Uyghur Muslims offering the afternoon prayer (Asr) (two dark shapes bottom right of frame). The low houses behind them are the same ones as in figure 0.4. May 2009

INTRODUCTION

0.6 The same two Uyghurs offering prayer, on the same occasion as in figure 0.5. The two most prominent buildings of the city skyline just visible through the haze behind them are the head office building of the Tarim Oilfield Company (left) and the most high-class hotel in Korla (right).

with intra-ethnic politics than they are with inter-ethnic politics. Uyghur absence is palpable throughout the ethnographies in this book. Poorer Han, like the family in figure 0.4, are more likely to live physically close to Uyghur people than are the residents of apartment buildings because of the segregated nature of the city space. However, even Han and Uyghur who share social space tend not to interact socially. Uyghur cultural influences on Han people in Xinjiang are increasingly weak and now exist primarily as reified claims for the distinctiveness of Xinjiang Han vis-à-vis *neidi* Han. Uyghurs provide a background of difference and potential instability. In doing so, they mark out Xinjiang as exceptional and uncertain and help to justify special policies toward the region and the people, including Han people, who live there.

The Anthropology of Experience

My aim in this book is neither simply to paint in broad strokes the politico-economic situation in Xinjiang nor to dissect Han society and social groups in any definitive way. Rather, I want to explore what it means and how it feels to live as a Han on China's frontier. I am mindful that the object itself is dynamic: like any ongoing experience, the experience of being Han in Xinjiang is continually formed and renegotiated at micro-, meso-, and macro-political levels.

"The anthropology of experience" was initiated, according to Victor Turner, by Wilhelm Dilthey's distinction "between mere 'experience' and 'an experience.'" "An experience" forms the basis of a narrative—it "does not have an arbitrary beginning and ending." Rather, the beginning and ending are chosen by the teller (the person who had the experience) to be meaningful in the particular context in which she tells it. The resulting mini-story is what Dilthey called a "structure of experience" (1986, 35). A person's collected "structures of experience" form her net experience, or her life history. In retelling someone else's life history, the mini-stories are what I need to get right. To quote the biographer Plutarch, "In the most outstanding deeds there is not always a revelation of virtue or vice, but often a little thing, a phrase or some joke reflects character more than battles in which tens of thousands die, and the greatest marshalling of forces, and sieges of cities" (Haase and Temporini 1992, 3, 832).

Plutarch was calling attention to nuance, the value of studying small things to understand larger things. He was making a distinction between biography and history, but classic 20th-century sociology came to regard these two, along with social structure, as fundamentally interrelated. C. Wright Mills writes, "We have come to know that every individual lives, from one generation to the next, in some society; that he lives out a biography, and that he lives it out within some historical sequence. By the fact of his living he contributes, however minutely, to the shaping of this society and to the course of its history, even as he is made by society and by its historical push and shove" (1959 [1974], 6).

Mills positions history, biography, and social structure as the three "co-ordinate points of the proper study of [men and women]" (ibid., 143). He goes on to list some questions that can be asked in investigating these areas in relation to one another:

1. What is the structure of this particular society as a whole? What are its essential components, and how are they related to one another? . . .
2. Where does this society stand in human history? . . . How does any particular feature we are examining affect, and how is it affected by, the historical period in which it moves? . . .
3. What varieties of men and women now prevail in this society and in this period? And what varieties are coming to prevail? In what ways are they selected and formed, liberated and repressed, made sensitive and blunted? (ibid., 6–7)

INTRODUCTION

Mills's prescription made immediate sense to me. Everyone who ever told me anything about themselves related their story to the social structures and historical discourses of their time and place. Mills's logic also fit in well with the anthropology of experience. While individuals have unique experiences of life, the building blocks of any given narrative can usually be found in other unique narratives. It is as if the blocks themselves are part of a common pool of dynamic and contextual mini-stories, or structures of experience. Almost by definition, a structure of experience is something shared. Other tellings of this shared experience will, whether by default or by design, situate themselves in relation to this dominant narrative—it becomes either a truth to adopt or co-opt, or a story to reject.

History is not so simple that it can be described by a single narrative: contrasting and complementary narratives tell a more nuanced story. "Narrative representations . . . are the very stuff of politics in Xinjiang," says Gardner Bovingdon (2010, 7–8). For Fernand Braudel, "history is the sum of all possible histories—a set of multiple skills and points of view, those of yesterday, today, and tomorrow" ([1958] 2009, 182). Although I cannot claim to cover the entire range of possible histories that circulate in Korla, I follow C. Wright Mills in applying the recognition that individuals' experiences of life can be simultaneously unique and speak of the broader historical-spatial contexts in which they and their contemporaries are embedded.

Reading Images with Experience

My approach to incorporating image and text as communicative equals in this book is to leave something in the image that the word does not say, and that is essential to the argument. I try to give space to the image and, to at least some extent, to depend on the image. To the very same extent, I am therefore depending on the reader of the book. I do not include these images simply as evidence for something which has already been stated in the text. I present the use of images in argument as an alternative to "the academic trap of starting off with what heuristically comes last: words and concepts" (Runia 2006, 307). While academic argument tends to start with a conceptual statement and proceed through a reasoned and selective justification, the argument of visual images proceeds by layering up ideas and imagery that are *not entirely controlled* and that move toward the conceptual. In particular, visual images demand the subconscious intellectual participation of the reader.

Life histories are comparable to photographs in the way that they make argument and provide insight. First, photographic snapshots are to an event, physical space or person as biographical excerpts are to a life. They are both selected representations of a much bigger whole, and are thus both snapshots. Despite their specificity, snapshots have the potential to encapsulate important aspects of that whole and are able to make a confident statement about it. Second, both operate in close conjunction with memory. Third, it would be incoherent to take up on all the points of departure that a given life history or photograph has to offer. I have to choose the tangents that make the point to which I wish to give the most relevance, and choose to pass over, or make only brief reference to, certain other themes that come up in the narrative. These tangential connections (between life histories, between images, and between life histories and images) confirm their great utility for the study of broader sociohistorical processes. Each of these multiple connections is a commonality that different people share. Moreover, it is not only the lives and experiences of the subjects of the study that these tangents intersect with. Part of the value of these *not entirely controlled* modes of re-expression is that many different possible points of departure provide ample scope for the recognition (conscious or otherwise) that our own lives also intersect with those of the people on the page.

The aspects of a given image that readers recognize may vary depending on their own past experiences. Past experiences, especially from early in life, are often stored as images in the eidetic (visual) memory (Rose 2003 [1992], 120, 122), so it is visual stimuli that causes these memories to be recalled. Readers' potentially divergent responses to the same stimuli mirror the diverse and divergent responses that people in Korla make to their surroundings. It is less the case that images are truthful *despite* this diversity and these possible contradictions, than it is that images are truthful *because* of this diversity and these possible contradictions.

Living among the Colonists

Viewing everyday life in all its complexity requires an extended period of fieldwork—to take photographs, build up trust, and steep in the subtly shifting mood of the place and the people. However, even before the violent turning point of July 2009, it was difficult or impossible for foreigners to obtain official permission to conduct social scientific research in Xinjiang. I reasoned that the most accessible way to ensure a long-term stay in the region was to get a job as an English teacher. Fortuitously, a job opened up at the Tarim Oilfield Company's Bazhou Petroleum Number One Middle School. The very name of the school, and the

INTRODUCTION

0.7 An old area of the inner city, looking toward the riverfront. Korla. April 2008

brief position description, hinted at the existence of a powerful institution based in an exclusive urban enclave; my imagination was piqued. The few pictures I saw before I got to Korla—of 10-yard-tall fake flowers, apartment buildings next to desert, and school parades in a 100% concrete environment—gave me an image of Korla as an out-of-place fairyland. On arrival, I was not disappointed (figures 0.7 and 0.8). I remain fascinated by the saccharin-and-dust aesthetic of the ever-changing urban space and its haunting postindustrial, postsocialist surrounds.

While most of the non–oil company people that I met were fairly immediately open and forthcoming with stories of their experiences, I had been known around the oil company compound for over two years before oil company employees began to offer their assistance with my research. This reluctance demonstrates the secretive paranoia that is created and cultivated within the company. In general, I avoided directly requesting interviews, finding it more productive to chat informally when people were less guarded, and to build up to a semistructured interview that filled in the gaps. Much of the information in this book could not have been obtained without first creating trust between myself and my interlocutors over the long term. I eschewed gift exchanges and emphasized nonmonetary exchanges such as language, cultural knowledge, and recreation such as hiking. I refused to give private language lessons for money, despite frequent and often desperate pleas, but I was always available for free informal consultation. When I did hold a small group private language course in the summer of 2009, I emphasized that gifts were not appropriate. My message was that I was interested in all people's experiences, ideas, and knowledge and that a price could not be put on those things. In other words, I built up affect with my interlocutors that transcended, or at least proposed to transcend, a purely instrumental exchange of favors.

The tight constraints that the oil company tries to keep on its foreign employees paradoxically turned out to be liberating, and invaluable to the conduct of my research. My Canadian colleague and I lived in separate apartments in a 12-unit stairwell that was occupied only by us, the headmaster of the school, and our minder. The minder recorded the identity card numbers of everyone who visited us, and made a note each and every time we left home and when we returned—even if it was only for two minutes. At first I resented this monitoring but soon came to realize that it afforded us a degree of protection from less explicit forms of surveillance and arbitrary restrictions, and was thus a kind of limited freedom: the oil company was deemed to be responsible for us, so the local authorities left us alone. Basically, I had freedom of movement within the city and, since everything that I intended to research (with the exception of the *bingtuan*) was within the Han areas of the city, my

0.8 Brickworks outside Tashidian, a dying industrial satellite township 15 kilometers north of Korla. November 2009

research was effectively unrestricted. It probably would have been a different story if I spoke Uyghur instead of Mandarin, had a higher proportion of Uyghur friends, and frequented the Uyghur area of town. As it was, rather than trying to escape surveillance and thus raise suspicions or offend people's trust in me, I made sure that I stayed clearly on the radar at all times. Furthermore, I was fairly (albeit selectively) open about my motives for being in Xinjiang and the topic of my research.

The reason for my tendency to avoid the Uyghur areas of Korla, especially at times of heightened ethnic tension, is that it was only by making it clear that I was not interested in "the ethnic question" (*minzu wenti* 民族问题) per se that I could gain the trust of my Han interlocutors and minders (not to mention avoid trouble with the authorities). My long-term performed-avoidance of this sensitive question became even more important, and paid invaluable dividends, in the ethnically polarized atmosphere that pervaded Xinjiang following the violence of early July 2009 in Urumchi.

I began my fieldwork in July 2007 and stayed in Korla until late August 2008, then returned for another full year from February 2009 until February 2010. My first period of fieldwork in Korla encompassed the 14 months of turmoil and increasing hype in China that culminated in the Beijing Olympics. Significant events included the 17th Party Congress, the intense late-winter blizzards across eastern China in early 2008 that stranded millions of workers traveling home for the Spring Festival, the March 2008 riots in Tibet and the subsequent crackdown, the May 2008 Sichuan earthquake, and a few sporadic events of antistate violence in Xinjiang—to say nothing of the pervasive Olympic-induced atmosphere of tension, anticipation, and apprehension. Even as a foreigner, I felt like China was under some sort of siege.

But if 2007–8 was a stimulating and tumultuous time in China, 2009 was more so. On July 5, 2009, Urumchi streets were witness to some of the worst inter-ethnic communal violence to hit Xinjiang since 1949. This became known in Chinese as the "7/5 incident" (*qi-wu shijian* 七.五事件) or just "7/5." Angry and frustrated Uyghurs rioted, burned buildings and vehicles, and randomly beat any Han person unlucky enough to be in the path of the mob. Police CCTV camera footage shows that some of the violence at this stage was shockingly casual. The footage was also revealing for what it didn't show: security forces were nowhere to be seen, although their awareness of what was going on is confirmed by the human-controlled actions of the video camera shooting the footage. Thousands of Han retaliated two days later, destroying Uyghur property and beating (again, often to death) any Uyghur witless enough to be present on the deliberately lawless streets—the Han security forces were bunkered down in pockets or, as word on the street has it, had thrown off their uniforms and were participating in the retaliation. Protecting Uyghurs and their property was far down the list of conflicting priorities, if it was a priority at all.

Battle lines in society were drawn clearly along ethnic lines. Everybody in Xinjiang knew that there existed a clear choice: either you side with the Uyghur or you side with the Han. And everybody was equally clear that siding with the Uyghur was not in their own best interests. Hui (Chinese Muslim) people, a traditional barometer of conflict between Turkic Muslims and Han Chinese because of their ethnic proximity to the Han and their Islamic faith (cf. Forbes 1986), shifted perceptibly in the direction of being "Chinese" and away from being "Muslim." As Han retaliation began on July 7, a Hui grandmother rang her son in Korla and spoke directly: "The Han have risen up; throw away your white cap. We are Han now."

A massive crackdown from the embarrassed and embattled Xinjiang authorities was imminent, violence past and violence-to-be hung heavily in the thick summer air, and fear and loathing was visible on the eerily quiet streets of Xinjiang's cities. The only thing in Xinjiang that was not at least semiparalyzed was rumor, which spread like wildfire. July 2009 to February 2010, in particular, was a crucible of politicized storytelling, fired by heightened emotions and unconstrained by the mannered niceties of peacetime. A certain kind of talk became briefly allowable as the assumptions of settler loyalty to Xinjiang and the precepts of Han occupation of the region lost their lock-hold over public discourse. The 7/5 riots precipitated great changes in economic relations between the core and the periphery. Chapter 7 argues that a significant politico-cultural shift also occurred, at least temporarily, in that relationship. The period between July 5, 2009, and April 2010, which was the culmination of my fieldwork and the temporal position from which all of the longer autobiographies herein are narrated, can be seen as a decisive moment in Xinjiang's recent history.

A Map of This Book

The main chapters of this book are arranged according to the vernacular categories of Han in Korla. Vernacular categories are terms of identity that circulate in everyday conversation. They are formed in this case with reference to the Korla region's three most influential civilian administrative institutions—the oil company, the *bingtuan*, and the local government. The resulting social groups are oil company employees, *bingtuan* or ex-*bingtuan* people, and people administered by local government (*difang ren* 地方人). The rest of the urban Han population are sojourning migrant workers or recent settlers (*wailai renkou* 外来人口). People from any one of the three former social-institutional groups may (or may not) also be descendants of the colonizing firstcomers of the Korla region—Korla "locals," or *bendiren* (本地人). The majority of the people whom I quote at length are either oil people or *difang* people, and about two-thirds of them grew up on the *bingtuan*. All but a couple were born between 1959 and 1971, and most are *bendiren*. Since I am primarily interested in the long-term experience of life in Xinjiang, recent migrants' voices feature only in chapter 1, as an essential part of the urban context.

The first chapter places the contemporary manifestation of the long-running statist project to "civilize" the periphery and its populations in a historical perspective. This image-rich chapter documents Korla's ongoing urban and social transformation. Similar processes are being repeated in small and midsized cities across China. Thus, what we see in Korla reflects a particular Chinese bureaucratic sense of what urbanization and modernity ought to entail, and also what they ought not entail. These latter are the objects of the civilizing project—and they include Han people, practices, and places. The claim to be one of those doing the civilizing, a constructor, is most important in this environment because it implies entitlement.

Chapters 2–4 look at Tazhi from the inside, through the lives of oil company employees. The life journey of an oil company cadre, depicting his social rise from a peri-urban *bingtuan* regiment to his present elite condition, forms the backbone of chapter 2. With the advantage of hindsight and a confidence conferred by status, he reflects on the rise and decline of institutions and populations. His story makes one of the many human connections between the *bingtuan* and the oil company—the defining institutions of their respective eras. By defining eras, these institutions also define people. There is not a single person living in Korla whose life has not been touched by at least one of these two institutions.

Chapter 3 explores status and social mobility within the oil company. As the spatial and ideational core of "civilization" in Korla, Tazhi models a society in which harmony and hierarchy are mutually productive. The formal internal structure of the Tarim Oilfield Company clearly delineates the rights, responsibilities, and opportunities that are associated with each position in the hierarchy. Employees "knowing their place," and knowing that wherever they are in that hierarchy they are above the vast majority of society, helps to harmonize relations within the company. For people immersed in China's economy of uncertainty and instability, the stagnant safety of the socialist-era work unit, or *danwei* (单位), is itself highly attractive. Stability becomes a status symbol. This chapter begins an extended consideration (chapters 3–6) of how people balance dull but necessary certainty against the risks inherent in pursuing greater possibilities.

Chapter 4 examines how the political economy of national memory affects the legends propagated and aspirations pursued by the Tarim Oilfield Company and the way that people within the institution deploy these legends in the pursuit of their own aspirations. Daqing oil field, in northeast China, is a significant element of Tazhi's institutional genealogy. Daqing became a defining icon of Chinese self-strengthening nationalism during the Cultural Revolution, and spawned an elite political lineage that only showed signs of fading with the CCP leadership transition in late 2012. The Tarim Oilfield Company has now assumed what I term the "legend of potential," once attributed to Daqing. Legends of potential are typically frontier, having a prospective orientation and holding a promise of salvation. Legends of potential may also be attributed or denied to people. The biographies of the now-elite permanent employees show that not all of them have access to this legend, and even a small generational difference can result in vastly different life chances. Socio-structural positions formed on the battlefields, wheat fields, and oil fields of northern China since the middle of last century echo in the classrooms and boardrooms of the early 21st century. But structures are not straitjackets: the oil workers' biographies also highlight their own agency, and the role of chance.

Chapters 5 and 6 focus on the experience of non–oil company Korla locals (*bendiren*), all of whom grew up on the *bingtuan*. Chapter 5 shows the specifics of the many different ways that informal "connections" (*guanxi* 关系) operate in Korla, arguing that affective or instrumental ties to agents of the state are perceived and experienced as a "necessity," not merely as a mode of being corrupt. I contend that such *guanxi* networks play a role in normalization, further infusing the periphery with the informal social structures of the core. Moreover, *guanxi* networks help to give the local Han community a cohesiveness which increases their collective political relevance. The social, economic, political, and cultural embeddedness, and thus influence, of these networks makes *bendiren* an interest group that the central state must take account for and maintain the loyalty of.

Chapter 6 looks first at how young people's marriage prospects and choices are influenced by their socioeconomic status. Nonelite people blame corruption, the exclusivity of Xinjiang's state enterprise–dominated industrial structure, and ultimately China's one-party system, for their lack of social mobility. Later in the chapter, two cadres discuss the very same problems from their elite perspectives. Their strident critiques from within the system, and the limitations that they themselves place on reform, demonstrates the key role that social structural position plays in both creating and constraining agency. A common reaction to such structural constraints is to accept a nonideal solution while attempting to maintain the possibility of moving closer to the ideal at some later stage. This strategy may be termed "pragmatic hoping."

Chapter 7 is a case study on the July 2009 inter-ethnic violence in Xinjiang and its aftermath. This chapter draws together two of the main arguments that run through this book. The first is the centrality of the Han population of Xinjiang, and their mutually dependent relationship with Beijing, to the political, socioeconomic, and cultural dynamics of Xinjiang in the 21st century. The second is the role of commercial enterprises in shaping and governing the periphery, essentially on behalf of the core region. The *bingtuan*, and central SOEs like the Tarim Oilfield Company, are the most prominent incarnations of this long-running imperial tradition.

The conclusion reflects on the historical leftovers that exist in the social time of the frontier, and their coexistence with a perennial sense of anticipation, as both individuals and institutions orient their gaze toward the future. Such asynchronicity is an integral part of the condition of modern China. The book ends with a challenge to the almost universally held assumption that integration of the periphery is the deep motive of all the core's actions and policies in western China. I argue that persistent "imperial thinking" in the core not only makes such integration impossible, it also makes it undesirable.

ONE

Constructing the Civilized City

"pioneer"

I am a constructor (*jianshezhe* 建设者), and so is my husband. A constructor is somebody who has their own goal, and their goal is very clear, and they relentlessly pursue this goal through their work. . . . A constructor is perfectly happy to contribute all their energies and wisdom to achieving this goal. . . . There are many types of constructors . . . but every constructor's goal is identical. For example, my parents are *bingtuan* people, and my husband's parents are cadres, but we are all constructors. What sort of constructors? Constructors of Korla! Although the work that we do is different, our goal is identical: we all aim to make Korla even better, even more beautiful, even more prosperous and strong. That is a constructor.

Idle people, or people who come to Korla only to play around and make a bit of money, are not constructors. Let's say somebody from *neidi* hears that Korla is good fun, so they come here to get a bit of work, and to play in the karaoke bars in their time off. Then they go back home after a year or two, or even less. Did they come to Korla? Yes, they came to Korla. Did they expend effort for Korla? Yes, they expended effort. [However], we don't call these people constructors—they don't have the consciousness (*juewu* 觉悟) of a constructor.   YANYAN, A KORLA *BENDIREN*, 2009

The title *constructor* implies entitlement and incites emulation, and is at once broadly attributed, widely claimed, and hotly contested in contemporary Xinjiang. This chapter deals with constructor discourse and the social and physical spaces that it creates—and is created by.

Implicit in much of the state and public discourse on construction is an assumption that the physical labor that a constructor does is part of a deeper and further-reaching project of sociocultural transformation. The stated endpoint of this transformation is a "harmonious" and "modern society"—arrived at through eradication, rather than acceptance, of difference, and molding to a particular statist ideal. The aims of construction in 21st century Xinjiang take the cultural and political aesthetics of the Chinese metropole as their guide. The object of construction here is not just Xinjiang-the-place but also the "undeveloped" peoples and cultures of the borderland: there are intimate connections between social and spatial engineering. Constructors are both inter-ethnic and intra-ethnic civilizers (Harrell 1995).

Constructor discourse is a useful optic through which to view social divisions because individuals and groups define and deploy the term *constructor* to serve their own interests and the interests of people who are "like them," or allied with them. Many recent Han in-migrants deploy an ahistorical *discourse of inclusion*—"we [Han] are all constructors"—that is premised on Xinjiang's current and continual need of construction. On the other hand, the settlers of the 1950s and '60s and their descendants speak a *discourse of distinction*, explicitly basing their demands for preferential treatment on the contribution that they or their forebears have made in the past. Old Xinjiang people claim and leverage firstcomer status in an attempt to marginalize recent arrivals. This notion—of inherent and justified firstcomer privilege—is "a quintessentially frontier idea" (Kopytoff 1987, 53). The narrator of the epigraph to this chapter, Yanyan, seeks to further narrow the category of constructor by insisting that only those with a certain "consciousness" are deserving of the title, regardless of time of migration. Yanyan is contracted by the local government to deliver compulsory mass lectures on civilization and etiquette to the staff of large government work units, and private companies in the service industry. She thus not only reflects the view of many Han in Korla that the act of construction must be a conscious one, but also shapes it. Without consciousness, the argument goes, they cannot be constructors, and only constructors are entitled to the fullness of state patronage.

Bingtuan *Construction*

The ever-changing picture of construction in [Xinjiang] is marked with our writing. This is our greatest happiness.
SHANGHAI "SENT-DOWN YOUTH" LEADER (SCMP, #3697, MAY 9, 1966, 27)

The *bingtuan* claims—for itself and its population—archetypal constructor status. It is a well-supported claim. After 1949, the first group to be spoken about as constructors of Xinjiang were the soldier-farmers of the

Xinjiang Wilderness Reclamation Army, the immediate precursor to the *bingtuan* (see Tian 1953). They were directed in 1950 to "defend the border and open the wasteland" by establishing agricultural colonies in strategic locations in Xinjiang. The victorious Communists saw Xinjiang as a tabula rasa, just as the Qing did before them (Millward 1998, 110). The fact that, at the establishment of New China, Xinjiang was already a diverse and dusty palimpsest of cultures, conflicts, and polities—both imagined and extant—presented no obstacle to this time-honored conceit. It was, after all, the conqueror's prerogative: each new regime in history has depended on the discursive construction of future potential for its own salvation. Since the *bingtuan* was formally established in October 1954, its evolution has framed the social, political, and economic milieu of Xinjiang; any understanding of contemporary Xinjiang must take the *bingtuan* into account.

The *bingtuan* was the main force behind Han in-migration to and cultural transformation in Xinjiang until at least the end of the Mao era. For example, an estimated 50,000 "sent-down youth" from Shanghai were in Xinjiang by 1965 (White 1979, 505–6), and the number reached 450,000 by 1972, of which at least 160,000 served on "army farms" (Bernstein 1977, 69, 191) that were almost all part of the *bingtuan* system. The *bingtuan* today is almost entirely civilian, and is both a SOE group and a parallel "quasigovernment" (*zhun zhengfu* 准政府) in Xinjiang (Zhou and Chen 2012, 38). It has a population of 2.5 million, 12% of Xinjiang's population, but it occupies 30% of the arable land of the region. Although the physical spaces that the *bingtuan* governs are nested within Xinjiang, it has a separate budget, its own police force, and its own court system—a sort of bounded sovereignty.

Internally, the *bingtuan* is arguably the least reformed physical and bureaucratic entity of comparable scope in China today. The resilience of the organization is related to the fact that it is still seen by the central government as playing an important role in maintaining social and political stability in Xinjiang. In part, this is because the *bingtuan*'s 94% Han population occupies key peri-urban, rural, and border regions. Moreover, the legal parameters governing this settler population remain different to those that govern non-*bingtuan* populations throughout the rest of rural China, including Xinjiang. These differential modes of governance result in a significant socioeconomic and politico-legal divide between the *bingtuan* population (especially the newcomers) and the non-*bingtuan* population (Cliff 2009).

The *bingtuan* becomes even more important when studying the personal histories of the Han community in Xinjiang because the *bingtuan* always has been almost exclusively Han populated and a large proportion of old Xinjiang people were themselves raised on *bingtuan* farms. Everybody who lives in Xinjiang is, in some way, affected by the presence and past of the *bingtuan*.

Korla's initial urban urge came from the *bingtuan*. When Korla people claim that "before liberation [1949], there was nothing much in Korla, just a dirty little river and a few Uyghur farmers; even the Uyghurs came after the Han started to build the city," they are claiming constructor status for the *bingtuan* pioneers. In 1949 Han people amounted to only 1.4% of the population of Korla. At that time, Korla was a small county town of less than 30,000 people. A few small Uyghur villages spread out to the south of the township and were enclosed and somewhat protected by a large bend that the Peacock River makes after it passes the Iron Gate Pass, and before it enters the hard stony desert en route to extinction in the wastelands to the east. After 1955 the in-migration of over 55,000 Han tripled the total population and by 1965 Han people constituted a 56.4% majority (XJ50N 2005, 505). An administrative reshuffle helps to explain this rapid growth: Korla took over from the nearby county of Yanqi as the administrative center for Bazhou in 1960 (Bazhou Government Net 2004) and the *bingtuan*'s Second Agricultural Division shifted its headquarters to Korla at the same time (Bingtuan Second Agricultural Division 2006).

The *bingtuan*'s unequaled transformative influence on social space and economy in Korla region began, however, during 1950–51 with the construction of the 18th Regiment Grand Irrigation Canal. The 35.2-kilometer-long canal took 7,000 people just nine months to build. In 750,000 person-days, laborers removed 375,000 cubic meters (490,000 cubic yards) of earth and stone. The unlined canal initially flowed at 7.5 cubic meters (9.8 cubic yards) per second and enabled an irrigated area of 50,000 *mu* (8,330 acres) (Jin 1994, 497).

The 18th Regiment irrigation canal initially reached to Wuwa village on the northern, uphill side of the 18th Regiment. The 18th Regiment was later renamed the 29th Regiment, and Wuwa township now serves as its regimental headquarters. Figure 1.1 (map) shows the geometric organization of space in the newly opened areas associated with the *bingtuan*—compare the straight outlines of the *bingtuan* irrigation channels and fields to the scribbly lines of natural seasonal watercourses and the still relatively organic-looking irrigation deltas of the villages (many populated largely by Uyghurs) to the south of Korla. Although these are both recent images, the organization of rural space—land and water resources—shown in them dates from no later than the 1960s. The

CONSTRUCTING THE CIVILIZED CITY

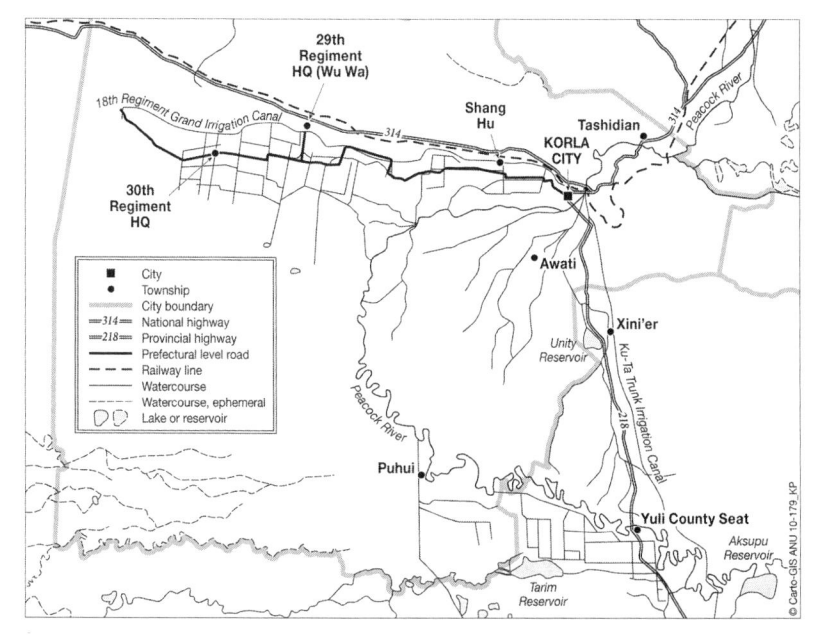

1.1   Korla city administrative region map. The irrigation channels of the 29th and 30th regiments can be seen in the top left quadrant of the map. The Uyghur-populated rural areas are south and west of Korla city, around Awati village. Korla city itself is in the top right quadrant.

flat land presented no physical obstacle to the ordered geometric arrangement seen in these images; irrigation enabled large-scale agriculture; Maoist ideology labeled the land as wasteland and positioned nature as an "enemy" to be conquered through violent struggle (Shapiro 2001). For the demobilized soldiers turned *bingtuan* pioneers, the new "war" was at least as arduous as, and promised an even less-glamorous conclusion than, the civil war that many of them had been fighting for most of their adult life. Subsequent waves of *bingtuan* settlers, most of them civilian, came to Xinjiang through the 1950s and '60s as what Mette Hansen calls "subaltern colonisers" (2005, 7). They established their sites of settlement "at the margins of civility" (Workman 1993, 179). In Korla, this meant attempting to farm the salty and inhospitable desert-fringe to the west of what was then a small agricultural settlement and postal waystation. The *bingtuan*'s survival today depends on convincing funding authorities (the center) of its continuing relevance and thus the necessity of maintaining the institution into the 21st century. In practice, this means demonstrating that it plays an important role in constructing the sacred dyad—"stability and development"—and indefinitely sustaining the notion that Xinjiang is in need of such construction.

State Constructor Discourses, 1949–2011

In state terminology, *constructor* is a flexible and polysemic term, especially when looked at over time. The 135,000 demobilized troops that became the *bingtuan* have also been referred to as pioneers (*chuangyezhe* 创业者) (Wang 1985, 2). Since these "reclamation warriors" constituted less than 4% of the total population of Xinjiang at the time and the vast majority of them were Han born outside Xinjiang, (XJSYB 1955–2005, sec. 2-3; Yao and Zhang 2005, 29), it is clear that both *constructor* and *pioneer* were culturally specific, even implicitly ethnicized, terms.

Physical construction on China's borderlands has long been associated with the construction (or *realization*) of the notion of the *Zhonghua minzu* (中华民族), a sort of pan-"Chinese" nationalism that takes the Han as the core ethnic group with the most advanced culture.[1] In the Republican era, Liang Qichao and others argued "that the unitary yet multi ethnic nature of the Zhonghua minzu was defined by a complex, unfolding national consciousness (*minzu yishi*)" (Leibold 2011, 347, 358–59). Within the 21st-century PRC geobody, the notion of *Zhonghua minzu* correlates to territorial and ethnic unity.[2] An August 2011 article in the *Bingtuan Daily* stated, "In the early days of the pioneering *bingtuan* undertaking, developing Chinese national spirit (*Zhonghua minzu jingshen*) and revolutionary tradition, and transforming the old rivers and mountains was driven by the pioneers' own initiative" (Wang L. 2011). The article thus also attributed to the *bingtuan* pioneers an agency that they did not possess and an ex post facto voluntarism that was seen as lacking at the time. Officers and troops of the 25th Division, for example, spent the first 50 days of 1950 in political study sessions that were aimed at convincing them to accept that they were in Xinjiang, to protect and to construct, for the rest of their lives. Raising these soldiers' "class consciousness" was an equally important aim of the political study. Indeed, the two were interconnected. Only after this first political study did the physical aspect of construction—"opening wasteland"—begin (Xiyu Wang 2010). Bachman writes that the CCP's attention to voluntarism was born of similarly precarious conditions during the Yan'an period (1991, 134–38). The voluntaristic impulse has seen a resurgence in recent CCP discourse relating to construction on the frontier and can be found in words and phrases like "consciousness," "*bingtuan* spirit," and "Chinese national spirit" (see, for example, Wu 2007; Liang 2009; Zhang Zhenhua 2009; Wang L. 2011).

The title of constructor, in the absence of some tangible occupational title, did not and does not necessarily attract material benefits. A group of some 7,000 young women from Shandong were outraged to discover in 1954 that they had joined a "women's construction unit" and not the PLA. Their disappointment was justified: regulations passed down on October 28, 1953, stipulated that "women who are sent to Xinjiang by the central government after today . . . should not be given military status" (quoted in Yao and Zhang 2005, 29). A 1965 intragovernmental document explained, "Because the women did not join the army, but rather went to Xinjiang to construct, these housewives [*jiashu* 家属; lit. "family members"] should not enjoy the preferential treatment due soldiers and workers" (quoted in ibid., 30). As "housewife-workers" (*jiashugong* 家属工),[3] these women were not entitled to state pensions. Construction, in this and related cases, meant being a wife. Nevertheless, a constructor was successfully set up as something to aspire to be.

Later in 1954, the *People's Daily* self-consciously broadened the scope of the term, approvingly quoting a law student: "When we resolve the case of privately owned companies cutting corners in workmanship, [and thus] guarantee the nation's economic construction and smooth development, we feel that we are not only constructors revolutionizing the legal system, at the same time we are engineers constructing a new society" (Luo 1954, 3). True constructors are thus agents—albeit also objects—of social engineering.

Attribution with the title constructor has continued to be used by the state as a motivational device at key times since the early years of the PRC. In 1985 the secretary of the Xinjiang Communist Party Committee (CPC), Wang Enmao, called on the newly mobile and aspirant population of China to support Xinjiang by migrating to and settling the region: "Xinjiang is a place where constructors engaged in opening-up can make the best of themselves" (Wang 1985, 2). In recent years, both former president Hu Jintao and secretary of the Xinjiang CPC from 2010, Zhang Chunxian, have used the term in relation to people in Xinjiang—including *bingtuan* people, oil workers, and road workers (CNPC 2008; 2011; Luo 2011). Hu Jintao referred repeatedly to people who have constructors as forebears—literal or figurative—as "defenders" (*hanweizhe* 捍卫者) or "successors" (*jiebanren* 接班人) (*Xinjiang Bingtuan Jianchayuan* 2011; Hu 2011, 2; Qiushi Lilun 2011).

Consistent with the current approach to integrating Xinjiang into the core area of China—by "normalizing" it, trying to make it more like *neidi*—culture now overshadows ethnicity as the key attribute of a constructor. The once-powerful Zhou Yongkang (周永康), then party secretary of the Central Politics and Law Commission (the organ responsible for internal security),[4] called on Uyghur high school students in Guangdong to "make a great effort to be models of upholding ethnic unity, be the backbone of accelerating the development of Xinjiang's social economy, and be constructors bringing about the great resurgence of the Chinese nation" (Zhang Zongtang 2009). He delivered a similar message to Uyghur migrant workers in a nearby factory. Uyghurs can, it seems, be constructors par excellence once they have been transformed by the disciplinary regimes of Han-run institutions such as the school and the factory.

Other keywords of the state discourse indicate the roles that Han (and, potentially, some Uyghur) constructors in Xinjiang are portrayed as playing, and the context in which they operate. Through "arduous struggle" (*jianku fendou* 艰苦奋斗), constructors "contribute" (*gongxian* 贡献) to nation building in an "ethnic region" (*minzu diqu* 民族地区)—or, more suggestively, a "special region" (*teshu diqu* 特殊地区)—that is "remote" (*pianyuan* 偏远) and both culturally and physically "barren" (*huang* 荒), requiring "opening up" and "leapfrog development" (*kuayueshi fazhan* 跨越式发展) to "catch up" to eastern China.

The physical and ideological/cultural aspects of construction overlap with the reform-era discourse of "civilization." In contemporary PRC discourse, civilization has both material aspects (*wuzhi wenming* 物质文明)—urban space, the built environment, consumption, and standard of living—and spiritual aspects (*jingshen wenming* 精神文明). This latter aspect is what Chinese state discourse means by "civilized people." Civility in personal qualities and behavior, the opposite of being uncouth, means being properly educated, with good manners, taste, language, and accent, and a loyalty to the official concept of nation. Civilization in contemporary Chinese terms is measured by the habits, habitat, and habitus of the population. Construction is thus a process whose aim, in 21st-century urban China, is the realization of all-round civilization.

Urbanization as Civilization

Civilizing the city is a teleological process in that it has a series of stages which must be passed through to reach a final destination. The final destination is often idealized and is assumed to be imminent—reflecting what Immanuel Wallerstein calls "the enormous subterranean strength of the faith in inevitable progress" (1983, 8). But what comes first in this process—material or spiritual civilization? A small but significant change

1.2   Billboard #1, roughly 90 yards wide and 10 yards high. New City District, Korla. July 2007

1.3   Billboard #2, roughly 90 yards wide and 10 yards high. New City District, Korla. November 2007

in a billboard produced by the Korla City Civilization Office (*wenming bangongshi* 文明办公室) hinted at the inherently political nature of this question. In July 2007, the 90-yard-long, 10-yard-high billboard read "创文明城市,做文明市民,建和谐家园" in Chinese, and "Create a Civilized City, So Civilized People, Harmonious Society" in English. By November, the English translation had changed to "Create a Civilized City, *Be* Civilized People, Harmonious Society." The (philosophically) materialistic and strictly teleological interpretation—*so*, not *be*—discursively undermines the Civilizing Authorities because, in effect, it relieves the population of primary responsibility for their own behavior. Many Korla residents with whom I spoke in late 2007 and early 2008, including some of those who claimed that the act of construction must be a conscious one, nevertheless assumed that mind followed matter: "Chinese people will naturally become civilized (like the West) once our material civilization reaches a certain level." The assumption was understandable: although the authorities continually exhort the population to be civilized, most of the money and effort goes into the superficial aesthetics of the urban environment.

Having experienced more rapid growth than anywhere else in Xinjiang since the establishment of the Tarim Oilfield Company headquarters in the early 1990s, Korla is now Xinjiang's "second city" and by far the most modern and economically powerful county-level city in South Xinjiang. This relatively high political and economic profile, combined

CHAPTER ONE

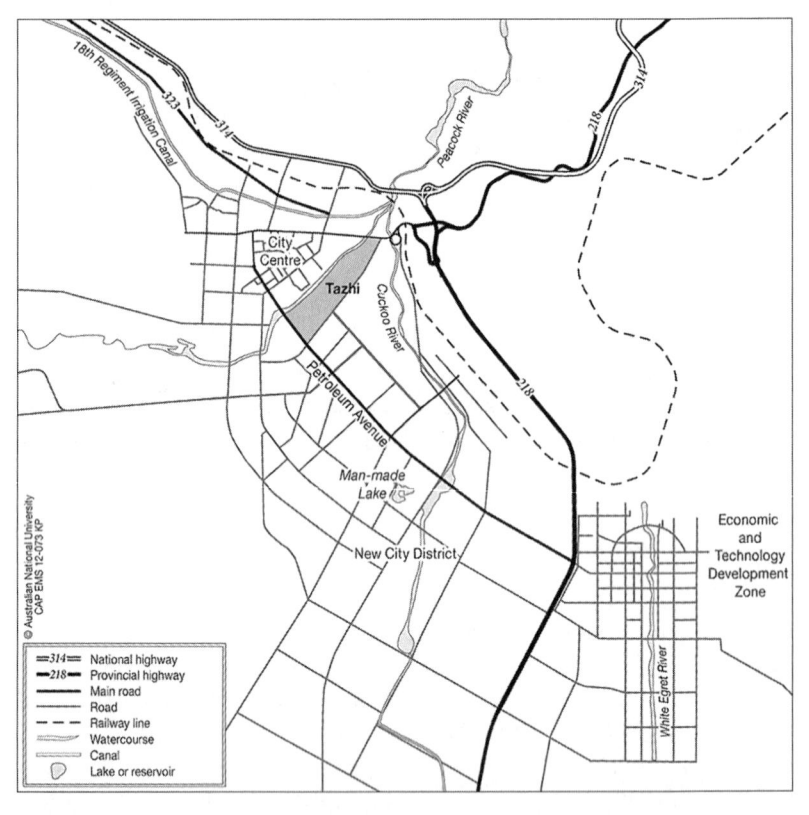

1.4   Korla city map, 2012. The three rivers of Korla City—Peacock, Cuckoo, and White Egret

with the importance of Xinjiang to China's economy and sense of domestic social stability (Xinhua 2009d; Zhang 2011), make it a political priority that Korla be seen as a model of urban development. As tools of governance, city-planning models are the physical manifestation of preconceived ideals and need to be replicable. James Scott's analysis in *Seeing Like a State* is useful here: "A far-flung, polyglot empire may find it symbolically useful to have its camps and towns laid out according to formula as the stamp of its order and authority. Other things being equal, the city laid out according to a simple, repetitive logic will be easiest to administer and to police" (55). Scott considers this formula to be part of a "high-modernist ideology," and he notes that the "carriers of high modernism tended to see rational order in remarkably visual aesthetic terms" (4). It follows that I use visual and spatial analyses to recount the development of this model.

CONSTRUCTING THE CIVILIZED CITY

The photographs and maps in this chapter illustrate that the built environment of urban Korla is increasingly in accordance with the "administrative ordering of nature and society" that Scott terms "legibility" (1998, 5–6). Until the early 1990s, all but the *bingtuan*-dominated "old" city center of Korla was effectively still rural land in terms of how it was organized and utilized (figure 1.5). The fields, irregular boundaries, and homes of extended families shown in the bottom half of figure 1.5 are typical of a rural organization of space. In the past, the relative proportions and positions of agricultural land, courtyards, and low adobe-style dwellings depended on the economic and population growth of these individual (mostly Uyghur) family units. Figure 1.6 illustrates Korla's transformation from a rural center to an urban model. These two photographs show that in the 21st century, Korla increasingly conforms to a planned, geometrically ordered layout imposed from above. Materials too have changed—from being predominantly brick, earth, and wood to being predominantly steel, concrete, and bitumen. The acceleration toward a geometric organization of space—both on the two-dimensional map and in the three-dimensional built environment—is also a transition toward legibility. Although it was the *bingtuan*, not the Tarim Oilfield Company, which initiated the project of legibility, Tazhi's

1.5   Korla, late 1980s. The land which becomes the Tarim Oilfield Company compound is in the foreground this side of the Peacock River. Picture © Hou Jian. Used with permission

CHAPTER ONE

1.6 Newer Korla, circa 2004. As in figure 1.5, this side is all the Tarim Oilfield Company compound. Picture © Hou Jian. Used with permission

political and economic gravity has enabled and led an intensification of legibility and ideal modernity in urban Korla. Legibility and a modern façade are, in the context of contemporary China, conditions of being civilized.

Korla city government and party committee began a push to claim the title of "Civilized City" in 1996, declaring April 2 Founding Spiritual Civilization Mobilization Day (Wenmingban 2007, 1). In the following years, Korla was awarded a series of increasingly prestigious awards, culminating in 2009 with the award of "All China Civilized City" (*quan guo wenming chengshi* 全国文明城市). Korla was the first city in Xinjiang (and one of only three county-level cities in China) to be awarded the title (Xinhua 2011a; 2011b). Such awards explicitly set up models for other local governments and populations to follow. These models need to be dispersed geographically around China as well as to be varied in the size-type of city they are modeling. Places in greatest need of transformation, South Xinjiang being one of them, are seen to be in greatest need of models to guide them. That is to say, the award of Civilized City status is as much a *statement of intent* as it is a *statement of actuality*—the city becomes the model and the model becomes the city.

Perhaps unsurprisingly in this future-focused environment, there remains a sense among Korla officials and residents that the ideal is never reached; the objective is a moving target that is always up ahead. A still-higher award, which is yet to be attained, is "Ecological City" (*shengtai chengshi* 生态城市), described as an urban area in which humans live in harmony with nature. Moreover, *cultural* transformation is the ultimate arbiter of colonial success: the civilizing conceit that nothing, or nothing of value, existed in Korla prior to the arrival of Han constructors also underpins a common Han lament that present-day Korla "has civilization but no culture." Constructing this culture, both retrospectively through the imposition of a particular historical narrative (Cliff 2013) and in the ever-present future, thus becomes the ultimate goal.

Urban Transformation, Uyghur Dislocation

Korla underwent a period of especially accelerated physical construction during 2007–9. When I got there in July 2007, I was struck by the large number of advertisements for as-yet unbuilt residential estates. Their promotional strategies drew on a perceived desire for European, metropolitan, and executive lifestyles—images of parkland, middle-class consumption, and technology predominated. The prospective orientation was again strongly present: a high-profile development named Future-Zone (*weilaiyu* 未来域) is one example (see color plate 5). Many real estate advertisements also associated high-status with proximity to centers of administrative power and key urban watercourses. For example, one residential development was named *Qianxi* (迁徙), which means "to migrate," and is a homonym of *qianxi* (前席), meaning "advance one's seat (to get closer to the speaker)." *Qianxi* was located midway between Peacock River and the grand new building housing the Korla City Government, located in the New City District. The four main public bodies of water in the urban area are Peacock River, Cuckoo River, White Egret River, and Man-Made Lake. These water features are modernist monuments, claiming victory over nature and claiming the technological supremacy of the Han: the location (but not the form, since it has been widened considerably) of the Peacock River is the only element of these watercourses that is not entirely artificial. Particularly in this desert region, water is both a symbol and a tool of power. Residential districts often also advertised their own water feature within the compound. Such for-consumption water features have displaced an earlier network

CHAPTER ONE

of irrigation canals that were primarily utilitarian and were associated with small-scale agriculturalists—most of whom were Uyghur.

The following series of photographs (figures 1.7–1.10) and plates 1–4 and 6–8 (following page 44) show the redevelopment of socially and spatially porous urban villages on the eastern side of Korla into gated residential compounds. In 2013 most of the landowners in the older urban villages were Uyghurs. If they had not rebuilt and rented out their property to Han sojourners, these Uyghurs lived in single-story adobe and brick dwellings that they had progressively added to as their family size and wealth grew. Their economy was semisubsistence: most families grew vegetables for their own consumption, and some raised a few sheep or goats which they then consumed or converted into cash; the landed families tended cash-crop orchards of the nationally famous Korla fragrant pear. Compensation (calculated per square meter) for this agricultural land is less than one half of the compensation for residential land whose buildings are not declared "illegal." This was a point of great tension and an opportunity for corrupt and coercive behavior on the part of state actors. For their part, Uyghurs living in villages in line for demolition hastily extended the floor area of their dwellings. Although some professed to be quite happy with their compensation, most Uyghurs were (and are) extremely reluctant to leave their extended family compounds for the sterility and atomization of a distant apartment complex. It is not just family life that is upset—many Uyghurs are self-employed and run businesses that rely on a base close to the city center. For them, relocation means unemployment. On the whole, Korla's urban reconstruction means a disruptive change in the practices of inner-city Uyghurs' everyday life—including cooking, eating, cultural production, and social reproduction.

The Uyghur residential buildings that were being demolished in Korla helped to sustain Uyghur community life, though it cannot be said that the buildings and layout of the villages represented some fundamental symbol of Uyghur-ness. These villages did not develop organically over hundreds of years—as in the case of Kashgar, for example. Instead, a regular diamond latticework of roads—clearly a product of a preceding round of state-led construction—was being drawn over. The inner-city Uyghur villages had developed in relation to these roads, and the overall layout appeared to result from a relatively recent but nevertheless quite complex process of accommodation and adaptation between mainly Uyghur agriculturalists and the mainly Han state. The large new boulevard-type roads, designed for the car and arranged on a grid pattern, make "no compromise" (Scott 1998, 104) with the preexisting spatial form, regardless of whether it was shaped by Han or Uyghur people.

1.7   First comes the plan—a redevelopment of Korla's pay-to-enter Peacock Park and the Uyghur residential district nestled behind it. The park once featured a few fairground attractions, an artificial lake with boats and fishing, and a small zoo—animal attractions included a sick-looking tiger and a sad-looking fox, both housed in tiny and bare concrete boxes with bars on the viewing side. The old Uyghur residential district is tactfully obscured by mist and forest on the left-hand side of the plan above, making it easy for the rest of the city's residents (or at least the non-Uyghur ones) to put the demolition of the urban village out of their minds as well. The sign says, "Peacock Park landscape engineering project construction office."

1.8   Then comes the relocation. The sign says, "Peacock Park demolition and relocation office." This is in a small building in the middle of the to-be-demolished village and is the face of the state for the people living in the village—it organizes compensation and the relocation schedule. Demolitions like this are often impending for many years—facilities and services are gradually downgraded or cut off entirely—but are carried out rapidly when they do start.

1.9 Dispossession and disorientation. Inside a yet-to-be-demolished section of the Uyghur residential area.

1.10 Salvage and relocation. Another former Uyghur residential and fragrant pear-growing area of the old city.

The Human Element

The project to transform space and society is never complete. Apparently finished buildings rise out of rubble and artificial stream beds run weakly—if at all. Korla's "civilized" façade, impressive as it is, is in many places only skin deep: scratch the surface and you will find a provincial desert town. Urban planning policies require developers to construct tall signature buildings on highly visible street corners and along major thoroughfares. The old urban villages are walled-in, out of sight, before being demolished altogether and their residents relocated.

A stroll through these back alleys reveals the diversity of the population—a diversity stemming from when they came to Korla, where they came from, why they came, what they do now, and how they identify themselves. The stroller meets groups of disoriented migrant laborers from central and eastern China, old *bingtuan* people and their children, old Korla people who never quite recovered from the final collapse of state enterprises during the 1990s, well-off employees of state enterprises that *are* doing well, Uyghurs whose families have lived around Korla for generations, and other Uyghurs just arrived off the slow bus from Kashgar. Every urban resident actively awaits something—a demolition, a compensation, an opportunity—while adjusting their habits to accommodate the actual changes in the city and in their lives.

Urbanization reshapes habits in both intended (civilizing) and unintended ways. In Korla, as in cities across China, habits are forced to change when villages are transformed into urban residential communities, when spaces of production are transformed into spaces of consumption, and when an assumption of peripheral behindness becomes an expectation of metropolitan modernity. Old pathways disappear under high-volume road grids, forcing people to modify the way they move through the city, and thus whom they encounter. Walter Benjamin's essay "The Work of Art in the Age of Mechanical Reproduction" clearly signaled how architecture and urban space have a corporeal impact on humans: "Buildings are appropriated in a twofold manner: by use and by perception." He goes on to claim that "the tasks which face the human apparatus of perception at the turning points of history cannot be solved by optical means, that is, by contemplation, alone. They are mastered gradually by habit." ([1936] 1969, 240). The very act of living in a constantly changing city works to transform the residents' habits of mind and body.

Han and Uyghur people respond to the disruption of habits in quite different ways. As shown above, it is usually Uyghur neighborhoods, and the roads running to and through them, that are destroyed to make way for the new plan. Relocated Uyghurs experience massive social and economic changes to their lives. Many Uyghurs justifiably see the destruction of old roads and neighborhoods as an imposition. Han, on the other hand, tend to see such destruction as a necessary condition of advancement, and an inevitable stage in the modernization project. Many Han honestly fail to understand why Uyghurs would prefer to stay in unheated, earth-floored houses than in modern apartments. For Han migrants, change is not only an aspiration but also a way of life—beginning with their migration from the core area and continuing with their role as agents and/or objects of civilization. As the epigraph to this chapter makes clear, the opposing claims to agency, and thus constructor status, made by different groups of Xinjiang Han often pivot on the issue of consciousness.

Contesting Constructor Status

The apartment salesmen in the FutureZone sales office, dressed in the standard black trousers and white shirt open at the collar, maintained their deferential tone even after they realized that we were window shoppers. My companion, Zhang Yonglei, a doctor from Gansu (see the introduction), began to question them aggressively about their reasons for migration. Yonglei had been living in Xinjiang for about six years at the time and had bought a house out at Korla's Economic Technology Development Zone (*jingji jishu kaifaqu* 经济技术开发区), where this incident took place in July 2009. The three young men explained that they came from Jiangsu and had done a short course in retail residential selling before being offered positions by a developer in Korla. "It is contract work—our base salaries are very low, but it is possible to earn 3,000, or even 6,000, *yuan* per month if you are a good seller," they said, with more hope than conviction. Then, somewhat apologetically, "anyway, there is no work in our home town, and no future for us there—we are just high school graduates, with bad marks—so we may as well come out here to try our luck."

Yonglei turned to me: "They are also constructors. They have come to make a contribution to Xinjiang's development." The boys protested modestly, and one of them asked Yonglei where he came from and what he did. "I am a medical doctor," Yonglei said proudly; they genuflected mildly. The questioner asked again. Haughtily, Yonglei looked directly at

1   Main thoroughfare of the New City District, looking northeast to Petroleum Avenue. On the opposite side of the large white building in the background are the massive billboards shown in figures 1.2 and 1.3. The low brick building in the left mid-ground is the same as that in the foreground of plate 2.

2   The New City District. August 2007. Reverse angle of plate 1

3 *Hua yu* residential development in the New City District, April 2008. The gray and white apartment buildings are the same as those in plate 2 and plate 4.

4 *Hua yu residential development. April 2008*

白鹭河畔 30 万平方米
人文生态亲水社区样板

5   This development, FutureZone, is in the Economic Technology Development Zone, next to the White Egret River.

6   Public space/state space in the New City District. Looking north from the Petroleum Avenue bridge over Cuckoo River. September 2009. A replica of the Beijing Olympic torch stands 30 yards high on its own pontoon in the middle of the widest part of the river.

7   No-man's-land. Inside Aktash, the urban village across the road from Tazhi. January 2010. Uyghur and Han landlords rent rooms to Han migrant workers from *neidi*. This is the boundary between the blocks of two landlords.

8   A corner store on the fringe of an urban village. June 2008. All the buildings connected to this one were marked for demolition with the symbol *chai* (拆), but 18 months later they were still standing.

him and said, "I'm from Gansu." It was a challenge of sorts—Gansu is one of China's poorest provinces, and Gansu people tend to be looked down on. A fleeting smirk, and a slight shift in the Jiangsu boys' body language on hearing this news betrayed their deeply held prejudices. Yonglei flinched, and his voice rose: "I am a constructor of Korla, and I am here to contribute to Xinjiang's development. I am supporting the border.... You are also constructors."

The boys protested: "No, we are not constructors. We are just here to make some money, then go home." Yonglei insisted that they were constructors. "No, we are not," the boys said equally firmly. "You are a doctor; we are just high school graduates. We are not constructors." The doctor's voice rose: "It doesn't matter what you are doing: if you are out here working, you are contributing to Korla's development, and you are constructors. You should realize that; you have a responsibility to realize that!" He lectured them for a couple more minutes without encountering any resistance, then summoned me and we left.

Outside the sales office, Yonglei was still furious, and he continued to criticize the Jiangsu boys for lacking "consciousness." He explained how important it was for in-migrants—border supporters of the 21st century —to have an awareness of what they were doing. Echoing state discourses, he stated that construction was not only, not even mainly, about building a Civilized City in the material realm—it was about building a Civilized City in the spiritual realm.

This brief interaction is a rich example of constructor discourse and its deployment in Xinjiang. It contains a number of elements. First, there are hierarchies among the Han in Xinjiang that depend on (1) origin place, (2) time of migration, and (3) structural conditions of migration. The fourth element is the concept of "consciousness" as a factor in the construction of a moral hierarchy. Finally, this interaction signals the critical role of the state in producing and perpetuating these discursive and material hierarchies.

Hierarchies of origin-place map directly onto a given location's "level of development." Urban takes precedence over rural, metropolitan over regional, and rich over poor. With regard to time of migration, firstcomers claim a higher status than newcomers. Structural conditions of migration depend on the following set of questions: Was the migrant self-sponsored or state sponsored? If self-sponsored, was it (predominantly) push or pull factors that took them to Xinjiang? To the first generation of Han "pioneers" to settle Xinjiang after the founding of the PRC, only those who came in the 1950s and '60s are "real" constructors. A group of *bingtuan* pioneers now living in urban retirement asserted that

CHAPTER ONE

"constructors are people who were sent here by the government. . . . They are not people who decide to come here of their own accord, just pick up their bag and set out. . . . It is different now." A retired "Third Front" worker sent to Xinjiang in 1964 explained, "We were constructors because we produced for the whole country, our production and our labor benefited the whole country. Today's China is different, it is now made up of capitalism and socialism melding together. . . . Yes, there are still constructors . . . but they are not constructors in the way that we were constructors, there are no present-day constructors like we were."

Yonglei is below the Jiangsu boys on the origin-place hierarchy but above them on the time of migration hierarchy. In the bigger picture, however, all of them are seen as recent migrants by the local Han people, and this helps explain why Yonglei became so frustrated with the Jiangsu boys' refusal to lay claim to constructor status. By thus refusing, they undermine his own claim to be a constructor. Conversely, if these uneducated young men are constructors, then a doctor like himself, particularly since he often works in less-developed and peripheral regions of Xinjiang, is an even higher grade of constructor. He was tutoring them to emphasize selfless pull factors such as frontier construction and national development, rather than selfish push factors like unemployment in place of origin, in their own telling of their migration story, and thus lay claim to constructor consciousness.

Yonglei would have been happier with the inclusive definition of constructors presented by another young apartment salesman. This young man had been in Korla for about five years at the time (August 2009) and had clearly internalized, or at least learned, the most recent version of the state discourse (and what it had to offer him): "Constructors are people who construct a harmonious society . . . that means everybody is a constructor—we are, building site workers are, farmers are—whoever helps to construct this society's environment and make it better and better is a constructor. . . . Even you are a constructor. Nobody is not a constructor."

The epigraph to this chapter also draws attention to the intimate relationship between a constructor and their consciousness in the discourse of Korla locals. Yonglei's frustration with the newly arrived Jiangsu boys shows that he has formed a picture of the rhetorical landscape of the frontier, more or less as described by that quote. He has recognized that identities, which tend to be firmly attached while an individual stays in their place of origin, are made more flexible by the act of migration. Migrants have the (limited) opportunity to remake themselves. He has understood that, in Xinjiang, the most useful identity to him is that of a construc-

1.11   A thoroughfare of the old urban village network, between a minor irrigation channel and one of the earlier (and more exclusive) gated residential developments in Korla. The road leads toward the migrant settlement of Aktash. January 2010

1.12   Migrant construction workers in the Economic Technology Development Zone. May 2008

tor, but that this title has multiple different levels of value. Thus he understands that it is necessary for self-sponsored in-migrants to bolster the weak state attribution of them as constructors—that is, to lay claim to this identity by stating that their motives are not only selfish and economic. This logic is premised on the assumption that it is by realizing (becoming aware) that they are the agents of an advanced culture that they can best help to realize (actuate) cultural change in Xinjiang. To come full circle, it is by doing this that they can claim a value above and beyond that of their labor and physical presence in Xinjiang.

A Han Periphery

The coercive forces of urbanization most dramatically affect the lives of inner-city Uyghurs, but non-Han ethnicities are not the only objects of the civilizing project in Xinjiang. Han people may also be seen to have "nasty habits."[5] Although the final objective—integration of the ethnic periphery created by the Qing dynasty and inherited from the Qing by the Republic and then the People's Republic—has not changed markedly over the course of the past 60 years, the social and political context that this colonial endeavor is unfolding within, and creating, certainly has. Han migration to Xinjiang today is predominantly voluntary, rather than state-sponsored and coercive as in the past; many migrants are self-employed or work in services or the construction industry in the urban centers, and these days, most migrants are not members of large formal state institutions like the *bingtuan* and the oil company. To say nothing of urban culture, economy, or politics, demographics alone complicate notions of Xinjiang as a Muslim borderland: in the 21st century, Xinjiang is as much a Han periphery.

The changing context has necessitated an adjustment of the methods and processes of peripheral integration, part of which is an increased focus on urban development in both the cities and the rural town centers of Xinjiang. In a sense, the lure of the city is taking over part of the role that formal state institutions performed in the past—in attracting, regulating and transforming the (Han) in-migrants—as well as in regulating and transforming the lifestyles of the Han, Uyghurs, and others already in Xinjiang.

Korla is being shaped in the currently dominant nationwide ideal of urban Chinese modernity (Kipnis 2012, 742–47). In Xinjiang, these grand plans of engineering are far less constrained by history, culture, or space than in *neidi*. The plans and their implementation are also inflected by the need to present a particular set of nested images—of Korla and its truncated history, of the center and its power and benevolence, and of the nation and its unity. But, unlike some other Chinese cities that lie "Beyond the Great Wall," the urban morphology and architecture of Korla pays (at the most) only the most superficial tribute to the history, culture, and aesthetics of the local non-Han (Gaubatz 1996; Perdue 2005). And although Korla today takes the aesthetic of the core region of China as its model, it does not precisely replicate that of the core. Rather, an aesthetic is emerging that is associated with the Han—and with the core that they implicitly represent, whether or not they have ever been there—but is peripheral. This aesthetic is framed by a different history and looks forward to a different future to that of the core aesthetic.

Urban Han society in Xinjiang interfaces the Chinese metropole, the *bingtuan*, and both internal (non-Han within Xinjiang) and external (non-Chinese) neighbors. The tones of *bingtuan* discourse, in a somewhat diluted form, seep into the discourses circulating on the frontier, and leave their mark on the fabric of frontier society. This can be seen in the strength and ubiquity of constructor discourse in the pioneering and exemplary-modern city of Korla. Contemporary metropolitan-originated ideals and aesthetics—of civilization and harmony—also color the discursive and physical space of the frontier. Sandwiched socially and spatially between the *bingtuan* and the metropole, Han society in Xinjiang is most strongly influenced by discourses originating from these Han-identified neighbors.

New arrivals, such as the Jiangsu boys, stand out because they tend to be less conversant with how these discourses manifest in Xinjiang— especially the relatively strong emphasis on voluntarism and collectivism. The question of whether these new arrivals, or others like them, can successfully lay claim to constructor consciousness determines whether they are seen as the *agents* or the *objects* of construction. The intensity of such claims and counterclaims within the Han community of Xinjiang shows that, for these people, intra-ethnic relations are at least as much of a concern as inter-ethnic relations.

Non-Han on China's borders tend to be automatically positioned as the objects of construction, and are thus a central tenet of the entire discursive realm—if all China were Han, and accepted themselves to be such, there would be no need for the idea of a *Zhonghua minzu* or its unifying imperatives. Apart from this, they play no greater role than the Han subalterns in producing (and a considerably smaller role in *reproducing*) the dominant discourses that circulate in the frontier space or the monuments under whose shadow they live.

TWO

The Individual and the Era-Defining Institutions of State

The process of becoming human and the nature of the human itself were fundamentally transformed in the passage defined by modernization. ANTONIO NEGRI, *EMPIRE* (2000, 285)

The transformations of space, society, and economy in the Korla region are closely linked to what I call the "era-defining institutions" of post-1949 Xinjiang. All these institutions have, to date, been SOEs or enterprise groups that dominate the local political economy during their particular era and thus shape the aesthetics, aspirations, and life chances of the frontier population. The largest of them have also been part of regional or nationwide "*danwei* systems"—state bureaucratic systems comprising a large number of separate and all-encompassing "work units" (*danwei* 单位) under the administrative supervision of a ministerial-level organ. Such direct connections to the central state lend them powers and motives that are quasi-independent of the Xinjiang Uyghur Autonomous Region government. The *bingtuan*'s Second Agricultural Division (*nong er shi* 农二师) and the Tarim Oilfield Company are the two key institutions of state in Korla and in Xinjiang for the period 1949–2012. Both of these institutions occupy spaces that are exclusive and bounded, and both also operate in a "contact zone" with the surrounding space, society, and economy. Thus, they both transform the frontier environment and, to some extent, are transformed by it.

Since 1949 spatial and demographic engineering has had an immense impact on Xinjiang. No other province-level region in the PRC has seen such transformative ideals carried out to the same extent, nor with such lasting significance. James Scott has argued convincingly that empire-builders and high modernists always see the organized chaos and complexity of the naturally developed city as a threat to external political authority (1998, 53ff). Today, the Mao-era effects of high modernist ideology in Xinjiang can be seen most clearly and are most widespread in the *bingtuan*'s construction of industrial-scale agriculture and irrigation, "greenfields" farming townships (now mostly in various stages of decay), and cities that rose "like desert flowers" from the stony wasteland (*Straits Times* 2000). Beginning in 1950, the *bingtuan* pioneers inscribed the space of Xinjiang with a new aesthetic—an aesthetic that, viewed today from ground level, looks distinctly rustic, uncomfortable, and passé.

Now the Tarim Oilfield Company, the paradigmatic representative of 21st-century PRC developmental modernism in Xinjiang, is writing over and in between the inscriptions made by the *bingtuan*. Tazhi is at the spatial core of Korla and is the main economic power behind the city, but it is administratively and socially distinct from the surrounding city. At the same time, Tazhi self-consciously exerts a strong aesthetic and aspirational influence on the city of Korla and its residents: as Korla is to other cities in Xinjiang, Tazhi represents an ideal. In this chapter, I juxtapose the *bingtuan* and the oil company with a life history which spans both of these institutions. The subject of this life history, Mr. Jia, grew up on the *bingtuan*'s 29th Regiment west of Korla, and is now a departmental director (*chuzhang* 处长) in the Tarim Oilfield Company. Many such human links exist between the *bingtuan* and the oil company.

Mr. Jia: From the *Bingtuan* to the Oil Company

Although he had rural roots, Jia's family was positioned just slightly but significantly above the ordinary *bingtuan* settlers. As he tells it, the original *bingtuan* settlers in Xinjiang were "a bandit army," cobbled together mainly from Wang Zhen's untrained forces, former Nationalist soldiers (many of them conscripts), and people who fled the post–Great Leap Forward famine in the early 1960s. Jia's father, a PLA radio operator, was sent out from northeast China in 1965 with many other low-level officers of that northeast army to "instill some discipline into the rowdy semimilitarized *bingtuan* farmers." At that time in their early 20s, Jia's father and mother settled on the *bingtuan*.

CHAPTER TWO

2.1 Jia's mother and father. 1963

Jia himself was born in 1966, so the first 10 years of his life coincided with the Cultural Revolution decade (1966–76). He did the college entrance exam in 1984, along with more than 600 students from the 29th Regiment alone. Student numbers at *bingtuan* high schools 25 years later were far lower, yet high school attendance rates had multiplied many times over, giving some indication of the significant demographic shift from the *bingtuan* toward the urban centers. Sitting in his large office in the Tarim compound relating his life history to me, he described the mood among his "*bingtuan* first-generation" peers in the early 1980s:

At that time, *bingtuan* children's greatest wish was to get into university—to leave the *bingtuan*, to shake off the *bingtuan*, because life on the *bingtuan* was very hard: it was a very arduous life; rural work makes you very tired; and income was unfairly distributed. At the same time, [non-*bingtuan*] people looked down on you and discriminated against you.

There were three types of people in Xinjiang at that time: city people were the first grade; rural people, the second grade; and *bingtuan* people were the third and last grade.... So we studied hard—it was the only way out.

Neither he nor his classmates had seen much of the world beyond the *bingtuan*, and so they had no idea to which university they should, or could reasonably, apply. So their teacher did it for them, matching up their average grades with the rank of the tertiary institution.

In July 1984, the 18-year-old Jia went to Korla to do the exam. This was the first time he had been to the city for nine years, despite it being only 50 kilometers down the road. He pointed out that a return bus trip to Korla from the 29th Regiment cost almost one week of his father's wages. Now he makes that trip in a white Toyota Land Cruiser. In Xinjiang, the Land Cruiser is the vehicle of choice for leaders: *bingtuan* leaders have green Land Cruisers and oil company leaders have white Land Cruisers.

The college entrance exam determined his fate and that of his cohort.

You did the test—three days: seventh, eighth, ninth of July. Then you went home and waited. If you didn't get the notice of acceptance by the end of August, you "fear

2.2   Jia and his younger sister, studio portrait. 1969. He holds Mao's "Little Red Book."

CHAPTER TWO

death." . . . After that, you just go to work, go down to the villages. You get allocated a piece of land by the *bingtuan*, and you just work there. . . . That's good enough for you. It's like gambling: either you make it or you don't—[and if you don't] then you just work on the *bingtuan* your whole life.

The children of his generation on the *bingtuan* knew little or nothing beyond the *bingtuan*, but they were convinced that anything was better than the *bingtuan*.

Take me for example. This university that I got into: I'd never heard of this university; I didn't know where this university was. What this major was all about, I had no idea.

He laughed and leaned back in his comfortable office chair, then went on, telling me how at midday on August 23, 1984, he was at his next-door neighbor's house, watching the opening ceremony of the Los Angeles Olympics. Although the neighbor was only a deputy company commander, and Jia's own father a full company commander, the neighbor got a salary that was three times as much as his father. This is because the neighbor was an "old revolutionary" (*lao geming* 老革命)—a soldier who joined the PLA before the Communist declaration of victory on October 1, 1949. The neighbor's monthly salary of 120 *yuan* in 1984 meant that his household could afford a black-and-white TV.

During the opening ceremony, Jia's younger sister came over with his acceptance notice to the Jianghan Petroleum College in Hubei. Jia noted that he should have been happy—university intakes in China in 1984 were less than 3% of high school graduates (ZGJYTJNJ 2009, 15). Furthermore, urban students made up 84% of those enrolled in the early 1980s (Seeberg 1998, 213), meaning that on average less than 0.6% of rural high school graduates were admitted to tertiary institutions during the period that Jia was competing for a position. Instead, he was disappointed: he wanted to study ocean shipping so he could see the world, but he got drilling engineering. Jia had seen films of the oil industry model worker Wang Jinxi (王进喜), and the hero's life looked even harder than life on the *bingtuan*. Even the supposedly worldly "old revolutionary" neighbor didn't know where the Hubei university was. Jia recounted:

My mood went even lower: this man, whom we respected and thought of as experienced and knowledgeable, didn't even know of the place I was going to. I didn't feel like going to university. . . .

Then my teacher said the Hubei University was "a little better than [the *bingtuan*-run] Tarim University." He just said that, nothing else. If somebody wanted to insult you, they would say that you had graduated from Tarim University. So I got even more depressed . . . and thus, muddled and confused, I went to university.

Even a small difference in social standing and income received made an absolute difference in opportunity. To feed and clothe himself each month for the four years of his degree, Jia needed 50% of his father's 40 *yuan* salary to supplement his 11 *yuan* government stipend. The remaining 20 *yuan* of his father's salary had to feed his father, mother, and two younger sisters back on the *bingtuan*. Jia told me, "My father was a company commander . . . but other families couldn't afford to send their children to university." An ordinary *bingtuan* worker at that time received between 26 and 29 *yuan* per month.

Jia's reluctance to work in an oil company tells us a lot about the reward structure in 1984. Oil was not considered a good job. But by 1992, nobody in Korla region, not even the poorest *bingtuan* farmer, could be unaware of the absolute social and economic primacy of the oil company and its employees.

Jia got into the oil company because the oil industry needed young, top-scoring graduates and told the universities to recruit some. He agreed to return to Xinjiang so that he could better care for his family. The officials at the Xinjiang Oil Management Bureau (*Xinjiang shiyou guanliju* 新疆石油管理局) in Karamay sent Jia to the progenitor of the Tarim Oilfield Company, the tiny South Xinjiang Oil Exploration Company (*Nanjiang shiyou kantan gongsi* 南疆石油勘探公司) that had its base just outside Korla. In 1988 the company had only 300 employees but had just struck oil in the Tarim Basin.

Jia grew with the oil company, working his way up to his current position as the fire chief of the oil company compound. The fire chief sprinkled tea in my disposable paper cup and casually told me how expensive and exclusive the leaves were. I asked him about the social divisions in Xinjiang today, and whether they were still the same as the three levels that had existed in the 1970s and '80s, the social divisions that he had opened his narrative with.

Much of Xinjiang is still the same: first city people, then rural people, and at the bottom, *bingtuan* people. But Korla is slightly different: the first-class people are us in this work unit.

He chuckled, and went on:

CHAPTER TWO

People say this: here, on this side of the Peacock River, in the Tarim compound, we call that Hong Kong. The other side, the old city center, represents mainland China. One country, two systems.

In pointing out that the oil company is to Korla as Hong Kong is to China, Jia implicitly recognized that physical and spatial structures both signify and help to determine social, economic, and political structures. He is well qualified to make this observation about the spatial hierarchy of opportunity and privilege. In 2010 Jia lived in "PhD building" (*boshi lou* 博士楼)—an apartment tower in the oil company compound that is reserved only for cadres of full director rank and above. The apartments in the building are considerably larger and better appointed than others in the Tarim compound, and the building itself is located by the river and away from the main group of apartment towers. The residents of PhD building are the elite of the elite in Korla, a socioeconomic position which is emphasized by the spatial conditions of their place of residence. Furthermore, as well as having the luxury of observing social structure from this elite perspective, Jia's narrative is also informed by earlier experience as a child of the *bingtuan*. He has seen the rural/urban division from both sides, and not only that, he has seen this division from close to the extremes of both sides. The *bingtuan* is a periphery, an Other, and a past in Jia's life story, and in the prevailing discourse of many Han people living in 21st-century Korla, especially the children and grandchildren of *bingtuan* pioneers. People with current or former connections to the *bingtuan* constitute a significant proportion of the population of Korla today. *Bingtuan* people are also well represented among the early cohorts of oil company employees and are now mostly in managerial roles.

Ms. Jing, a mid-ranking oil company cadre, explained how a relatively high proportion of graduates from certain *bingtuan* high schools during the early 1980s made their way into respectable, or even elite, social positions. In doing so, she highlighted how small differences in spatial and temporal positioning can dramatically influence an individual's life course. Jing was born and raised on a relatively developed *bingtuan* regiment close to the *bingtuan* capital Shihezi, in North Xinjiang. She entered university in 1985 and has been with Tazhi since 1990.

[Current oil company leaders who are] Xinjiang people . . . probably had a family background and living conditions similar to mine. But if they came from the countryside of *neidi*, their circumstances were much tougher than mine when I was young. In fact, when I was young it really wasn't that tough. At that time nowhere in China was really that developed, and the *bingtuan* [townships around Shihezi] had a standard of life equivalent to a small or medium-size city in *neidi*.

In the early 1980s, a small absolute advantage in Xinjiang (in terms of social, cultural, or economic capital) translated into a much higher relative advantage. Each provincial-level region had a quota of university positions allocated to them, so Xinjiang high school graduates were not competing directly with those from *neidi*; they competed only among themselves. Consequently, graduates from high schools in relatively well-off *bingtuan* townships, like those around Shihezi where Jing and her husband Ren grew up, were afforded chances that may be characterized as above their position when compared to a child with a similar family background who grew up in *neidi*. "Over 80%" of Ren and Jing's fellow students were allocated university positions, in an era (early 1980s) where the average nationwide intake was less than 3% of applicants. All former classmates whose career Jing is still following are comfortably well-off with at least above-average status jobs. In 2010 Jing herself was a section chief (*kezhang* 科长) in the Tarim Oilfield Company, and Ren was a vice director (*fu chuzhang* 副处长). Combined with the tendencies of job placement to put the graduate back where they came from, along with many Xinjiang graduates' own preference (or at least willingness) for returning to Xinjiang, the above-listed factors help explain the disproportionate number of *bingtuan* children who got into the Tarim Oilfield Company in the first few years. Later *bingtuan* cohorts did not enjoy the same relative advantage: as standards of living in eastern China crept up through the 1980s and 1990s, even on Xinjiang's better *bingtuan* farms, they stagnated. *Bingtuan* areas in South Xinjiang, where most ex-*bingtuan* Han in Korla hail from, have always lagged behind those in North Xinjiang.

Back to the Bingtuan

In January 2010 I took a trip out to the 29th Regiment with Jia and his daughter, Jing, and Ren. The three adults were old friends, having met at university. We drove out through the salty semidesert in Jia's white Land Cruiser, and a minor *bingtuan* official met us at an empty crossroads in a newly developed part of the regiment. It was explained to me that this was the New Regimental Headquarters and that the museum we were first to visit was at the Old Regimental Headquarters. "There is also an Old Old Regimental Headquarters," said someone, and someone else explained, "Yes, it has moved twice." Always, the move was further up

CHAPTER TWO

2.3 The cinema at the Old Regimental Headquarters. The woman foreground and the man to the left are *bingtuan* residents, and the group near the Land Cruiser to the right are the oil company people I was with—Jia, Ren, and Jing.

the very slight slope toward the mountains, the railway, the main Korla-Kuche Road, and the canal, and away from the geographical center of the regiment. The places Jia located his memories were all down there on the perfectly flat land, with its derelict buildings and discarded people.

According to my ex-*bingtuan* now oil company guides, in the late 1970s the 29th Regiment boasted "the best cinema south of the Tianshan—better even than the cinemas in Korla city." The cinema is located next to the Old Regimental Headquarters building, and both are apparently unused. The two or three people I saw did not exchange words with us or with each other. Individual personal space was expansive, respected, and jealously guarded. The Old Regimental Headquarters was surprisingly dust free, and there was an almost cryogenic stillness to the place and the atmosphere it produced. It was like a theme park out of season, a sort of underworld.

We visited a couple of abandoned schools. The primary school apparently had people living in parts of it. Some of them watched from a distance while Jia described how the classroom had never had any glass in the windows. In winter, it was the students' responsibility to replace the newspaper in the windows when it got blown out. One of the residents, a short man dressed in an army tunic and walking with a limp, was following us around the primary school. Everybody in our party ignored him, but when we made to leave, he protested. It seemed that he wanted some explanation of our purpose. The mood of figure 2.5 comes from the tension created by this man confronting something that he has no explanation for. Our visit could mean change—and change, for this man and other ordinary rural members of the *bingtuan*, has rarely been positive for the past three decades.

We got a similar response when we visited the shop near where Jia's mother and father used to live. There was a palpable suspicion on the part of *bingtuan* locals until Jia's connection with that place was established—then it was all "have a seat," and "would you like something to drink?" But we left quickly after that, and the locals, a couple of them of Jia's age cohort, watched us go. Again, it seemed like they were watching from a great distance. The distance was made greater by the physical proximity

2.4 Jia in his Land Cruiser in 2010, looking at his old high school on the *bingtuan* 29th Regiment. All aspects of the two worlds shown in this picture seem opposed to one another: outside is dusty and exposed to the elements, a derelict building, and a lack of human activity; inside is clean and climate controlled, a comfortable and spacious vehicle that will take us wherever we want to go that day, and the quiet chatter of memories being recounted. None of us wound the window down or got out of the car; as one, we welcomed the barrier between us and that particular ruin.

CHAPTER TWO

2.5 Jia's old primary school. The limping man at right foreground is quintessentially *bingtuan* of his generation—dressed in an old army tunic with a military haircut and a suspicious, defensive air.

of where each lived (Korla is only 50 kilometers up the road), and the childhood experiences that they shared. We left them standing on the dusty road outside their shop and returned to the city.

Fortress Tazhi: Spatial and Social Differentiation

Until 1992, the Tarim Oilfield Company Headquarters had been located 15 kilometers west of Korla, at a place known as Da'erxian (大二线). In the late 1980s, when the South Xinjiang Oil Exploration Company was looking for a place to set up their headquarters, they were considering both Aksu and Korla. A senior manager in the oil company told me, "Aksu offered the company a piece of bad land far out of the town center. . . . but the Bazhou government was very nice. They were very accommodating. They said, 'Whatever place you want, it's yours.'"

The Tarim Oilfield Company secured the prime piece of residential land in Korla, on the east bank of the river directly across from the center of the city. Part of the agreement that the oil company had with the city government was for the two parties to cooperate to design, fund, and construct the riverside parkland which stretches the length of the Tarim compound on both sides of the river. The farmers got moved out, first to a low grid of newly constructed concrete houses nearby, and then, when the oil company needed that land also, to a couple of six-story apartment buildings further down the road. The latter is still known as their "village." The Tarim compound today is split into three districts, numbered 1, 3, and 5, respectively (there is no district 2 or 4; see figure 2.6). Districts 1 and 3 were included in the initial bequest by the Bazhou government, and the oil company then bought out the Uyghur farmers who occupied the current district 5 for what was at that time seen as "a large sum of money."

The most significant aspect of the compensation given to the Uyghur farmers was their (partial) inclusion in the ever more exclusive oil company. Each family that had previously occupied the district 5 land was provided with one oil company job, for either a son or a daughter. Now in their late 30s to early 50s, these compensated former farmers' children are virtually the only Uyghur employees in Tazhi, and their own sons and daughters the only Uyghur children in the Tazhi school. With a few notable exceptions, they rarely hold high positions, but their

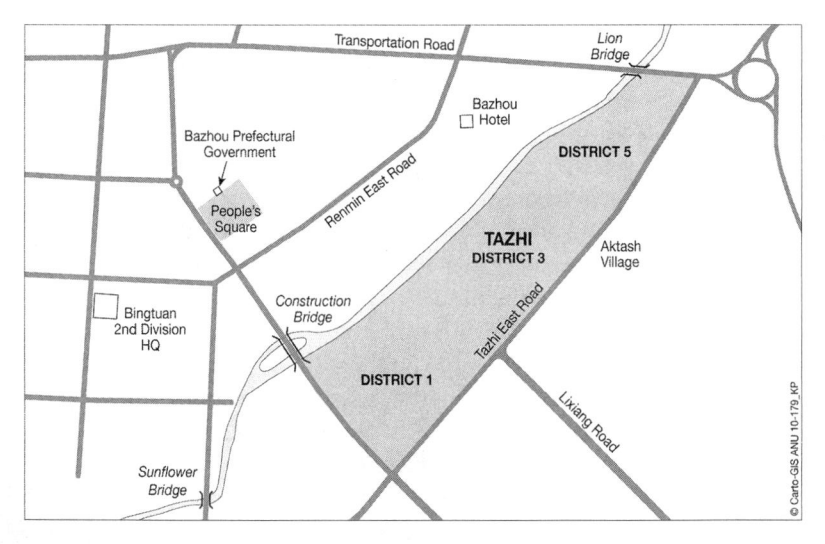

2.6   Map: Tazhi in Korla. Tazhi is enclosed on three sides by major roads and on the fourth side by the Peacock River. It is a distinctly bounded space. Southwest over the road from District 1 of the compound is the formerly Uyghur village where the photographs in figures 1.7, 1.8, and 1.9 were taken.

CHAPTER TWO

jobs are generally undemanding and, since they have been in the company a long time, they receive quite reasonable salaries. The apartment blocks of almost all the Uyghur employees are grouped together, close to a Uyghur restaurant in district 3. Although beside the river and surrounded by trees, the apartments are small and old—a reflection of these employees' low bureaucratic status.

Model Suburban Exclusivity

Even before the encircling of the Tarim Oilfield Company compound by a high steel fence in early 2009, Tazhi was an exclusive space in social, spatial, and economic terms. Today, outsiders cannot even get into the Tarim compound without passing through a police checkpoint where identification is validated. At times of heightened security tensions—increasingly frequent and bordering on arbitrary since the riots in Urumchi in July 2009—only people with company-issued identification are allowed in. The archetypal *danwei* has always sought to enclose itself in this way (Perry and Lu 1997, 11; Bray 2005, 5), so perhaps more surprising is the fact that it took 20 years for the oil company to completely wall itself in, and others out, in a physical sense.

The social space of Tazhi is suburban. Although there is no urban sprawl and Tazhi is located in the heart of the city, suburbia here is expressed through and represented by an attitude and an aesthetic. In figure 2.8, Tazhi children explore a newly built and, at the time (May 2008), unoccupied 40-story high-rise apartment building. The "snakeboards" they are riding were at that time the latest craze from South Korea. Everything about this activity and the way in which they are doing it screams "Suburbia!"—the soft drink, the snakeboards, the sports fashion clothing, and, not least, the way that these five 11-year-olds move through the space of the Tarim compound. They are "hanging out." The base of this apartment tower is 150 meters from the public play park and exercise area in district 5. The play park is built on top of a large underground parking garage, hinting at the high proportion of car ownership among Tazhi employees, especially relative to any other social group in Korla. Tazhi is the only residential district in Korla to have underground parking. "Rush hour" happens four times a day in Tazhi, most noticeably at the start of the midday lunch break, and consists of a long line of newish cars moving sedately from one end of the compound to the other. Groups of schoolchildren meander slowly homeward, dropping snack wrappings and playing swap-card games on low walls and manhole covers. Uniformed police are stationed at every intersection to prevent gridlock and

2.7 Play park and exercise area in District 5, Tazhi. This is built on top of a large underground parking garage.

2.8 Tazhi children exploring a newly built and (at the time, May 2008) unoccupied 40-story high-rise apartment building

ensure superficial order. Tazhi then returns rapidly to silence and stillness within 20 minutes of the lunch gongs sounding simultaneously in the classrooms and offices of the compound. This suburban ambience is modulated and reinforced through the daily and weekly rhythms of life: dressed-up women on Saturday morning shopping trips; the brief crush

CHAPTER TWO

2.9 Tazhi Main Street, looking toward the school and the earliest-built cluster of medium-rise apartment buildings

of the mealtime queues at the company canteens; and children playing, watched by a grandparent or two, in the late summer evenings.

Tazhi acts as a transplanted model of the suburban lifestyle associated with eastern metropolitan China and the developed Western world, and something to aspire to for those outside Tazhi. Life in Tazhi is quiet, regimented, physically and economically very secure, and, above all, exclusive. Jing noted that "once you get into this SOE, you are set for life." According to a director of the city landscape architecture department, "Tazhi is the only successful residential district in Korla" because the watercourses and gardens of the commercially built (i.e., non-Tazhi) residential districts are unmaintained, and are now dried-out and decrepit. Tazhi is widely recognized as "the best work unit in Korla," yet the oil company almost never takes on locals as permanent employees. New permanent employees are sourced from among the best and brightest young graduates from universities across China, causing locals (both Han and non-Han) to feel "left-out" of the wealth and privilege associated with the oil company. Tazhi's exclusivity is at least in part an attempt to demonstrate difference—to take Tazhi "out-of-place" and locate it in the civilized metropolitan east. Suburbia is a metropolitan aesthetic. However, Tazhi and its population are themselves products of where they are specifically located. Walls may keep people out or in, but they cannot completely exclude context.

Tazhi in Korla in South Xinjiang

Tazhi is out-of-place because it is ahead-of-time in a place that is seen as behind—South Xinjiang. Almost everybody I know in Korla has pointed out to me at least once that South Xinjiang is "behind" (*luohou* 落后). Regardless of which era we are talking about, or which aspect of life, anything that may lead to a comparison between South Xinjiang and North Xinjiang leads also to the positioning of South Xinjiang as behind North Xinjiang. They are mainly referring to material aspects of civilization, such as the built environment (see above) or the industrial and employment structure (see below). Xinjiang is in turn posited as behind *neidi* (cf. Fan and Zhou 2000; Fan, Wu, et al. 2001), and China posited as behind the developed world.

Certain aspects of Korla have, since the early 2000s, presented an exception to this general spatial hierarchy. These aspects include public space, consumption levels and styles, and a proliferation of leisure service industries which cause Korla to stand out as the opposite of behind in the context of South Xinjiang. In these respects, Korla also compares favorably to anywhere in North Xinjiang and to a great many similar-sized cities in *neidi*. Similarly, Tazhi stands out as advanced and developed in the context of Korla.

Tazhi is what has brought Korla to the level of urban spatial and economic development that it is at today. Notably, it was consumption by the highly paid oil company employees, rather than oil and gas production per se, that drove the city economy to these heights. Taxes levied on oil and gas production went primarily to the central government at least until the new resources tax law came into operation in July 2010. A local who grew up in Korla, and who is now a bureau director (*juzhang* 局长) in the city government, explained in January 2010,

> The Tarim Oilfield Company [directly] pays the city government some tens of millions of *yuan* in tax . . . but it's nothing for a big company—the real contribution which they make to the city is through their consumption, both as individuals and as a company. . . . Look around Korla, all these restaurants, massage parlors, karaoke . . . expensive jewelry shops, et cetera—that's all to service Tazhi and Tazhi people. . . . Last year, tax on manufacturing and resource extraction was 5 billion *yuan*, but tax on

services and retail was 6.9 billion *yuan*—that's a massive difference. We can say Korla is a consumption city [*xiaofei chengshi* 消费城市].

Furthermore, apart from the real estate companies that help to drive these consumption figures (real estate sales count as retail), Korla is almost completely devoid of large private enterprises.

The Industrial and Employment Structure of Korla

Xinjiang's industrial structure has historically been dominated by state-owned units (*guoyou danwei* 国有单位), a category that includes administrative government (*zhengfu* 政府) and redistributive agencies (*shiye* 事业), as well as government enterprises (*qiye* 企业). Using data from Chinese sources up to the year 2000, Calla Wiemer has argued that "the economic ties linking Xinjiang and the central government remain stronger than for other provinces" (Wiemer 2004, 174). Wiemer shows that in 1999 the central government share of investment in capital construction in Xinjiang (59.7%) was almost twice that of China's national average (32%), and the state share of gross industrial output in Xinjiang (77.2%) over 1.5 times China's national average (47.3%). She also pointed out "the weakness of local entrepreneurial activity," based on the relatively small contribution that private enterprise made to gross industrial output in Xinjiang (6.7%) compared to China as a whole (18.2%) (ibid., 174–76). This shows the historical preponderance of the state, especially the central state, in the region's economy. However, because capital-intensive extractive industry constitutes a high percentage of Xinjiang's industrial output figures, employment figures are a better gauge of the effects on individuals and their psyche.

The 2009 data presented in table 2.1 show how strong economic ties to the central government translate into employment tendencies in Xinjiang. China-wide, Xinjiang ranks fourth highest in the percentage of urban workers employed in state-owned units. Within Xinjiang, only Urumchi, Shihezi, Karamay, and Turfan report a lower percentage of urban workers employed in state-owned units than Korla. However, few people in Korla would consider comparing their city to anywhere in Xinjiang but Urumchi, Shihezi, or Karamay (respectively, the Autonomous Region capital, the *bingtuan* capital, and the base of the Xinjiang Oil Management Bureau). The cultural, economic, and political status of every other city in Xinjiang is deemed far too low to warrant consideration. The popular perception of Korla's employment structure is thus that it is state dominated by the standards of comparable cities in Xinjiang. The data

Table 2.1. State employees (*guoyou danwei zaigang zhigong*) as a percentage of working population (*jiuye renyuan*) (all/urban only), by region[a]

China-wide (%)			Xinjiang-wide (%)		
	All	*Urban only*		*All*	*Urban only*
China	8.2	20.6	Xinjiang	21.9	47.8
Beijing	14.8	20.3	Urumchi city	27.7	33.3
Zhejiang	5.4	**13.8**	Karamay city	21.9	**22.1**
Shandong	7.9	29.3	Shihezi city	31.7	37.2
Liaoning	12.9	27.9	Hami pref.	25.7	50.8
Henan	6.4	35.7	Altay pref.	**32.8**	64.1
Xinjiang	21.9	47.8	Bazhou	24.8	46.5
Heilongjiang	19.8	47.1	Kashgar pref.	13.1	57.2
Gansu	10.5	49	Hotan pref.	**11.1**	57.9
Shaanxi	12.7	**53.1**	Yili A.R.	25.1	**63**

Sources: China Statistical Yearbook 2010 (no. 1213, sec. 4-2); Xinjiang Statistical Yearbook 2010 (no. 1212, sec. 3-18).

Note: I use these official Chinese statistics with great caution, as they may be inadvertently or deliberately misleading. These figures retain the most veracity when they are compared with each other rather than treated as absolute. To check for inconsistencies within the published results, I compared these figures to other official data. To highlight overall skewing (e.g., through systematic misreporting or differences in categorization), I compared them to my own empirical data on worker numbers and wages in the oil company.

[a] 2009 figures; lowest and highest percentages in bold. The figures for regions of Xinjiang show that the more peripheral a region, the greater the state dominance of urban employment. The same is not true when rural areas are included ('All' column), primarily because of the vast differences in the urban-rural population ratio in the prefectural-level regions being compared.

presented in table 2.1 takes "urban Bazhou" as a proxy for Korla because more complete data is available at the prefectural level.

Tazhi is the latest of a line of large SOEs that have shaped Korla and driven the local economy during specific eras. In official terminology, these large institutions are called "key enterprises" (*longtou qiye* 龙头企业), and they tend to have a monopoly status. They comprise *danwei*-within-*danwei*: for example, CNPC, Tazhi, and units within Tazhi are all referred to as *danwei*. People "outside" these institutions have always been aware of the privilege of those "inside" and have directed their social and economic resources toward getting themselves or their children "in." The overlapping golden eras of these institutions have been the *bingtuan* (1954–1970s); the Third Front factories (1964–80); the Fourth Transport Company (*si yun gongsi* 四运公司; mid-1960s–late 1980s); the Southern Railway Bureau (*Nanjiang tielu* 南疆铁路局; 1979–mid-1990s); and Tazhi (mid-1990s–present). Commonly, these are not the sole key enterprise of an era but, as the most prominent, represent *groups of enterprises* which dominate the social, economic, physical, and political landscape at any one time. The workshops, offices, and residential complexes of the *bingtuan*, the Fourth Transport Company, the Railway Bureau, and of course Tazhi each exclusively occupy separate large tracts of Korla. Single-*danwei* domination is equally clear across Xinjiang—outside Urumchi, the region's major cities owe their existence to the *bingtuan* (Shihezi) and the oil company (Karamay, Korla).

Today, people compare formerly powerful institutions with Tazhi, iteratively confirming prior findings (Lin and Bian 1991; 2008) that the particular *danwei* that a person is employed in—their "workplace identification" (Bian 2002, 105)—is an even more important determinant of socioeconomic status than one's job position in that *danwei*. This perception arises because the paternalistic care that a given *danwei* is able to provide to its employees depends on the resources that it has discretionary power over, and the resources that different *danwei* have access to can vary greatly and change quite quickly. For example, I was strolling with a railway employee and his wife when she pointed out the decaying Railway Park and explained that in the past "it was very beautiful, with lots of trees and water—the best in Korla, better than the Tarim compound." In 2003, the Korla-based Southern Railway Bureau was subsumed under the Urumchi Railway Bureau and all the leadership and revenue went to Urumchi. Consequently, she said, her husband and the other workers on the Southern Railway had "nobody here in Korla to care for them." A Tazhi employee born to parents who worked for the Fourth Transport Company (his parents used their company connections to get him the Tazhi job) related how the transportation system in Xinjiang was divided up into protected markets for local state-owned transport companies. "Everything which came through Bazhou was transported by the Fourth Transport Company from here to the next prefectural center—Aksu [westbound] or Turfan [eastbound]." In the early days, before Tazhi's own transport company reached capacity, the Fourth Transport Company thus did lots of business with Tazhi. "The Fourth Transport Company's monopoly was very profitable, and they passed these profits on to their employees in the form of salaries and other benefits. . . . Tazhi is the Fourth Transport Company of today."

Central Administrative Space on the Frontier

Aesthetically and socioeconomically distinct, and ultimately controlled from afar, Tazhi is seen as a part of the core transplanted to the periphery. A number of people told me, "Tazhi, that piece of land, does not belong to Bazhou or to Korla, it belongs to the nation [the political center]." The Tarim Oilfield Company is a party-government-enterprise unit. It is directly under the jurisdiction of CNPC, itself a vice-ministerial level unit that is officially under the auspices of the State-owned Assets Supervisory and Administrative Commission (SASAC). SASAC, in turn, is a "special unit" that reports directly to the State Council (Naughton 2004, 12). The Tarim Oilfield Company has a bureaucratic rank equal to the prefectural-level government and higher than the Korla city government. Tazhi executives negotiate as equals with these governments on areas of common interest, and enjoy de facto autonomy within their own patch of ground and areas of operation. The company thus performs a range of administrative and service functions which are nominally the concern of government proper (see chapter 3). A stronger, but essentially similar, form of extraterritoriality applies to the *bingtuan*—described as a "party-government-*army*-enterprise" unit (Jin, Huo, et al. 2001, 13–14), reflecting its military origins. The Second Agricultural Division has the same bureaucratic rank as Tazhi and is answerable to the *bingtuan* headquarters in Urumchi. *Bingtuan* headquarters is also of vice-ministerial status, beneath the State Council.

The elevated bureaucratic status of these two institutions in Xinjiang is attributable to their effective monopoly control over certain resources. For the oil company, these key resources are in the first instance simply oil and gas. The Tarim Basin's domestic reserves have self-evident value to a China that is ever more voraciously consuming energy and concerned about the dependability of foreign-sourced oil and gas (Kennedy 2010, 137). The *bingtuan*'s key resources are arable land, water resources, and a rural Han population. The power and influence of the oil company stems from the strategic and economic value of the resource it produces, while the *bingtuan*'s influence derives primarily from the provision of a service—maintaining the presence of and social order among an increasingly subaltern Han population in Xinjiang's rural areas. This is why the *bingtuan* is imbued with a degree of actual governmental power over its population and land area, while Tazhi has an administrative, but not a legislative/judicial, relationship with its population. Both operate with the authority of the central government and are thus, to a significant degree, free to go about their respective tasks without hindrance from local or provincial authorities. The *bingtuan* does its primary job by *occupying* and *controlling*, and the oil company does its primary job by *extracting* and *modeling*.

Institutional Continuity and Complementarity

In the Korla region, the Tarim Oilfield Company and the *bingtuan*'s Second Agricultural Division are complementary—they perform similar functions or possesses similar characteristics but do so in a different space or in regard to a different subpopulation. The *bingtuan* farms and the Tarim Oilfield Company compound both occupy exclusive and bounded spaces. Although, at ground level, spatial aesthetics differ quite dramatically between planned rural and planned urban areas, the Mao-era layout of the *bingtuan* bears many similarities to today's preferred urban form when seen from on high (as a planner does)—a "legible" organization of space, arranged on a grid pattern, and separated from or overlaid on the previous system of pathways, waterways, and buildings.

Both the *bingtuan* and the Tarim Oilfield Company have had, and continue to have, significant effects on the nature of society and economy in South Xinjiang. The oil company contributes handsomely to local government coffers (Bazhou Government 2007; SeekingAlpha 2011; Yaxin 2011; Pathway to China 2012; Reuters 2012c), but most of its profits and the resources that it extracts go eastward. The oil company has established, and now models, the guiding aesthetic for the city. It is a metropolitan, future-oriented aesthetic. The *bingtuan* exerts a psychological influence on Han society in Xinjiang that is more subtle but no less powerful. Although the *bingtuan* also occupies part of the contemporary urban space, it is always associated with the rural past; although still held up as a political and ideological model by state actors keen to inspire voluntarism and self-sacrifice, the population sees the *bingtuan* lifestyle and aesthetic as an anti-ideal. At least 80% of the *bingtuan*'s budget has been supplied by the central government since the early 1990s (Becquelin 2000, 80), and recent reports suggest that this subvention is getting closer to 100% (Liu Yong 2010, 46). For the past 40 years the economically inefficient bingtuan system has been more or less on the verge of collapse, yet it has to date always been resuscitated by central government subvention. This cycle—of collapse and resurrection—is typical of the core-periphery relationship. Among Xinjiang Han people (and institutions), such cycles reinforce a sense of dependence on the core region, but also of their own indispensability to that core (see chapter 7). This mutual dependence has come to define one of the most significant aspects of their collective subjectivity.

Both the *bingtuan* and the oil company have been, and are, responsible for bringing large groups of people from *neidi* to Xinjiang, whether to settle permanently with no chance of return, to stay indefinitely for economic or political reasons, or as seasonal migrant workers. In general, *bingtuan*-related in-migration is to rural areas of Xinjiang—differentiating it from the rural-to-urban migration that predominates in China. Korla's economic boom since the mid-1990s, a direct result of the growth and consumption of the oil company and its population, has attracted hundreds of thousands of self-sponsored economic migrants from *neidi*. Xinjiang was the second-most popular destination for interprovincial migrants in China from 1953 to 85 (Yuan 1990), and only the major urban conglomerations on China's east coast recorded a higher level of net in-migration than Xinjiang from 1990 to 2005 (Chan 2008, 11). It has long been relatively easy and inexpensive for self-sponsored migrants to transfer their *hukou* to Xinjiang. Unlike the *bingtuan*, the oil company has no official employment relationship with the majority of the migrants that its presence attracts. The migration pattern and the type of employment that is stimulated by the oil company are quite similar to the dominant form of intranational migration in China: rural-to-urban, self-sponsored, temporary or indefinite stay, and industrial or commercial, rather than agricultural labor.

Jia's early life story emphasizes the human continuity between these two key institutions. *Bingtuan* children of his age cohort are disproportionately represented among the Tarim Oilfield Company pioneers, and thus many of them hold quite high positions in the oil company. For a few years in the 1980s, multiple biographical connections were made between the *bingtuan* and the oil company as the elite of the former were transformed into the elite of the latter. Just as the *bingtuan* pioneers stake out an institutionally supported and widely recognized claim to be the original constructors, Jia and his cohort of *bingtuan* children-turned-oil-company-workers emphasize their own roles as successors in the *bingtuan* context and as pioneers of the oil company: "We came to Tarim when there was only 300 people here. Now there are 12,000 permanent employees, and 30,000 if you include the contractor employees, . . . so you can say that we are pioneers." It is unnecessary for these permanent Tazhi employees to publicly claim they are constructors. Confident of the social and political status of the institution that they are associated with, they tend to assume such an attribution. Media reports habitually refer to frontline oil company workers as constructors (CNPC 2010b; International Oil Web 2010), and public-facing calligraphy that is part of a monument celebrating the Tarim Oilfield Company exhorts the reader to "Pay great respects to the constructors of Tarim" (see chapter 4).

The *bingtuan* and the Tarim Oilfield Company are the bookends, the era-defining institutions of state, in post-1949 Korla. These two institutions reflect the social, political, and economic context in which they were formed, have developed, and currently exist. In a frontier setting, new institutions may be "fashioned from the materials at hand" to replace the old institutions that are weakening (Parker and Rodseth 2005, 24). This chapter has suggested that such new institutions may take over the roles of their predecessors, perhaps inventing new roles, and usually modifying the old ones. Moreover, in 21st-century China, new frontier institutions tend to be fashioned from imported "material"—both tangible and intangible—as well as that which is produced locally. In Tazhi, these characteristics interact to form something that is both explicitly transformative and has itself been transformed by its presence on China's western periphery. "Frontiers," to quote Parker and Rodseth once again, "are the quintessential matrices of change" (2005, 9).

THREE

Structured Mobility in a Neo-*Danwei*

We don't worry about our future, because we are in an SOE. . . . [In fact] we haven't thought carefully about our own future yet, because I have to work another 15–16 years. DIRECTOR REN, 2010

The socialist-era *danwei* lives on in contemporary, ever-reforming China (Tang, Tomba, et al. 2011). Ironically, the processes of reform helped to perpetuate the traditional *danwei*'s paternalistic practices by concentrating monopoly power in selected, partially market listed, centrally owned enterprise groups. The Tarim Oilfield Company is an outstanding example of this balancing act between socialist and market structures—a neo-*danwei*. Like the socialist-era *danwei*, the oil company produces dependency and constrains social mobility. Yet, even amid the present-day glorification of creativity and individual achievement, the desire to enter the *danwei* is as strong as ever. In this chapter, I use multiple viewpoints and life-course episodes to explore the formal and informal structures that shape (and are sometimes shaped by) social mobility, aspiration, and expectation in the Tarim Oilfield Company. The story that an ambitious temporary employee named Mary most wanted to tell, which frames this chapter, first alerted me to how distinctions between different categories of employee help to sustain a *danwei* ethic in the midst of marketization.

Mary desired and resented status. She suggested that we meet in an expensive coffee shop with a Western menu for our first interview and insisted that we speak in English. To people outside the oil company, Mary's institutional identity marked her out unequivocally as one of the elite, but Mary saw her position as unsatisfactory. Other temporary employee women were working as waitresses before they "married into" the oil company, but she was educated at a good university and held a professional job before coming to Korla with her PhD husband. He was sent to get some practical experience in Xinjiang before returning to the headquarters of CNPC in Beijing to continue a career in research management. Mary told me that they had decided not to take an offer that her husband had received from a foreign oil company because the behavior of expats in Beijing had convinced her that foreigners were not really as "civilized" as her teachers at school and university had led her to believe. Moreover, the competing offer from CNPC promised him rapid promotion and them both a lifetime of high status.

Mary explained that, in the Tarim Oilfield Company, "your [employment] status decides everything." She noted the "really quite different" way in which temporary employees are treated, compared to permanent employees:

For example, a few days ago the secretary of my office told me to pick up a box of mooncakes before I went home for the mid-autumn festival. That day, I finished my work early, picked up a box of mooncakes, and went to my car. Just then, my telephone rang. It was my leader. He said, "You are not a [permanent] worker—you must return the mooncakes." You know, now I am nearly 30 years old—I've never had that kind of feeling. I got tears in my eyes; my self-respect fell. . . . I was hurt deeply. I was really really angry. . . . When I returned back and met my leader, I shouted, "I don't care about a box of mooncakes, but you need to be clear."

Mary noted that similar conflicts often break out around her, and she placed the blame on "the system of the company." The following day, the secretary of Mary's unit called her to announce that all temporary workers would also be allocated mooncakes, as a direct result of her "making a fuss."[1]

In this case, "the system" created a social stability problem that managers clearly felt compelled to respond to: disgruntled temporary workers have the potential to affect the permanent workers to whom many of them are married. Maintaining social stability is a primary requirement of any leader in China, and mooncakes are not expensive, so the response from the leaders seems explicable. But why the distinction in the first place? If such low-level conflicts are not uncommon, why are materially insignificant entitlements such as mooncakes so bitterly disputed?[2] On the other hand, Mary's angry words, "I don't care . . . but you need to be clear," imply an acceptance (albeit, perhaps, a grudging one) of differential treatment, as long as the entitlements and opportunities associated with different statuses are clearly defined and consistently applied. Mary's reaction to the misinformation, and then about-face, regarding the entitlement to mooncakes suggests that expectations play a large part in attitudes toward entitlements at the *danwei*. That is, the expectations that employees have of the system, and whether or not these expectations are met, directly affect social stability within the work unit. Of particular relevance here are employee expectations of treatment according to status and opportunities to change this status through social mobility, and how these expectations interact with the institutionalized constraints on such opportunities.

Yanjie Bian's 2002 survey article "Chinese Social Stratification and Social Mobility" asserts that "post-1978 market reforms and the rise of labor markets [have made] social mobility a living experience for almost everyone" (Bian 2002, 104). However, as Mary noted in her conversation with me, even in this relatively high-status work unit, many ordinary employees do not seem to aspire to "move up the ladder" and, moreover, discourage such aspirations in other employees: "When I first came and used to recite English material, many people around me were surprised. [They asked], 'Why do you study? Your salary is not related to your labor.' If I work hard, at the end of the month, I will get 2500 yuan salary. If I sleep in the office, I can still get 2500 yuan salary. This is because [the Tarim Oilfield Company] is a [state-owned enterprise]."

The distinctions between permanent and temporary employees, and an apathetic "*danwei* mentality" among certain groups of employees suggests that elements of the low-social-mobility "status hierarchy" (Bian 2002, 104) of the Mao era persist in the Tarim Oilfield Company. Yet Mary's husband has already been rapidly promoted and is seemingly being groomed for an even higher position in the Beijing head office. The two members of this family live in different socioeconomic worlds, a situation that highlights some of the key concerns of this chapter. Who has access to interfirm mobility or career mobility within the firm? What is the effect of gender on social mobility? How are transitions from "outside the system" (*tizhi wai* 体制外) to "inside the system" (*tizhi nei* 体制内) achieved or obstructed? These questions have also been central to earlier studies of social mobility in postreform China. More broadly, and as a start point that references the epigraph to this chapter, to what extent has the social and institutional structure of the prereform-era *danwei* been modified in the Tarim Oilfield Company, and to what effect?

An Artifact of Transition

Tazhi is the most recently established of all CNPC's regional oil companies. The difficulty of extracting oil from the Tarim Basin—due to both shifting-sands desert conditions above ground and complex geology below ground—meant that exploration teams in the 1950s, '60s, and '70s all failed to locate and tap a viable source. The discovery and exploitation of the Tarim number one well in 1986 is a point of great pride for the pioneers of that day, who are the oldest of the oil company permanent employees. Their success was made possible by imported technology that only became available after the start of China's reform and opening up (see chapter 4). The desert's unforgiving physical conditions thus played a key role in determining the historical moment of institutional emergence.

The Tarim Oilfield Company's institutional structure was, in turn, influenced by the time of its establishment. The reform era transformed China's already compromised and internally contradicted social contract; among other things, downsizing the workforce became both desirable and permissible (Tang and Parish 2000, 3ff). The Tarim Oilfield Company accounts for only 12,000 of China's approximately one million permanent oil company employees, while older oil fields like Karamay (North Xinjiang, began production in 1955) and Daqing (Heilongjiang, established in 1960) have over 100,000 permanent employees.[3] Tazhi did not need to lay off staff to produce this relatively lean condition—building from a base of fewer than 400 employees, managers had only to limit the number of permanent employees taken on each year. Tazhi is an artifact of the transition from *danwei*-type employment conditions to a reform-era type of social contract. By this I mean that partial transition is embodied in the formal structure of the company, as well as in the informal structures of expectation and practice, or "moral economy" (Thompson 1971), that the company and its employees create in their interaction. The formal component of this institutional structure is known as the "Tarim model" (*Talimu moshi* 塔里木模式). The Tarim model is lauded as "completely new" and a "successful practice" on the official website of the Tarim Oilfield Company's parent, CNPC (2009b). In economic and technical terms, the latter claim is fairly well founded.[4] Claims of structural novelty, however, require a more complex assessment. This "new industrial model" was built with the shards of the old.

Neo-*danwei*

Tazhi resembles a traditional work unit—a *danwei*—at its core. In the socialist era, the *danwei* "provided all essential services [including housing, food rations, education, and so on], produced economic and political dependency," and was the primary way for employees to interact with the state (Walder 1986; Tomba 2008, 51). In Tazhi, these "essential services" have been updated to the modern era and adjusted to an elite level commensurate with the company's strategic and monopoly status. Along with the company's administrative headquarters and office blocks, the Tarim compound contains a hospital with the best equipment in town, a school, a cinema, a cultural center with free or heavily subsidized activities, an expensive sports complex and swimming pool, and even a city district–level police station. Human and capital resources are concentrated in Tazhi. Although Tazhi is not an official level of government, it is seen as governmental and performs many governmental roles. Offices within the Tarim compound provide services such as security, fire protection, hygiene, central heating, education, family planning, and household registration. It is theoretically possible for an entire family to go about a normal life without ever leaving the Tarim compound.

The common statement that the Tarim Oilfield Company is "Korla's best work unit" signals that many people in Korla think primarily in terms of "workplace identification," rather than "the occupation of wage work," when assessing attained status (Lin and Bian 1991; Bian 2002, 105). Faced with limited prospects for social advancement (or even material security), many young local women of marriageable age act this out in their preferred choice of marriage partner. As a teacher in the oil company school, I was asked on a number of occasions to act as a matchmaker for local women who wanted to marry an oil company employee: "He can be divorced, that's OK, and he doesn't have to be good-looking, he just has to be kind—or even *reasonably* kind—and not too old." At the opposite end of the educational status spectrum, some of China's top-scoring students in oil exploration engineering, geology, and other relevant fields compete for acceptance into CNPC—one of the most economically powerful (and, at the time of this research, politically influential) SOE groups in China. New recruits, predominantly male, strut proudly around the oil company compound, knowing full well that they have laid the groundwork for their future economic security and privilege. A job in, or marriage into, the Tarim Oilfield Company is seen as an "iron rice bowl," and more.

The oil company does not carry out the paternalistic and all-encompassing role of the socialist-era work unit for all employees and their families. Rather, it classifies employees into three basic types—permanent, contractor, and temporary[5]—to which varying degrees of entitlement are granted. Permanent employees, the true elite of Tazhi, are the only ones to get the full benefit of the services; contractor and temporary workers are not considered full members of the "*danwei* family." Both permanent and temporary Tazhi employees have a direct employment relationship with one of the subcompanies of the Tarim Oilfield Company. However, temporary employees are not eligible for promotion, and their insurance benefits are limited to the health, unemployment, and retirement benefits dictated by national-level regulations for all SOEs. At best, these insurance benefits come out at about one-third of the value of what permanent employees of the Tarim company are covered by. Those in the contractor workforce are employed by one of the many state- and privately owned companies that provide specific services to Tazhi—these are known as *yifang fuwu danwei* (乙方服务单位) or "contractor service companies" (hereafter, contractors). They must depend on their own, external work unit for salary and benefits. Neither contractors nor temporary workers have the right to buy a (company-subsidized) apartment in the Tarim compound. This classification system is called "three modes of employment" (*san zhong yonggong* 三种用工). Naturally, a hierarchy also exists among the permanent employees of the Tarim Oilfield Company. Although technological skill, level of education, length of service (*gongling* 工龄), and area of operations are important factors in determining remuneration, bureaucratic rank is the preeminent marker of social distinction here.

The classifications outlined above are not a new phenomenon in China. Forms of outsourcing were the rule, rather than the exception, in certain large industries in Republican-era China, and SOEs used temporary workers even at the height of the socialist era (Walder 1986, 30, 48–56). Contractors are now once again a common phenomenon in workplaces across the country (Chan and Unger 2009, 4). There are specific and identifiable precedents for many of the component parts of the neo-*danwei*, but there are no examples in the literature of them all existing simultaneously within the one institution. The term "neo-*danwei*" implies a resilience of traditional socialist forms of enterprise organization and its social structures, adapted to the new economic conditions.

The Tarim Model

The core of the Tarim model is an operating principle known as "two new and two high" (*liang xin liang gao* 两新两高). The two "high" aspects are high standards (*gao shuiping* 高水平) and high returns (*gao xiaoyi* 高效益), while the two "new" aspects are new technology (*xin jishu* 新技术) and new company structure (*xin tizhi* 新体制). A senior oil company manager, Department Director Xie, explained to me that high standards means setting a high standard for employment of permanent personnel and requiring that they finish the job to a high standard. Since the early 1990s, new permanent personnel have been sourced exclusively from among college graduates. Today, Tazhi takes only the cream of these graduates. The company smugly points out that they have gone from a situation where they "request people" (*qing ren* 请人) to one where they "choose people" (*xuan ren* 选人) (CNPC 2009b). High returns means a high return on investment. New technology means mechanization and computerization, with one of the main aims being to reduce the workforce: "In the past we would have about 30 people in the control room, but now we only need two. This technology . . . means that we can cut off lots of employees." As he said this, Director Xie made a slow chopping action with his right hand, as if shearing meat off a doner kebab.

The "new company structure" of the Tarim Oilfield Company is unique among the CNPC regional oil companies and refers specifically to the practice of subcontracting tasks as diverse as exploration, high school teaching, and entertainment to "contractor service companies." The primary reason for such a structure is to reduce the number of permanent employees maintained by the Tarim company and thus reduce the total payout of retirement and nonsalary benefits. "To maintain our current level of production, we employ [12,000] people, but if we used the old company structure, we would have to employ 100,000 people," Director Xie told me. Tazhi outsources on a far greater scale than any other regional oil company in China. Contractor employees account for 60% of the workforce, and 75% of the contractor service companies are not directly subordinate to the Tarim Oilfield Company. While it is not uncommon for permanent and temporary employees to work side-by-side in the same small team or work unit, the teams of contractor employees tend to work quite separately.

CHAPTER THREE

Tazhi outsources a wide variety of different responsibilities, and contractor employees' socioeconomic status varies greatly depending on the type of services provided to Tazhi by the company that employs them (as well as their occupational position and their employment relationship with the contractor). Among the elite and the most highly skilled of the contractors to Tazhi are teams belonging to other regional oil companies; the teams set up companies within the Tarim compound and compete for tenders put out by the Tarim company. These teams are found in greatest concentrations at the "front line"—that is, the desert, where they work on exploration, drilling, production, and oil field construction. There are over 170 teams from other regional oil companies working for the Tarim Oilfield Company, and they make up the bulk of the contractors (CNPC 2009b). These contractors employ both permanent and temporary employees, whose employment relationship is not with Tazhi but ultimately with one or another of the "parent" regional oil companies. The permanent employees of these contractor exploration companies are well paid by their own parent company—as long as they keep winning contracts from Tazhi—but they are not eligible for all the benefits of the Tarim compound. Despite the fact that some of these contractor employees have been living in Korla and servicing Tazhi since its inception 20 years ago, they do not fall under the paternal umbrella of the Tarim Oilfield Company. The profits of these exploration contractors eventually flow back to the parent regional oil company. In other words, much of this outsourcing happens between regional oil field companies within CNPC. This system is enabled by the fact that, while there is potentially still quite a lot of resource exploration and exploitation to be done in the Tarim Basin, the output of many oil fields in other parts of China has plateaued or is declining. Consequently, many of the other regional oil companies retain excess employees, even in skilled occupations like exploration.

Many contractor employees, however, are in far less lucrative lines of business. Although these employees may enjoy slightly inflated wages compared to somebody doing a similar job for a non–oil related, local company, many have no job security and receive little more than their wage in compensation. Employees of the contractors providing hospitality and entertainment services at the "front line," for example, may be migrants from elsewhere in China, or may be locals, and they tend to be young and ethnically Han. Still other parts of the Tazhi workforce that are broadly classified by the oil company as "contractors" (*yifang* 乙方) do enjoy a degree of job security but did not choose to come to Korla. Like the exploration contractors, they were sent to Korla by their parent company or institution. The parent is usually linked in some way to the oil industry. For example, Jianghan (江汉) oil field in Hubei (run by SinoPec [*Zhongguo shihua* 中国石化]) has an arrangement with Tazhi to supply high-school teachers to the oil field school. Teachers of all ages from Jianghan generally come on three-year rotations. They receive very little extra salary, and if they refuse to come they lose their jobs back at the Jianghan oil field school. For young teachers with saleable skills, quitting and returning east remains an option—especially for unmarried young women, or those who are recently married and want to have children. For older teachers who are close to retirement, however, quitting would mean a loss of their coveted permanent status at Jianghan, along with their retirement pension and other benefits. These latter have no choice but to stick out the three years in exile.

The newly arrived high-school teachers are broken in by sending them to pick cotton for one to two weeks. For the physically weak among them, this experience borders on the traumatic. They return with welts on their arms, allergic reactions to the chemicals sprayed on the cotton, sunstroke, sore legs and backs, and darkened skin. The cotton-picking excursion is framed by the oil company as character-building—teaching the soft eastern urbanites how to bear hardship. However, it is more often received, first, as a demonstration of the oil company's ability to exercise arbitrary authority and decision-making power over the lives of these conscript-teachers, and second, as a crystal-clear statement of the new teachers' place at or near the bottom of Tazhi's internal hierarchy.

The Jianghan teachers are housed in basic hotel-style accommodations, alongside other seconded personnel (from petroleum research institutes and universities elsewhere in China, for example) and unmarried graduate employees (who spend most of their time at the "front line"). The building is not set up to be homey—it is simply a place to sleep between work shifts. All the people who live there are expected, first and foremost, to labor productively, and the rooms are equipped accordingly. A double room simply means two single beds. Very few rooms have attached toilet and bath facilities, and none of the rooms include cooking facilities. The residents are expected to eat at the nearby canteen. By doing so, they save on food preparation time (leaving more time for work) and reduce the living space needed per individual. The combined effect of long work hours and the lack of a place to feel at home is that these secondments have very little opportunity to build up social networks in Tazhi or in Korla. The lack of cooking facilities is one of the most disturbing aspects of life in Tazhi for most of the female conscript-teachers. For them, cooking and eating familiar food is a central part of feeling at home, and they got very excited when my Canadian colleague and next-door neighbor invited them to use her kitchen. An entire troupe of them came over and cooked up a great variety of comfort food dishes. My colleague said that she had never seen them so happy. This deprivation of private socializing space is, at a very personal and gendered level, part of what it means to be a resident but without full citizenship rights in the Tarim Oilfield Company.

The seconded employees, the teachers from Jianghan being the largest group, are not "of the Tarim company"; they are simply being supplied (as if, or even as, a commodity) to the Tarim company in a business deal with another company. Although they have some degree of belonging to this latter company, and may even be permanent employees entitled to full benefits, these rights do not apply to their relationship with the Tarim Oilfield Company. Tazhi has no paternal responsibility toward these contractor employees, and since they are seen as replaceable, they are treated as expendable.

Selective Paternalism: Distinctions, Dependency, and Discontent

Tazhi's paternalism covers a range of benefits and services for permanent employees that surpasses what SOEs are officially allowed to provide. The popularly understood justification for this is the company's location on the frontier, where certain services and opportunities are scarce or unavailable. In other words, the yardstick by which an acceptable standard of living is judged is that of Beijing, not Korla. Aside from the cash salary, the benefits granted to permanent employees include an in-house pension scheme, subsidized housing, K–12 educational facilities and reserved university positions for their children, jobs for their spouses, and, since 2008, jobs to graduated children who pass an "internal examination." Note the strong focus on family members' social mobility. These arrangements could be characterized as a form of occupational welfare, and they clearly produce dependency on at least two scales—first, of the family on the work unit and, second, of the family members on the permanent employee.

Salary and Bonus

The salary package the Tarim Oilfield Company provides to its permanent employees demonstrates the all-encompassing paternalistic socioeconomic role the company plays in their lives. Various sorts of bonus form the major part of an oil worker's cash income. The largest of these is the twice-yearly "productivity bonus" (*xiaoyi gongzi* 效益工资), which in 2009 amounted to 60,000 *yuan* yearly for an unranked permanent employee. A low-level cadre received roughly 90,000 *yuan*, and the bonus increased considerably with rank. In comparison, even the official average salary in Korla only reached 28,000 *yuan* per year (*Ku'erle Wanbao* 2009d, 1).

A veteran Tazhi employee explained that salary is paid according to bureaucratic rank:

It doesn't matter if you work hard and he works little. If your bureaucratic rank is the same, then your salary is the same. It's only in the bonus, when the leaders appraise you, that the difference is made. But they dare not make it too big—they are afraid of creating contradictions among the people, and of the people quarreling (*pa qunzhong you maodun, chaojia* 怕群众有矛盾、吵架). So the total income difference is still very little [at the same bureaucratic level]. A little difference in bonus is enough to demonstrate the leaders' recognition of one person and warning to another.

Even distribution of bonuses was the norm in SOEs in the early 1980s and was at that time associated with "worker solidarity." Solidarity was said to depend heavily on workers' close personal ties (*guanxi* 关系) with other workers and managers (Tang and Parish 2000, 128–32). Such a conclusion may be less appropriate for Tazhi, where distribution practices apparently reflect workers' aversion to criticism by others. Workers' Union cadre Mr. Tai, who describes his own role as "making the workers feel looked after," told me, "Loss is disgrace, but a gain doesn't mean much to an already well-off Tarim employee. If you give them 1,000 *yuan*, they won't say much, but if you take away 100 *yuan*, they will be up in arms." As with the mooncakes, something expected and then taken away causes an outcry. Expectations are in turn driven by a strong sense of "natural" entitlement that is relative to one's place in the hierarchy. Workers' jealous guarding of such (perceived) entitlements reveals their dependence on the company as their sole source of both income and personal legitimacy.

The productivity bonus is not paid after retirement, but the company runs an in-house retirement benefits scheme to supplement the nationwide scheme. Retirement benefits are just one of many examples in which the Tarim Oilfield Company circumvents national or PetroChina-level regulations to provide extra benefits to its permanent employees. Mr. Tai explained that Tazhi set up an "enterprise annuity" scheme

CHAPTER THREE

because the amount paid to any retiree by a retirement fund is not permitted to be more than 50% higher than the average retirement pension in the locality that they live—in this case, Korla. Because of their higher salaries, Tarim Oilfield Company employees would have to pay more into the retirement fund than do Korla townsfolk. "At the end, if the local average was, say, 1,500 *yuan*/month, we could only get 2,250 *yuan*/month"—which would be inconsistent with the far larger wage differential. To solve this problem, the oil company set up their own in-house retirement plan, concurrently reducing the official salary (*gongzi* 工资) component and increasing the bonus as described above. The way the retirement benefits scheme is set up also helps to explain the fairly even bonus amounts: a large proportion of the bonus is seen by company leaders and employees alike as a part of the entitlement due to a particular bureaucratic rank, regardless of performance—in effect, the basic salary.

Housing and Hierarchy

The general statement that "where a person lives is determined largely by their status" is particularly clear in the Tarim compound. As employees move up the workplace hierarchy, they are entitled to increasingly larger apartments in the Tarim compound. Most of these larger apartments are built toward the newer end (district 5) of the compound. Since these apartment towers are furnished with elevators, the most sought-after apartments are on the upper levels. Different buildings have different floor plans and different floor areas (the most outstanding example of this explicit differentiation is "PhD Building"). Thus, a glance at the three numbers (district, building, floor/apartment) that make up the address of a Tarim employee tells the viewer something very clear about that employee's status within the work unit.

Jing and Ren bought their apartment from the company in 1997. At that time, most people in Korla lived in *danwei* housing or in single-story houses on small plots of land. The commercial housing market only really began around the year 2000, so the idea of buying a house was alien to the vast majority of Korla residents. The heavily subsidized price of 260 *yuan* per square meter[6] that Jing and Ren paid was based on the official size, not the actual size, of the apartment.

[The company] built the apartments a bit bigger. You see, the national regulation was that an employee of a given bureaucratic level was only entitled to a certain size of apartment. That is a regulation set by the Beijing Oil Ministry, but our oil field found a loophole: although they call it "65 style," it is in fact built to be over 90 square meters.

They allocate housing to employees according to the "style" [the official designation of its size], not its actual size. If housing allocation was done according to the actual size, even those "65 style" apartments would go to section chiefs. All of the houses in the Tarim compound are like that—look at this one, for example. It is "85 style," but in fact it is over 140 square meters.

Until the late 1990s, the company provided these apartments to employees free of charge, but nationally mandated enterprise reforms sought to streamline SOEs by divesting them of their massive social obligations. One aspect of this nationwide reform required that employees purchase the apartments they lived in. Enterprises would thereafter no longer be required or permitted to provide housing for their employees. The Tarim Oilfield Company began to implement these policies relatively late, in 1997, and it took a second round of housing reform in 1999 to complete the transition. Even then, employees were initially granted a lump sum from the company to "purchase" their apartment. They paid lower than market rates per square meter of floor area despite the better quality of construction and the vastly superior environment of the Tarim compound. Elsewhere in China, much former work-unit housing can now be sold freely on the open market: the five-year moratorium on private sale ended in 2002 (Tomba 2004, 17). In contrast, although Tazhi apartment owners can rent out their properties to anybody who can afford to pay the premium of living in the best residential district in South Xinjiang, the apartments can only be sold back to the company. "Outsiders" cannot buy in, and renters can be easily evicted.

Company Schools

Education is significant because of the particularly high value Chinese parents put on their child's education as well as its strong correlation with status attainment in reform-era China (Bian 2002, 99–105). Inside the Tarim compound is the relatively small, but extremely well resourced, Bazhou Petroleum Number One Middle School. Very few SOEs in China today play such a direct role in the education of their employees' children. The school was eventually transferred from oil-company to local-government operation in 2010, almost a decade after the original ruling that prohibited SOEs from running their own schools, hospitals, and other social services. The delay can primarily be attributed to parents' (oil company employees') extreme reluctance to cede the indirect control that they enjoyed (via the oil company) over the school: school leaders complained to me that, before 2010, they "could not do anything that the parents did not agree with," so the transfer was "not all bad."[7] Despite the loss of complete ownership, the company still heavily subsidizes education for children of oil company employees. In 2010 construction finished on a completely new Tarim Oilfield Company high school in Korla's "New City District," which the company then promptly handed over to the prefectural Education Bureau. Director Xie explained that education remains "a large portion" of the noncash benefits that the company provides to its employees.

Gendered Career Paths

Perhaps one of the most important, revelatory, and socially complex benefits that the company provides to its permanent employees is to guarantee employment for their spouses. The latter are usually women who marry a male Tarim employee.[8] Sometimes these are local Korla girls; sometimes the boy finds a partner in his place of origin; and sometimes these girls are service personnel at the hotels and restaurants out in the desert where the newly arrived graduates spend most of their time. The latter category makes up such a significant proportion of the women who marry into the Tarim compound that there is now a minor industry in positioning young marriage-age women in service jobs out in the desert. This practice of guaranteeing spouse employment can be seen as the genealogical successor to the mass state-organized[9] migration of young women to the borderlands of Xinjiang, Heilongjiang, and Inner Mongolia in the 1950s and '60s in order to provide wives to the pioneers of the *bingtuan*, the Forestry Bureau, and other state *danwei* systems. The goal—providing wives for state workers involved in nation building on the frontier—is the same. Only the tools have changed, from being purely state coercion to a form of market coercion augmented by the oil company's state-granted monopoly position. The party secretary of one of two subcompanies which employs these women (postmarriage) explained, "Our work unit's main responsibility is not to seek profits. The main goal is to arrange [work] for oil workers' wives. This is the form of our work unit. . . . Every year they give us some tens of people to find work for. We just have to arrange work for them in our company, and as long as our company doesn't go bust, we are doing our job . . . As long as this oil field continues to operate normally, this practice will remain."

The party secretary insisted that other regional oil companies in China do not, and do not need to, take care of this aspect of workers' lives as well as Tazhi does. It is necessary in a small place like Korla, he said, because there are few opportunities for "appropriate" and well-paid work. Conversely, he argued, if a male worker at an oil company in a large city "can't find an appropriate wife" with a decent job, then that is his own problem: "Nothing to do with the oil company." The wives' jobs are guaranteed as a social service provided by the oil company to the permanent employee husbands. Conditions are quite good,[10] although the women usually remain temporary employees.

The distinction between a male permanent employee and his temporary employee wife reinforces the latter's dependency. I suggest that the initial decision not to grant mooncakes to the temporary employees (related by Mary at the beginning of this article) was not simply because it is an extra cost to the company. Rather, the decision was also driven by the perceived need to maintain distinctions between temporary and permanent employees. Permanent employees' sense of higher status and negotiating leverage in the domestic situation is reinforced by such policies (Tang and Parish 2000, 315–16). Furthermore, the exclusion of temporary employees from entitlement to mooncakes may even be a validation of some permanent employees' feelings on who should be entitled to what and when—namely, the everyday politics of distribution. The same pattern is then easily followed when it comes to managing and distributing other, perhaps more significant, entitlements and opportunities. More broadly, and undergirding everything mentioned above, such distributions are a restatement of what everybody already knows—that is, who is of the *danwei* family and who is not. Conversely, the mooncakes' real value to the temporary employee recipient is in their *symbolic* inclusion of the recipient in the "family" of the work unit, and in the entitlements' implied statement that the worth of the temporary employee is equal to that of the permanent employee whom they work beside—or are married to.

Oil company promotion practices also affect the career mobility, status, and domestic bargaining position of women who are permanent employees. Daisy, a permanent employee teacher whose husband is a rising oil company technician explained that women are rarely promoted to positions of leadership and responsibility, "because their first responsibility is to their family." The expectation that a woman will perform certain domestic duties on behalf of her husband and child means that "oil company leaders . . . cannot make women work as hard as men. If a woman is regularly home late, it will be bad for the harmony of the family." Managers appear to have succeeded in making this gendered inequality into something that is normal and acceptable, at least to the extent that it is not directly challenged: "I think this is bad, but it is right. . . . I accept my responsibility as a woman. . . . When I was young, my dream and my goal was to work in a university. . . . but now my goal has changed. Now my goal takes into account the reality of where I live and work. . . . I used to think that my career was important, but now I've given that up, and I live for [my husband's] success and for my son; his success is my success."

Daisy's sentiment was echoed by a number of other women in both permanent and temporary positions. Since they have no other option that they are willing to take, these women retreat into pragmatism. The notion that this patriarchal hierarchy is a way of maintaining domestic harmony in the work-unit compound also shows that it is perceived by the (almost exclusively male) leaders and male permanent employees as "the correct order of things" in a Confucian sense, and a sort of "benefit" (*fuli* 福利) that they provide to themselves.

Succession

Educational level is a key variable for intergenerational social mobility in the oil company, and it affects different micro-cohorts of the permanent employees in very different ways. In mid-2007 the company revoked its policy excluding Tazhi children from employment with Tazhi and, in early 2008, held the first "internal entrance examination." The policy aimed to keep positions available for the most qualified applicants, but the company had been under pressure for many years from parents concerned for their children's employment prospects and aware that other CNPC oil fields have always had a system of internal recruitment. To be eligible for the examination, a candidate must be the first child of a permanent employee of the oil company, must not have accepted a reserved oil company position at university, must be a recent graduate, and must have completed a four-year degree that is not irrelevant to the oil industry. Tazhi children with oil industry–related qualifications, such as petroleum engineering or geophysical prospecting, are accepted straight into the company. Otherwise unqualified Tazhi children who attain master's degrees overseas are also eligible to sit for the examination. The first internal examination attracted 23 candidates, and 19 of them gained permanent employment with the oil company. This satisfied most parents and was generally seen to be fair and reasonable, although many employees noted that the policy "happened to change just as the leaders' children were about to enter the employment market." I explore in detail in chapter 4 how some older employees, whose children had already been passed over, were exceedingly angry about this change in policy.

The exclusion policy reflected the reformist ideals that Tazhi was set up with, while its abolition seems to demonstrate an ongoing and intergenerational nostalgia for the cloistered security and surety of the pre-reform *danwei*. Compare this situation with that of CNPC's Daqing oil field, which inaugurated a very similar policy in April 2014 after more than a year of decreasing production and profits. The crucial difference was the policy context: previously Daqing had accepted any oil worker's child holding a higher degree. Thus, while Tazhi's implementation of an "internal entrance examination" was a concession to the permanent employees, Daqing's implementation of the examination was a limitation. In response, about 2,000 Daqing employees and some of their children protested outside the company headquarters, accusing the leadership of corruption and mismanagement and demanding that the examination requirement be dropped. The protesters expressed a strong sense of entitlement: "We are the children of the oil company; going to work in the oil company is as natural as returning home" (Chen 2014; *Renmin Ribao* 2014b). On the second day, hundreds of police were brought in from Daqing City and the protest met with a forceful crackdown. Emotions were running high: one side saw the reproduction of the family at stake, while the other saw the survival of the corporation at stake. This was a collision between paternalistic and merit-based ideologies of redistribution. The official line was published in the *People's Daily* more than three weeks later: "guaranteed job assignments for children of oil workers have not existed for a long time." However, the persistence of what the same author pejoratively termed a "strong oil field complex"—a sense of entitlement that combines the *danwei* paternalism of the Mao era with the high salaries and extra benefits of the reform era—was a result of Daqing's hiring practices, which amounted to guaranteed job assignments, irrespective of the official line (Lin 2014; *Renmin Ribao* 2014a; 2014b). These examples show how shifting policies at the oil field level influence intergenerational mobility (cf. Davis 1992a; 1992b).

In 2015 CNPC centralized the internal exam and the assignment of positions. Although the first round saw little change in practice, with successful Tazhi candidates being allocated jobs back in Tazhi, successful candidates nationwide are no longer automatically entitled to positions back at their home oil fields. There are two more immediately significant things about these CNPC-wide reforms. First, the reforms' dismissal of differences in the succession regime between regional oil companies provides an opportunity to impose the most stringent standards—in this case, those of Tazhi—across the board. Second, the reforms erode regional oil companies' independence from CNPC and from the central authorities.

CHAPTER THREE

In Xinjiang, such centralization of political and bureaucratic power augments normalization—even as, in certain respects, the frontier institution is itself the model.

Formal Distinctions

The complex social, economic, and spatial distinctions that separate the oil company workforce from its social surrounds and differentiate within that workforce were emphasized and formalized in early 2009 with the issuing of "smart" identity cards to all people who live or work in the Tarim compound. The card system is an accurate reflection of how the company sees its relationship with, and obligations to, the various sectors of its workforce. Socioeconomic and spatial boundaries had always existed, but prior to the card issue the social boundaries could occasionally be ignored, and the spatial boundaries had been porous.

The Universal-Use Card (*yi ka tong* 一卡通) is a technology that not only helps to monitor, control, and differentiate the population but also helps to create a desire in the population to be classified as internal to the system—*and thus to be controlled themselves*. The Universal-Use Card allows the user to enter the compound through the security gates that lead to the public area of the riverbank, permits access to that user's stairwell and to sporting and recreational facilities, and acts as a debit card for paying residential management and utilities fees, purchasing goods from the company supermarkets, and paying for meals at the subsidized company canteens. Each use of a card—when, where, and for what purpose—is recorded and compiled in a central database. Should the oil company leaders desire it, they could order the production of a constantly updated cadastral map of certain types of actions made by the Tazhi population. As "legibility is a condition of manipulation" (Scott 1998, 183), the information provided by these smart cards clearly has profound implications for the maintenance of social order.

Equally as significant is the card's explicit role in maintaining a *particular* social order by classifying and identifying their holders as either A-, B-, or C-grade citizens. The highest rank, A, is issued only to permanent employees of the Tarim Oilfield Company, and A card holders are able to use the full range of company facilities. B cards are subsidiary to an A card—they are for children and spouses of A card holders and have all the same rights as the A card, except that fees for certain services like the exclusive swimming pool must be charged against an A card. C cards are issued to contractors and others who need to access the Tarim compound to work, including the Jianghan teachers and the foreign English teachers. Besides access to the compound, the only distinguishing right that C card holders are entitled to is use of the company canteen. Bound up as it is with citizenship rights and an implicit hierarchy of worth, the card system immediately became a status structure and a source of resentment.

Intimate Distinctions

The Tarim model, particularly the "new company structure," is the key to enabling Tazhi to perform roles and fulfill responsibilities which appear, on the surface, to be at odds. Director Xie makes the Tarim Oilfield Company sound very much like a "market-oriented neoliberal" corporation in the US and British mold (Chan and Unger 2009, 3). In distinguishing Tazhi from the typical picture of a Chinese SOE, with massive amounts of employees and burdensome social responsibilities, he rearticulates company discourse. However, the social and economic value of the noncash benefits due to permanent employees of the Tarim Oilfield Company would appear to undermine the apparently genuine attempts to shed Tazhi's social responsibility and reduce employee numbers. These two apparently adverse characterizations can be reconciled thus: rather than the many types of benefits undermining the streamlining effort, the streamlining effort enables the benefits to be provided. At the core of the streamlining effort is the "three modes of employment" system of classification. Only a relatively small number of people, either working or retired, count as full citizens of the Tarim Oilfield Company. The streamlining is not a means to a single end—that is, greater profits—but a means to dual ends which are both important, namely, (1) profits and (2) benefits for permanent employees.

The structure of the Tarim Oilfield Company both distinguishes it from the socialist-era *danwei* and shows its origins in the mode of governance that the *danwei* exemplified. Tazhi is paternalism wrapped in a profit imperative. But while some of the paternalistic characteristics of the Tarim company are surprisingly persistent, others echo *danwei* tradition in their purpose but date from the reform era. These latter, including the internal examination and the in-house retirement benefits scheme, can be thought of as *reconstituted*—"the transformation of tradition" (Bøckman 1998, 311). Reconstituted benefits exist alongside change and continuity but take a new form that connects the world inside with the world outside. This dynamic combination contributes to making Tazhi a unique institution, a neo-*danwei*.

CHAPTER THREE

What might be called the outer and inner discourses of the Tarim Oilfield Company—respectively, corporate profit and corporate paternalism—converge in oil company cadres' explanations of this system of distinctions and related benefits. Mr. Tai argued that in order to "attract and keep skilled employees, we need to offer these extra salary benefits, because Xinjiang is not attractive to people to come and live." Director Xie explained, "We are profitable, so we are justified in passing on this affluence to our employees. . . . Another thing is that skilled people will stay on with the enterprise, not betray it." His argument unites the shareholder logic of the market with the "one big family" logic of the socialist-era *danwei*. But it should also be clear by now that the operationalization of this selective paternalism is closely tied up with certain intimate distinctions, within the immediate family as well as between coworkers. These distinctions shape the sort of social mobility available to different categories of people associated with the oil company.

Micro-cohorts and Mobility

There are distinct differences in the opportunities available to people in age cohorts that are separated by only a few years and thus differences in the degree of their present employment mobility. Take for example the story of Director Xie, who grew up in a small town in Gansu and gained entrance to Xi'an Petroleum College in 1988. He scored highly in the final exams and, instead of choosing to move up in the spatial hierarchy of China by choosing an assignment in eastern China (as most students of that era wanted), he chose to go to the Tarim oil field. He made the decision in 1990, two years before graduating, and he applied for a position in writing at that time.

I heard that a particular well, Tazhong No. 1, had a very high production of 1,000 tonnes per day, and experts were saying that this new oil field had a bright future. I thought, I'm from the North—why not work in Tarim? I think that it is suitable for me.

His foresight paid off. Combined with his unquestionable ability as a manager of people, his early and timely declaration of commitment helped him to rise quickly through the company ranks. In 2004 he was chosen to be one of 10 CNPC employees that year to receive postgraduate MBA education in the United States. Xie estimated the cost (Tazhi footed the bill) to be approximately one million *yuan*, without taking into account lost productivity during his three years of study leave. He signed a contract stipulating that he would work for the company for at least eight years after returning. Xie's potential mobility, and the company's risk of losing him, was greatly increased by his overseas education.[11]

Xie is only three years younger than Jing and five years younger than Ren, but his success in gaining the CNPC scholarship was in part a product of his age. Applicants had to pass the TOEFL test at a certain level, hold a rank of section chief (*kezhang* 科长) or above, and be under 35 years old. Since it takes time for individuals to work their way up in the ranks, the latter two conditions combined to strongly favor people who were at the upper end of the age limit—Xie turned 35 in 2004. The difference in emphasis on English-language training in universities in China when the cohort of Jing and Ren were attending university and when Xie's cohort went to university also helps to account for his relatively high level of skill in that area. Not least, Xie knew the value of information. He used the information he received about the projected growth of the Tarim Basin oil and gas fields to direct his career toward Tarim. He knew where he wanted to go. In contrast, Jia, growing up on the insular *bingtuan* and making these decisions three to five years earlier, was far less directed. He was only clear that he wanted to leave the *bingtuan*. In this sense, psychological as well as tangible structures, both shaped by specific times and places, contributed to giving Director Xie's age cohort a distinct advantage in competing for the career-making CNPC scholarships.

The Constraints of Privilege in an SOE

Expectations of social mobility among Tarim Oilfield Company employees are status-specific and vary greatly, but at some point, most people find their ambitions constrained—if not by their own aversion to risk, then by that of the company itself. The rhetorical question asked of Mary when she first arrived in Tazhi—"Why do you study? Your salary is not related to your labor"—highlights how little has changed from the ideal-typical *danwei* of the socialist era. To the lower-level temporary and permanent workers, "lifetime employment" means doing the same job for life. The question was, of course, also a warning to her: "Do not get out of line; do not rise above us." Her coworkers were desperate to make her like themselves, as comfortably immobile as they themselves felt.

The perception that almost insurmountable constraints act on social mobility is not limited to lower-level employees. Ren and Jing explained that they too are constrained by comfort, as well as age and educational level: "We work for a state-owned enterprise—it is extremely difficult to change locations." They assured me that they have little alternative but to stay with the company until they retire: "We would be hard pressed to find any workplace that offered us conditions as good as here—wouldn't such a good workplace accept only younger people, or people with MAs and PhDs? This is about knowing yourself. . . . You can't just run wild all over the place."

Many examples elsewhere in this book concur with a large amount of empirical research that educational level is a key influence on opportunities for social mobility in postreform China (Whyte and Parish 1984; Walder 1995; Raymo and Xie 1997), but Mary's view demonstrates that education alone is insufficient. The dynamic tension between social mobility and certainty is evident in the way Mary views the career pathways open to her. Although she has a master's degree, she would need to become a permanent employee before she could be promoted. Mary complained that temporary employees are given all the bad jobs, no matter how well they perform or how hard they work. At the same time, as the wife of a permanent employee, she can never be fired. She occupies a position inside the elite but outside the core. She told me that, on return to Beijing, she hoped to get a permanent job with the oil company, but even this ambitious and well-educated young woman did not rule out staying on as a temporary employee. An undemanding, dead-end job is abhorrent to her, but the security and relative prosperity remain attractive. Such an attitude is far from unique to China, of course, but the competitive nature of the employment market and an inadequate social security system constitute particularly strong incentives to seek personal material stability in the public sector.

Social mobility beyond the oil company is available only to the most outstanding (and courageous) candidates. A couple of examples illustrate this point. In more than two years living in the company compound, and under conditions of increasing desire to get out of Xinjiang because of the rising inter-ethnic tension, I heard of only one nonmanagerial employee who left his permanent position to take up a job elsewhere. Two different people mentioned his story to me, without prompting and with palpable respect in their voices, suggesting that such action was something of a local legend, not a common occurrence. The "escapee" was a highly skilled technician who emigrated to North America. Only after arrival did he secure a job with a large Canadian oil firm, and he is now apparently very well paid with "a large freestanding house" and "a number of children" (such are the symbols of masculine success).

A second instance was Director Xie. A few years after I first interviewed him, and just as his eight years was up, Director Xie secretly quit his job to "go it alone" (*ziji gan* 自己干) in east China. "Going it alone," in this case meant moving into an executive position with a private oil industry–related company. There was not much "upside" left for him in Tazhi; he had been further promoted soon after return from the United States. At that level of the Tarim Oilfield Company, however, his skills were underutilized; higher positions in the administration were increasingly political in nature. Xie lay low and was incommunicado for six months following his sudden (but obviously planned) resignation, suggesting that leaving the oil company is no simple matter for that small proportion of employees who *are* in demand elsewhere. Moving on, he had noted some years earlier, is seen as "betrayal."

The "Hard Target" of Stability

Bureaucratic incentives to maintain stability also exert a strong influence on activity, achievement, and aspiration in the oil company. Tazhi is known to be the most strictly governed work-unit and residential compound in Korla, and its governing practices blur the boundaries between the work environment and the living environment. For example, renting out an apartment in the Tarim compound is a riskier proposition than in Korla city because the owner of the compound apartment takes responsibility for the behavior of the tenants. If the tenants breach a safety regulation, or an accident such as a kitchen fire occurs in the rented apartment, the apartment owners and all the people in their work units, as well as the tenants themselves, will be penalized. They may, for example, lose one month or even an entire year of salary bonuses, depending on the severity of the breach. This system is officially known as "joint responsibility" (*liandai zeren* 连带责任) and more colloquially called "guilt by association" (*lianzuozhi* 连坐制). The system of "joint responsibility" is an integral part of the social control mechanism within the Tarim compound and the oil company's work units. A number of oil company employees independently asserted that the leaders "put joint responsibility into practice whenever and wherever they can." Although many of these employees seemed to resent the practice in some respects, most also reflected that the system of joint responsibility did serve a useful control function.

Along with safety and security, breaches of the family planning regulations are most heavily penalized. The careers of local police officers and work-unit leaders can be severely compromised if just one of the people that they are supposed to be keeping an eye on exceeds the birth-control quota or causes a major accident. These two hypersensitive areas are said to attract a "one-vote veto" (*yipiaofoujue* 一票否决)—that is, one mistake in either of these areas is enough to stop a career in its tracks. Hence, these areas are very tightly controlled, and all sorts of coercive measures (mostly, but not exclusively, focusing on penalties rather than rewards) are deployed.

Tazhi's own imperatives of social and economic stability temper the ambitions of its employees, as demonstrated by Party Secretary Zhang's story. Zhang's first major assignment after starting work in 1992 was a poisoned chalice: he was sent to manage a failing chemical factory that was producing an environmentally harmful product that nobody wanted. Zhang had no capital and only antiquated equipment, but by slightly changing the product the factory was making, he increased sales tenfold in the first year. Zhang claims that, by the time he left seven years later, the factory's economic output had grown by 52 times.

Zhang related with some disappointment how a cadre's promotion in the oil company depends less on making outstanding achievements than on avoiding outstanding mistakes. He explained that his leaders did not want him to further grow the chemical factory because "[they] seek only stability. There is no benefit to them in making [the factory even more profitable], and there is much to be lost in making it worse." Zhang reflected on this situation, commenting that although the speed of development is slower under this system, it does have the advantage of minimizing the risk of spectacular failures. Out at the factory that he currently manages, the conditions are good and the work is not hard, but he lamented the bureaucratism: "Anything that you want to do, you have to get approval from higher levels. . . . You can't just operate the factory as you see fit—that's not OK. . . . My feeling of success is not as good as at the old factory."

Right down to the microlevel of bureaucratic succession, the system is geared toward preserving the political status quo, a particular form of stability. Section Chief Jing explained, "We are an SOE. We have to be obedient to the party. If you are not obedient, the leaders may not punish you openly, but they will certainly make you uncomfortable every day—by giving you the bad work, withholding your promotion, and et cetera." Zhang lamented similarly that "promotion in an SOE is highly dependent on *guanxi*," then reflected, "It is possible that a private company is different, that the leaders may consider ability and achievement above their relationship with you." *Guanxi* in this workplace context is itself often predicated on a leader being convinced that an underling will carry on his legacy. Mary explained,

If the worker always agrees with and flatters the leader, then the leader will choose them to succeed him. When that worker gets to be a leader themselves, they will use the same method to promote those under them, because they are the sort of person who uses flattery in this way.

In this social order, there is thus an intimate connection between privilege and loyalty. Privilege is directly associated with bureaucratic rank, which in turn is dependent on showing at least perfunctory support for the CCP.

In spite of some resentment from mid- to lower-level oil company employees toward the strict governance applied to them, this elite group sees controls as valuable—worth sacrificing some of your own freedom to secure. Both explicit and implicit discourses assert that only top-down control, strict security measures, hierarchy, and rigid rules are sufficient to keep the destabilizing and unpredictable elements of society in check (including those close by and even inside one's own work unit). Thus the Tazhi hierarchy and the system of "joint responsibility" are accepted.

The people who live in the Tarim compound are, outwardly, models of a harmonious society. In this sense, they differ from the well-off residents of gated communities in Beijing, which Tomba described as one of the "most contentious and rebellious social groups in late socialist urban China" (2008, 57–58). But they are also similar, insofar as the Tarim compound provides a tangible model of socioeconomic aspiration. Although the model can create resentment, its presence at least creates an opportunity for administrative rhetoric to proclaim that material advancement is not only possible but also extant in Xinjiang and, further, that stability and (therefore) material privilege owe their existence to CCP rule and to the attendant political assumptions and behavioral expectations. The message is that if you want to be rich, you have to be obedient, high-quality (etc.) citizens.

Conclusion

All the attributes that we associate with the traditional *danwei* are present in Tazhi. These include the gated compound, the all-encompassing benefits and services due the permanent employees, the complex structures of dependence, the difficulty of getting in (and out) as an employee, and the low career mobility within the work unit. The oil company claims to have done away with more of the old *danwei* characteristics than it actually has. But Tazhi is not just a replica of the socialist-era *danwei*. Tazhi has abolished certain traditions and transformed certain others. Market practices and the reconstitution of *danwei*-like practices render simplistic characterizations inappropriate. Established in the first decade of the reform era, Tazhi is an artifact of transition.

Expectations are formed within this environment. The formal structures and managerial practices of the Tarim Oilfield Company are more or less accepted by the various classes and ranks of employees, and sometimes they are even internalized. For example, the views of some women who see their place as "primarily in the family" (Bian 2002, 103) are shaped by formal and informal structures that make them dependent by restricting, or denying altogether, their career mobility in the workplace. Second, even skilled male technicians and researchers do not expect to rise up much in the hierarchy unless they switch to a managerial career; this echoes the old worker-cadre distinction (Walder 1995). Third, Tazhi permanent employees expect that their children will be given preferential entry into the oil company, but their expectations are still lower than those of employees in the more traditionally structured Daqing oil field company. Fourth and finally, among the permanent employees, bureaucratic rank is widely accepted as a justification of sometimes quite widely differing material and status entitlements. Maintaining the consistency of the entitlements at each level of the hierarchy—rank-based equality—appears to be more important to the unranked employees than addressing the underlying logic of the hierarchy itself. Consistency and predictability are valued. For these unranked employees, being judged "not inferior/behind" by a superior is more important than being judged as "outstanding/advanced." I suggest that this is a direct reaction to the ranking system itself: employees need to know exactly how they stand in relation to the people they interact with on a daily basis. They need to know what to expect in terms of treatment, both material and social, from these people, and how they are expected to treat other people—and even whether they ought to be socializing with them at all. The ranking system provides a clear guide to these social and economic ambiguities. Thus, part of the explanation is structural: rules create expectations.

Similarly, many people choose to follow career and life paths that are constrained but allow them to reach a known, and for them acceptable, status. The path is predictable and safe. Often, they are unable to move very far beyond this acquired status. Psychological and formal dependence on the work unit makes the individuals more accepting of the rules that determine social mobility. Dependence makes people compliant and is accentuated in Tazhi by certain sociospatial factors: there are no employers out on the frontier, except other central SOEs, that offer comparable benefits; and Han people who are in this *danwei* all realize that they are at the periphery of their own empire-state. With regard to their work-unit status and material conditions, they have reached "somewhere," but culturally and spatially they are still in "the middle of nowhere."

Nevertheless, many people in China still really aspire to work in such a *danwei*, rather than in an environment where there is more potential for mobility, and more potential to shape one's own career and identity. I favor the simplest explanation: people who come into the oil company (and other work units with similar attributes) accept the structures of dependence and the constraints on their own future mobility as the price of privilege. Tazhi permanent employees are of course very well remunerated relative to those outside the *danwei*, and the search for (material and occupational) status plays a big part in this, but socioeconomic stability seems to be the most sought-after privilege. Such certainty allows planning and social reproduction in a broader environment (contemporary China) that has a history of, and is still seen as liable to, rapid change. Privilege, here, equates to certainty.

Individual, institutional, and statist desires for stability converge in Tazhi. People seek certainty in an uncertain world, and many are willing to trade off against potentially greater possibility—a bird in the hand. . . . In this way, material stability itself becomes an element of status, something to be envied. The state and the institutions of the state seek social and economic stability to perpetuate their rule or their paramount position. Social and institutional reproduction, respectively, are the nostalgic aspirations of postsocialism.

FOUR

Legends and Aspirations of the Oil Elite

[Although] there is only the bleak and desolate desert, [we] are not leading bleak and desolate lives (*zhi you huangliang de shamo, meiyou huangliang de rensheng* 只有荒凉的沙漠, 没有荒凉的人生). TARIM OILFIELD COMPANY SLOGAN

Legend and aspiration are linked because they are both expressed in the present. On one hand, the present is made up of all that is past: "The time of today is composed simultaneously of the time of yesterday, of the day before yesterday, and of bygone days" (Braudel [1958] 2009, 182). On the other, the past is written from the perspective of the present: "All history is contemporary history" (Benedetto Croce in Cox 2002, 1). The past and the present are mutually constitutive. Moreover, because "individuals live 'prospectively as well as retrospectively'" (William James in Bruner 1986, 14), past experience shapes aspiration in the present, and aspirations shape the stories people tell about themselves.

In institutions as well as among individuals, legends are selectively deployed to serve aspirations. The legend of a given institution at a certain point in time is shaped by the aspirations of that institution at that time. Similarly, the narratives that individuals construct about their lives are shaped by their structural positions and their aspirations vis-à-vis the audience at the time of telling. Since individuals' past and present experience is shaped by the institutions that they are involved with, individual legends and aspirations are also linked to the legends and aspirations of the institutions to which those people belong. Throughout the history of the PRC, this has especially been the case in peripheral regions like Xinjiang (White 1979; Frolic 1980; Rohlf 2003; Wang 2007b), where certain institutions may be era defining.

This chapter is built around the family biographies of three veteran employees of the Tarim Oilfield Company, all of whom were born and raised in Xinjiang and now have sons and daughters in their mid- to late 20s. The biographies trace the circumstances of their parents' arrival in North Xinjiang and their own relocation to South Xinjiang to participate in the Tarim Basin "petroleum exploration campaign" (*shiyou huizhan* 石油会战, hereafter "exploration campaign") in the late 1980s and early 1990s. Their narratives, driven by legend and aspiration, lead inexorably to their children and their children's life chances. Now in their mid-40s and 50s, the primary concerns of these comfortably well-off state employees are their children's education, employment, and marriage. Interwoven with their narratives are the state/institutional narratives of Tazhi, of the Chinese oil industry, and of the frontier.

The Cultural Revolution–era legends of the Daqing Oilfield have been adopted by the Tarim Oilfield Company and adapted to fit its current self-image. Two key legends emerge—a *legend of hardship* and sacrifice and a *legend of potential*. Legends of hardship claim rights or status on the basis of past hardship that was selflessly undertaken for the greater good. The legend of potential is fueled by hope: although by definition legends draw on (nostalgia for) a real or imagined past, the dominant legends of contemporary Tazhi are oriented toward the future, not the past.

Many life histories presented in this book resonate with legends of hardship or potential. These legends are all used rhetorically—as evidence for claims both fulfilled and unfulfilled. The lives of the Tazhi pioneers featured in chapters 2, 3, and 4 have been closely interwoven with the development of the oil company itself, and they project these experiences and expectations into the future. These people all began working at the oil company before the official end of the exploration campaign in 1992. They are all now in comfortable positions, but, being born between 1959 and 1971, the conditions under which they grew up varied immensely. Partly as a consequence, their educational attainment ranges from only two years of secondary school (Wu) to an MBA earned at an American university (Xie). Education is a primary object of aspiration and regret for people throughout this book (and many others in China) because it is seen as the key to attainment of high socioeconomic status.

Educational attainment is a particularly important, albeit complex, object of analysis because it is at once cause and effect in the life course. Moreover, as an effect, educational attainment has causal elements of both structure and agency: opportunity, however small, is a necessary but not sufficient condition for educational attainment, which depends also on what an individual *does*.

Along with educational level, key influences on the life courses of Tazhi pioneers include gender, time of entry into the workforce, age cohort or micro-cohort, and the informal connections and economic capital that their families could draw on. These individuals' respective places of birth modify the socioeconomic effect of the above factors—to be understood, cohorts must be spatially as well as temporally defined. All these factors are in some way structural, yet the narratives repeatedly demonstrate the exercise of agency *within* structure. Structures may also be unexpectedly twisted: in the final section, I draw again on the narrative of Mr. Jia to show that chance is sometimes perceived as a concept on the same level as structure and agency.

Ren and Jing: The Making and Remaking of Xinjiang People

The intersecting life-history narratives of Ren and Jing span the "major social and cultural transformations" (Fischer 1991, 25) of the past 100 or so years in western China, and are at once a victorious and a fatalistic retelling of these transformations. Ren began:

My father's older brother was conscripted into the Nationalist army and, because he was married, my father took his place. He was willing to do that for his brother. They both had exactly the same name—Ren Dashi. The Nationalists sent my father to Xinjiang. He took part in the September 25 [1949] mutiny and changed sides to the PLA, later becoming one of the first *bingtuan* pioneers.

In official as well as public discourse, the negotiated mass defection of Nationalist forces to the incoming Communists (led by Wang Zhen) on September 25, 1949, is framed as a "mutiny" (*qiyi* 起义) (Mu 2008, 157) that led to the "peaceful liberation" of Xinjiang. The frame of "mutiny" served to legitimize the mass incorporation of these 100,000 or so Nationalist soldiers directly into the PLA. The vast majority of these combined armies—the "bandit army" that Jia referred to—then became the very first *bingtuan* pioneers. Ren's father was settled on the 133rd Regiment near Shihezi in North Xinjiang. They built everything from

4.1 Ren's family, Shihezi, early 1980s, just before his father died. Ren's father is seated, center, with bald head; his mother is to the right of his father. Surrounding them are their children, including Ren's mother's children and stepchildren from her former marriage who fled with her to Xinjiang. Ren himself is back row, third from left.

scratch; the arid land was barely even worth grazing goats on. All around them, they saw threats—from the Soviet Union, the Uyghurs and other ethnic minorities, and from the physical environment itself. "They worked with a gun in one hand and a pick in the other" (*yi shou na qiang, yi shou na gao* 一手拿枪, 一手拿镐), Ren said, echoing an often-quoted *bingtuan* legend.

In 1960, after a decade of "arduous struggle" and at the age of 38, Ren's father was finally able to marry. The woman, Ren's mother, came from Gansu and was 32 at the time. Rejected by her father for being a girl, she was raised as a child bride by a local landlord family. They mistreated her, and she escaped by marrying a much older man whose first wife had died. She bore three children to her first husband, the youngest of which was less than two years old when the old man died during the post–Great Leap Forward famine. Ren's mother's older brother (also a Nationalist conscript settled in Shihezi) arranged for her to escape the famine by going to Xinjiang to marry an army comrade of his—Ren's father. She was to leave all her children with her dead husband's family, but just as she got on the train, she made the impulsive decision to take all three of them with her to Xinjiang. "If we are going to die," she reportedly said, "we will die together, as a family." Her stepdaughter, age 17 at the time, was in love with a boy that the former (now dead) husband's family would not permit the girl to marry. The young lovers (along with a male cousin) also jumped on the Xinjiang-bound train at the last minute, and they all settled down on the *bingtuan* farm outside of Shihezi, where Ren's father worked. The entire group of seven people were refugees—fleeing both the acute shortage of food and the restrictive social conditions of the Chinese countryside.

Ren himself was born in 1964, in a *diwozi* (地窝子)—a house dug partly into the ground. These houses, which are synonymous with the early years of the *bingtuan*, did not require lots of building materials to construct and were relatively warm in winter and cool in summer. (A super-basic version of the *diwozi* also forms part of the legend of Daqing oil field [Sun 2007, 105].) The facilities were exceedingly basic, and on those occasions when it did rain heavily, the houses tended to fill up with water. Ren explained,

It was a very hard life, so my father died soon after retirement, at the age of 60. We have a saying in China: "if you give your youth, you give your whole life; if you give your whole life, you give your sons and grandsons." For *bingtuan* people, this line is extremely representative.

Although Ren's father was a former Nationalist conscript, Ren was not significantly discriminated against (cf. Kardos 2010). He graduated from high school and tested into university in 1984, choosing to study electronic engineering "because it sounded very advanced to [a boy who] grew up in the backwoods."

Jing was born in 1966, to parents who arrived in Xinjiang in 1964 and 1965, respectively. She told me,

My father joined the air force. He helped to suppress the Tibetan uprising [in 1959]. Then his entire unit was demobilized and they were forced to go to Shihezi to join the *bingtuan*. . . . The common people [from *neidi*] were not willing to go to Xinjiang at that time—conditions were very bad. But soldiers had to obey orders, so they had no choice but to go to Shihezi.

Ren mused "by rights, we should be in a different place, *neidi* . . . Wuhan, or somewhere with luxuriant foliage like that."

Nevertheless, Shihezi in the 1980s was not only a relatively well-developed place compared to most of the rest of Xinjiang, it even had certain advantages over *neidi*. My *bingtuan* informants (all Han) main-

4.2   Jing, circa 1985

tain that, by dint of distance and the more pressing need to maintain social and political stability, Han areas of Xinjiang did not suffer as much as *neidi* from the Great Leap Forward, the subsequent famine, or the Cultural Revolution. The self-contained and insular nature of the *bingtuan*, combined with its role in internal and border security, made it yet another step removed from the two most self-destructive decades of China's recent history. *Bingtuan* leader Wang Enmao's conservative policies during the Great Leap Forward helped to ensure the survival of the *bingtuan*'s agricultural economy, leading to an influx of famine refugees from *neidi* to *bingtuan* areas in the early 1960s (McMillen 1981, 79)—the story of Ren's mother is highly representative in this sense. Although Seymour (2000, 173–78) makes it clear that the *bingtuan* did not escape the Cultural Revolution unscathed, the turmoil was fairly well contained in the urban areas and among the ranks of leadership, and the Cultural Revolution was officially "postponed" in Xinjiang following the "Shihezi incident," a clash of militarized Red Guard factions, in late January 1967 (Current Background 1968; McMillen 1981, 79–81).

Ren and Jing met and became lovers in high school. Graduating one year after Ren, Jing chose a major that she "thoroughly dislikes—accounting." This was in order to be readily employable in the oil industry and study alongside Ren at the Jianghan Petroleum College. "Oil fields were short of accountancy experts at that time," she said. Her good marks enabled her to choose her major and the college that she attended. Jing's informed confidence stands in strong contrast to Jia's confusion regarding university entrance, and emphasizes the differences in opportunity structure between the *bingtuan* farms near Shihezi and even the best of those around Korla. Furthermore, because "the quality of teaching and equipment in Xinjiang was relatively behind *neidi*," Xinjiang was allocated a quota for high school graduates to study in *neidi* universities. (A similar policy now drives a phenomenon known as *gaokao yimin* (高考移民)—*neidi* students attending the final years of high school in Xinjiang to increase their chances of a university position.) Jing said, "If we had had to compete with *neidi* students, we would probably not have been able to go to university." Especially for Ren's family, Xinjiang was a place of opportunity.

Return and Reproduction

China during 1988–89 had a job assignment system whereby the units seeking graduate employees would be listed by the university and the students, in order from highest scoring to lowest scoring, would choose where they were to be allocated work. The only place less popular than Xinjiang as a work-placement destination was Qinghai. It was an accepted practice for high-scoring students who wanted to go to less popular places—for example, if they came from that place—to help their lower-scoring classmates out by claiming a popular destination like Beijing and then swapping with their mate. Ren arranged to do just this with his friend, who had been put last in line by school authorities for being caught playing mah-jongg (which was strictly forbidden). Ren himself planned to go to Wuhan, where his father was born and he had close relatives, to look for work independently. He was already thoroughly sick of his major and the school bureaucracy. When the school found out about the swap, however, they vetoed it. "You can swap with anybody," the school told Ren, "but not with him [your mah-jongg-playing mate]—he's going to Qinghai." Since Ren had no intention of taking the quota position that he had been allocated in his friend's home town, he was now outside the quota. His original plan, he decided, was also unfeasible:

I realized that I couldn't go to Wuhan—if I did, the school would withhold my dossier [to punish me], and getting any job without documentation would be too difficult. I knew that I could only choose to go to Xinjiang. I told the school, "Apart from Xinjiang, I'm not going anywhere!" . . . I come from Xinjiang and I know what it is like here, so I was willing to come back. In fact, I really love Xinjiang. . . . *I really love Xinjiang.*

Two things made it possible for Ren to request and receive placement by the Xinjiang Oil Management Bureau. The first was that the school gave him his dossier—partly because he was a good student but mainly because national policy was to encourage people to go to Xinjiang. The second was that, being from Xinjiang, his family knew people who could help him get the complicated paperwork in order, bending a few of the strict regulations and overlooking the restrictions on employment from outside the quota. These connections of Ren's were in the right places, which was in this case more important than them being highly placed. As Jing put it, "Actually, even if you are 'going through the back door,' you still have to go through the formal channels to get in." Eventually, Ren was assigned a job in Karamay.

Jing graduated in 1989, and they got married immediately. They acted quickly because she had been assigned to work in Shenyang, in northeast China, over 3,000 kilometers from Ren. Work units would only consider uniting a husband and wife once they had been married for three years, so the earlier they married, the sooner they could start to request transfers. "We saw each other twice a year—him one time, me one time," Jing explained, and Ren added, "All our [expendable] income we gave to the railways!"

The Tarim exploration campaign began in earnest in 1989 (CNPC 2010a), concurrent with the formal establishment of Tazhi on April 10 that year. Regional oil companies all over China were sending teams to assist in the campaign to open up the desert oil fields. Jing volunteered for a tour of duty "because it was closer to Ren, and because the conditions of the exploration campaign were better—I was entitled to two family visits each year." She arrived five months pregnant, and their daughter was born in January 1991.

Meanwhile, Ren was busy negotiating with Karamay to transfer him to Korla, but to no avail. A degree of tension seems always to have existed between Karamay and the Tarim Oilfield Company. Mr. Tai, the Workers' Union cadre, told me,

When we [began to produce] oil in 1991, we needed lots of people. We asked Karamay to come, but they didn't want to. Karamay doesn't like here. South Xinjiang is a

CHAPTER FOUR

4.3 Ren and Jing on a visit back to the *bingtuan* regiment where they grew up, circa 1994.

"behind" place, and Karamay is very good, so they didn't want to come. So we asked Daqing. Daqing has very bad conditions: it is very cold; the wind cuts like a knife; the snow is very thick. They came.

After three years, the Shenyang team had finished their tour of duty, and the attendees were given the choice to stay in Korla or return to Shenyang. Jing said, "I chose to stay, and the [Tarim] company was then obliged to solve my family problems—to give me a house and bring my husband to work in Korla." Ren arrived in Korla in late 1993, and the family was assigned a "58 style" apartment in the newly founded Tarim compound.

As some of the longest-serving university-educated Tarim employees, Ren and Jing rose steadily through the ranks and now occupy respectable positions. Length of service counts for a lot in Tazhi: it is a factor in calculating redundancy payments, housing allocation priorities, and other nonsalary remunerations, as well as salary; of course, it also influences a person's informal networks. Nevertheless, in part because length of service alone does little or nothing to enhance an individual's educational status, some of the longest term employees harbor bitter feelings of having been "left out."

Wu's Story: The Legend of Tarim

The stories of two older employees who had transferred from Karamay even before the official founding of the Tarim Oilfield Company came out unsolicited one night over dinner in early 2010. They told their stories simultaneously, using the same hurt and slightly indignant tone. Although the details were different, they both felt that they had made sacrifices for the company and that their contributions were now not being sufficiently recognized. Their common complaint was the policy which disallowed their children from being employed in the oil company (see chapter 3). These older workers felt that the company was obligated to solve their children's employment problems.

Wu's story is remarkable for its consistent advancement of a commonly heard line of argument. In a formal interview a few days after the aforementioned dinner, he built a picture of generations of struggle and selfless contribution to the construction of Xinjiang and China. This is the stuff upon which the hardship legends of the Tarim Oilfield Company are based. Like an essay, the start point of being "left out" became the end point that he was working toward. Nestled within Wu's narrative are "structures of experience," which each reveal aspects of this man.

My father was a PLA soldier from 1938—he fought the Japanese and liberated China from the Nationalists. He fought in the Korean War and was demobilized immediately afterwards. The country needed people to help construct the Karamay oil field so he and many of his comrades in arms went to Karamay. At that time, their attitude toward life was different. If the country needed you somewhere, you went there. *The country was their hope.* He could have stayed in *neidi*, in a very good place like Beijing or Xuzhou, because he was a regimental-level cadre. But he enthusiastically volunteered to come to Xinjiang, to take part in the oil field construction in Xinjiang. . . . That was 1956.

Some months earlier, in my presence, Wu had told a Chinese colleague a slightly different story. He said that his father chose Xinjiang over Beijing or Xuzhou because the two latter were too close to his extended family, whom he expected would continually badger him for money and favors if he were nearby. Although the events of the story did not change, the tone of the story changes if you replace that patriotic fervor with an internecine economic squabble. It is likely that there is some truth in both versions.[1]

CHAPTER FOUR

I was born in 1959, born in the Karamay oil field. I graduated from lower middle school at the end of the Cultural Revolution, 1975. . . . At that time, our attitude was very simple: quickly start work; contribute to nation building; "one red heart, two types of preparation"; et cetera, et cetera. . . . Then there was the "Up to the Mountains and Down to the Villages" campaign . . . Mao Zedong was still around . . . so as soon as we finished school, we went to work on a farm near Karamay to temper ourselves and learn through hard work. We were there until November 1976, when we began work in the oil fields—we are oil children (*shiyou zidi* 石油子弟), after all.

We of this generation grew up in the Mao era. Our values were different from the youth of today. Our aim was first of all to make a contribution to the country, to the enterprise—to make this country prosperous and strong. At that time, our viewpoint was different.

Until 1983, I was a worker and a welder at the "front line." We endured a lot of hardship. But that experience made me and my comrades able to endure extremely difficult conditions, made us determined, and made us able to carry forward the Spirit of Daqing, the spirit of the petroleum exploration campaign.

When Tarim Basin oil exploration rebegan in 1986, they requested 22 administrative cadres from Karamay. South Xinjiang had very tough conditions. Most of my colleagues were not willing to come. So our work unit's party committee sent the 22 best, most skillful cadres, including me.

Our company did transport, and the biggest difficulty in the Tarim desert was transport. Just to get a start, you needed to get the drilling frame in, but in the desert, that wasn't possible with the equipment we had at that time. So China bought over 40 desert-going trucks from Mercedes-Benz—they were very expensive, over one million *yuan* each in 1986.

There was a phrase around at that time: "four step up, three step down" (*sishangsanxia* 四上三下). We were the fourth generation to try to find and extract oil from the Tarim desert: in the 1950s, the 1960s, and the 1970s exploration teams had all stepped up, but they had all failed and stepped back down. Now we had stepped up, but we had an advantage: China had already begun to reform and open up. We had advanced foreign equipment—those Mercedes trucks—so we could at least get in and out of the desert. Because the sand moved [unlike the hard, stony desert around Karamay], we had to remake the road every three to five days.

The first well in the Tarim was drilled for one year without striking oil. Finally, in early 1988, Tazhong No. 1 well struck oil. It was over 300 kilometers from the edge of the desert; [exploitation] became a task for transportation.

We flew in on a helicopter. On the way back, we threw a car tire out of the helicopter every 30 seconds . . . so we could find our way back to Tazhong when we made the road.

The oil company leaders held a meeting. They said, "You must not fear death—because when you enter the desert, maybe you don't come out. . . . This 300-plus kilometers [200 miles] is very tough."

I was young. I was 30. I shaved my head—to express being not afraid to die. We formed a "deserve death unit" (*gaisi dui* 该死队)—five trucks, six bulldozers, over 20 people—to find and mark out the road, and we set out from [that first unproductive well] in May 1988. It was tough going: the ground underfoot got to 57°C in the daytime; at night you had to sleep with a thick blanket. At best, we could go 30 kilometers a day. It took us about 20 days to reach Tazhong. . . . Many of my colleagues fell sick with diarrhea and fever. . . .

It is unthinkable, the changes to today. . . . I drove to Tazhong a few days ago and got there in less than three hours.

Wu's "personal legend" fits neatly into the "large-scale stories" of the Chinese oil industry, and of the Tarim Oilfield Company more specifically. "Large-scale stories," a term coined by Roger Abrahams, are defined by Edward Bruner as "the dominant narratives of particular historical eras, in the sense that during these periods they were most frequently told, served as guiding paradigms or metaphors, were the accepted wisdom of that time, and tended to be taken for granted" (1986, 18). State discourses and institutional self-histories are the large-scale stories of China. This is because, in China (and even more so in Xinjiang), the right to prescribe what constitutes official history and proscribe the telling of other histories is reserved solely by the CCP and its agents. Large-scale stories in China define the acceptable parameters of history; they define what Victor Turner calls the "consensually legitimate past" (1986, 36). Such "legitimate pasts" may also be successfully deployed by social actors in their negotiations with state representatives—witness the invocation of socialist values by the blue-collar victims of SOE reform, for example (see also O'Brien and Li 2006, 1–3, note 2; Wright 2010, 6–9). Wu directly associates himself and his family with the large-scale story—the institutional legend—of the Tarim Oilfield Company. Wu has internalized the assumption that current entitlement is implied in past sacrifice and relates this to his aspiration—his son's employment and thus marriage. Large-scale stories are thus a framework for defining how the past should be understood in the present, a tool of governing that can also be used by certain groups among those being governed to advance their own interests, and an important influence on how individuals and groups experience their lives.

Legends of Hardship and Potential

Oil has always possessed a political importance in the PRC that outweighs its simple economic value. The tension in the past revolved around the

CHAPTER FOUR

extent (perceived or actual) to which China needed to rely on foreign imports of oil; nationalistic concerns about the resources that a strong country *ought* to have under its own soil were thoroughly mixed in with more strictly pragmatic economic and political concerns (*China Reconstructs* 1956, 9; Yen Erh-Wen 1966; Lim 2010). In the 21st century the debate has changed only slightly to be one about the extent to which China ought to rely on oil purchased on the international market rather than exploited by its own state-owned companies—either at home or abroad. Put simply, the question in the minds of energy policymakers is "Do we need to own the oil fields or is it sufficient to simply purchase the oil postproduction?" The views on this differ at the top levels of government (Kennedy 2010), but China's concerted push to acquire stakes in foreign oil reserves, and the state-owned oil companies' willingness to pay top dollar for these leases (Evans and Downs 2006, 1; *China Daily* 2011; Platts 2011b; Reuters 2012b) indicates that the still-dominant policy direction at the top is based on the assumption that it remains important for China to own the means of production. Popular discourse reflects, and most likely also helps to reproduce, this assumption—national self-reliance in petroleum is a long-running and persuasive discourse in the PRC. Thus, oil reverberates with nationalism.

Important industries and institutions attract and create important individuals. As the petroleum industry grew in size and importance in China, the energy sector and the leaders associated with it became a powerful interest group in Chinese politics. The same goes for the legends that the oil industry created around itself. Although these legends grew up in pioneer oil fields like Yumen and Daqing, it is the areas of new exploration like the Tarim Basin that now carry the flag.

Legends of Hardship

The Chinese oil industry was born at Yumen on the Gansu-Xinjiang border (CNPC 2009a, 8) as a response to the Japanese naval blockade that began in 1938 and prevented foreign oil from getting to China. Initially, oil was required for the anti-Japanese war effort. Later, with Communist victory in the civil war imminent, Joseph Stalin linked Xinjiang's oil to the CCP's survival in the postwar era. Addressing Mao Zedong in a brief telegram dated June 18, 1949, Stalin wrote,

[We] advise to pay serious attention to Xinjiang, where there is oil in the subsoil. . . . It will be difficult to you without your own oil. If one were to begin work soon in Xinjiang, then after 2–3 years one could have one's own oil. . . . Therefore you should not delay for a long time the taking of Xinjiang. (Wilson Center 1949)

With Soviet assistance, oil fields were established in Qinghai and North Xinjiang by the mid-1950s, and in Sichuan in 1958 (*China Reconstructs* 1956, 7; Li 1958, 20; Frolic 1980, 60). Work began on the Daqing oil field—the star producer of the 1960s—following the first Sino-Soviet split in 1959.

With oil imports from the Soviet Union severed, the desire and anxiety for self-sufficiency in oil became even more acute in China. Refutations of China's "oil deficiency" became increasingly triumphant (and not a little bit shrill) through the late 1950s and 1960s (*China Reconstructs* 1956, 7; Li 1958; Tien Chin-Chi 1963; *China Reconstructs* 1964, 11). In April 1966, just before the official launch of the Cultural Revolution, a strongly worded critique of "the United States and British oil monopolies," and their use of oil as a weapon of "political and economic domination" against China was published in the English-language monthly *China Reconstructs*. The passage was attributed to an editor of the Guangming Daily (*Guangming Ribao* 光明日报) named Yen Erh-Wen. Quoting first from a British oil industry journal from 1938 which asserted that "no possibility of commercial oil deposits exists" in China, Yen declared with true *Zeitgeist* that:

China rose in revolt against the bullying of imperialism and the treachery of its internal allies. Swept out with the trash were the robber oil companies and their foreign oil. China will never produce oil, they had said. The Chinese people proved them wrong. . . .

The world learned that the days when China had to depend on imported oil were gone forever. And gone also was the imperialists' illusion that the Chinese people were incapable of locating, drilling or refining oil. (1966, 15)

Oil was given political and economic priority: when 70% of China's new investment in industry was directed to the construction of the "Third Front" between 1964 and 1979, oil was the only sector not to have resources taken away from it (Naughton 1988, 353). As the Chinese oil industry grew, so did the importance of individuals and institutions associated with it. Following the official announcement of the establishment of the Daqing oil field on February 13, 1964, the central government issued a statement that read in part "[Daqing oil field] has the capacity to rapidly alter the backward state of China's petroleum industry." The central government ordered "all regions and relevant departments to render maximum support" to the exploration campaign (*People's Daily* 2003). While agriculture was "learning from Dazhai," industry was exhorted to "learn from Daqing."

On February 16, 1966, again in the charged political atmosphere of the pre–Cultural Revolution months, Daqing model worker "Iron Man" Wang Jinxi (1923–70) stepped up to the podium in the Great Hall of the People and told the Daqing story to the 13,000 people gathered there. The lengthy address was broadcast nationwide by radio and television, and Wang Jinxi's name became synonymous with "The spirit of Daqing—Iron Man spirit." He began by relating the philosophy that drove him to get the job done regardless of injury, extreme cold, or lack of equipment:

> I am an oil driller. I know very well that without pressure you can't drill, even if the stratum is as soft as bean curd. . . . Without pressure beneath the earth, no oil will gush out. It's the same with men: if they don't feel pressure, they'll just float around and get nothing done that's worthwhile. But if they work under pressure, what they do will measure up to the highest standards and stand the inspection of our children and their children's children.
>
> It's not the kind of pressure from this or that leader. It's a kind of pressure the Chinese working class takes upon itself, the pressure of responsibility. . . . This pressure brings out the best in him. What a tremendous pressure it is for a country not to have oil! . . . I have never shed a tear in my life, but the sight of the [Daqing] oilfield made me weep for joy. "A whole sea of oil!" I cried. "Battle positions! Let's get the drills working." (Wang 1966, 2–3)

In the same vein as the Shanghai Youth Leader who labored on the *bingtuan* in Xinjiang (quoted in chapter 1), Wang went on, "hardships for a few of us would bring happiness for generations to come—this would be our greatest happiness" (ibid., 3). A former oil man who defected to Hong Kong in 1975 offered the opinion that "whether he really did everything that they said he did—well, that doesn't really matter" (Frolic 1980, 65). What matters, as far as this study is concerned, is how the legend that has been built up around him is appropriated and applied today.

Daqing's success was also due to the guidance of two pioneer leaders, and later key figures in the "petroleum faction," Kang Shi'en and Yu Qiuli (Lieberthal and Oksenberg 1988, 46). Both men had gone to Daqing in 1960 to initiate the exploration (*People's Daily* 2003). By 1964, they had both returned to Beijing to take up higher positions—Yu as the de facto head of the State Planning Commission, and Kang as acting Minister of Petroleum. Until 1967 Daqing was effectively run by the technocratic Kang, who "allegedly attached [priority] to production and expertise" (Lieberthal and Oksenberg 1988, 45). In part because of this ideological pedigree, by 1967, Daqing was at the center of a "struggle" over how to run industry in a revolutionary way that thoroughly refuted "China's Kruschev," Liu Shaoqi (*China Reconstructs* 1968, 42). Kang Shi'en came under attack and was purged, but he was back in a leadership position of the Jianghan oil field in 1969. Lieberthal and Oksenberg assert that the Ministry of Petroleum Industries (MPI) (and, by extension, the individuals associated with it) "did not suffer as severely during the Cultural Revolution and its aftermath as most other ministries," and attribute this to "the strategic importance of its product" and the support that the MPI enjoyed from top leaders like Mao Zedong and Zhou Enlai (1988, 84–85). Yu Qiuli and his "petroleum faction" continued to gain power and influence through the 1970s until the early 1980s, commensurate with the global rise of the oil industry (Lieberthal and Oksenberg 1988, 85; Downs 2008, 133).

The protégés of these early MPI powerbrokers continued to have a strong presence in Chinese politics at least until the ascension of Xi Jinping to power in late 2012. The political pedigree of Zhou Yongkang is particular relevant here: Zhou was the first commander of the Tarim Oil Exploration Campaign headquarters, from 1988 to 1996, and was helped to his highest position, secretary of the Central Politics and Law Commission (2007–12), by his connections with Zeng Qinghong.[2] Zeng Qinghong was himself a protégé of Yu Qiuli (Downs 2008, 134). After Xi Jinping began a concerted assault on the petroleum faction, Zhou's political fortunes changed accordingly. He was arrested and expelled from the Communist Party in December 2014 (BBC News 2014).

Legends of Potential

Daqing spirit is a key part of the corporation-wide image of CNPC (see Wang 2008), but Tazhi takes ownership of the Daqing legend to a much greater extent than other regional oil companies in China today. Although the Iron Man spirit will forever remain associated with Daqing, the primary part of the legend that made Daqing—the legend of potential—now belongs to Tazhi. Daqing became and remained a model oil field in large part because of the major role it played in making China self-sufficient in oil by the late 1960s and a net exporter of oil until 1993

(Downs 2008, 128). The steep rise in demand for oil to fuel China's development and reform in the early 1990s brought self-sufficiency crashing back to earth at just the time when the Tarim Oilfield Company was opening up deep and previously unexploitable reserves in the Tarim Basin. As hinted at in the stories of Wu and Director Xie, there was a great deal of excitement generated by the eventual success of Tazhong No. 1 well. With China's incumbent large oil fields like Shengli, Karamay, and Daqing in inevitable decline, new drilling technologies opening up new underground frontiers, and the vast space of the Tarim Basin to explore, Tazhi assumed the mantle "The Hope of CNPC" (*Talimu, Zhongguo shiyou de xiwang* 塔里木, 中国石油的希望) (CNPC 2006). As noted, Daqing had occupied this position from the early 1960s until at least the mid-1970s, and Daqing had delivered on the inherent promise of the legend. A legend of potential is less common, and a lot more valuable in material terms, than a legend of hardship. Under the inaugural top leader Zhou Yongkang, the Tarim oil field adopted this legend of potential, and in doing so drew another connection between Zhou and his political forebears Yu Qiuli and Kang Shi'en.

Self-image, institutions, and elite individuals are not the only connections between Daqing and Tazhi. Many of the Tazhi pioneers hailed from Daqing, and one of the six Contractor Exploration Companies permanently based in Tazhi is an offshoot of the Daqing oil field. There are also individual and institutional connections between Tazhi and a number of other regional oil fields (Jianghan, Karamay, Shengli, and Sichuan among them), as well as between Tazhi and the *bingtuan*. The Tarim legend, however, directly references that of Daqing, and the persistent notion that on the frontier the possibilities are boundless.

The Visual Iteration of the Tarim Legend

The Tarim Oilfield Company tells a localized adaptation of this large-scale story about itself. The story is told through a four-yard-high relief sculpture that stretches for a couple of hundred yards along the riverside walkway next to the Tarim compound.

The sculpture locates both the origins and the futures of key national-level legends in the specific bodies of the Tarim Oilfield Company and its people. This hyperbolic visual legend and mission statement is publicly proclaimed, but consumed with perhaps the greatest gusto inside the oil company (as in Wu's narrative). As such, the sculpture's narrative helps to shape the memories and aspirations of people both within and outside Tazhi. People are reminded of or educated about how their own stories fit into and help to form familiar national-level and frontier discourses—the pioneering spirit, the history making and future making, the spatial hierarchies between core and periphery, the fixed ethnic roles and inter-ethnic harmony, and the celebration of industrial modernity, to list the most overt (cf. Harrell 1995; Scott 1998). In this way, the sculpture draws direct and dialogical links between the legends and aspirations of individuals, of the enterprise, and of the nation.

The narrative opens with a strong male oil worker (Han, by dint of the fact that he displays no ethnic markers) carrying a flaming plate of gas and riding on a dragon (figure 4.4). Behind him on the wall (not shown) are camels and dunes representing the forbidding Taklamakan desert, which oil pioneers like himself have "stepped up" to "wage war on" in their attempts to find and extract energy resources to offer as tribute to the center. Flying swans and a winding stream represent the idyllic tourist spot Bayinbulak (Swan Lake), the spiritual home of a group of persecuted Mongols who settled there in the late 18th century. These people are now the titular minority of the Bayinguoleng Autonomous Prefecture, of which Korla is the capital.

The second panel (not shown) tells much the same story, dominated by Bayinbulak images—yak, swans, Mongols on horseback—on the right and, to the left, a more literal image of the Han exploration teams surveying the dry mountains north of the desert. The hard work of the Han pioneers is emphasized throughout the sculpture, contrasted with the friendly simplicity and stasis of other ethnic minorities.

Panel 3 (figure 4.5) shows teamwork between the modern, technically skilled Han oil explorer and the non-Han camel drover with his invaluable local knowledge. Time is compressed as the right-hand side of the panel suddenly erupts in a cacophony of oil fields and industry; the moon and stars icons show that men and machines work day and night. The pillar to the right contrasts this modernity, masculinity, and noise with the cool feminine comforts of welcoming Uyghur women harvesting grapes.

Panel 4 (figure 4.6) abstracts the narrative, drawing on the legends and symbols of the past to focus on the aspirations of the future. Led by a Han oil worker, four people stand shoulder-to-shoulder, ready to construct and embrace their (now common) destiny. Rather than a plate of flaming gas, the Han man now carries a plate of fresh yellow figs, a local specialty of the (Uyghur) oases of southern Xinjiang; his tribute symbolizes these most culturally and politically resistant peoples' submission to the will of the (Han) center. The five repeated shapes that dominate the panel are shaped like figs; they are also shaped like drops of oil. They are simultaneously receptacles of valued tradition and the fertile germ from which the future sprouts forth.

The center section features two panels of calligraphy, written by once-important leaders who visited or were involved with the Tarim Oilfield Company. Jiang Zemin and Wang Enmao have both made lengthy inscriptions; a sampling of more succinct examples are listed below. These are words of power—denoting and advertising, for public consumption, the oil company's pioneering status, and its cultural and economic importance to the center.

"Make war on the desert, develop oil and gas fields" (*Zhengzhan da shamo, kaifa you-qi tian* 征战大沙漠,开发油气田)

ZHOU YONGKANG (周永康)

"Pay great respects to the constructors of Tarim Oilfield" (*Xiang Tazhong youtian de jianshezhemen zhijing* 向塔中油田的建设者们致敬)

TIAN JIYUN (田纪云)

"Dare to transform the sea of sand into a new day" (*Gan jiao shahai huan xin tian* 敢教沙海换新天)

YANG RUDAI (杨汝岱)

Panel 9 (figure 4.7) is again about culture sharing (Han learning Uyghur dance) and harmony (the familiar motif of the white dove of peace). The pillar to the right of panel 9 is dominated by Shanghai's Oriental Pearl Tower—a reference to the west-to-east gas pipeline which both situates Tazhi on the frontier and defines it and its role in relation to the metropole. Some other pillars, as well as the Han man riding the dragon and a large plinth in the center of the calligraphy wall, feature a hand offering a flaming plate. This repeated motif appears to be a reference to the "contribution" of resources made by the Tarim Oilfield Company to eastern China. This contribution is framed as essential to nation building and economic development, and therefore to the creation of harmony: CNPC's main externally facing slogan is "Contribute Resources, Create Harmony" (*fengxian nengyuan, chuangzao hexie* 奉献能源创造和谐).

Korla people have a habit of walking or slow-jogging a circuit of the river and, consequently, many people pass the sculpture at least once a day. Tourists do the same, or part thereof. Many tourists take their time to examine the sculpture and read the associated calligraphy. In this way,

4.4   Han man on dragon, northeast end of the Tarim legend relief sculpture

4.5   Panel 3 of the Tarim legend relief sculpture

4.6   Panel 4 of the Tarim legend relief sculpture

4.7   Panel 9 of the Tarim legend relief sculpture

this particular retelling of Korla's nationally significant local history becomes a large-scale story.

Oh, Children! Cohorts and Education

The flip-side of the rhetorical Trinity outlined above—the legend of potential, Daqing spirit, and the opportunities of the frontier—is, for Wu, a counter-rhetorical Trinity of lived experience. It is a feeling that he and his son and his son's (future) son have been excluded from the *great potential of* the future, despite his own *Daqing-spirited* sacrifices in the oil fields and his selfless contribution to nation building *on the frontier.*

At that time we didn't talk about wages, bonuses, et cetera . . . At that time we believed in what we were doing. That is the spirit of our generation. And we consider ourselves responsible to our children.

At Da'erxian, there was no kindergarten, no facilities, no parks. . . . In Karamay there was everything. In 1988, when it came time for my son to go to school, there was no school for him to go to. In the end, he had to go to a *bingtuan* village primary school. The conditions were terrible. They didn't even have desks—they used bricks and a plank. That is to say, [our children] also had a hard time.

And at the end, we are now old, but our child has not yet secured a stable job or a decent position. He cannot be totally independent: he has not secured a permanent job with good benefits to support his life, and this affects his ability to get married. So we old people are unsettled. We feel that we have done wrongly by our children.

Wu's son was not eligible to be employed by Tazhi, even after the policy excluding employees' children was revoked in 2007, because he was not a recent graduate. Wu complained that "the leaders . . . won't solve the employment problems of us old oil workers' children. . . . They change the policies to suit themselves."

The Tarim Oilfield Company's policy of excluding employees' children is closely tied up with social and institutional assessments of the quality of education received by this first generation of children born to Tarim Oilfield Company pioneers. Embodied cultural capital (here, education) is reproduced in the children of university graduates (an elite group during the 1980s) far more easily than in the children of people like Wu, who left school at 15. The oil company's own school did not open until 1992, so Wu's son could attend it in only his later years.

Wu's narrative emphasizes how changing policies can privilege one micro-cohort at the expense of another, how the sacrifices made by one generation may echo in their offspring, and why cohorts also need to be spatially defined:

> You look at my colleagues of the same age in Karamay—many of their children now have really good jobs, really stable jobs. They themselves had regular work and regular work hours, and their children received a regular education. We here are different: when you go to the desert, it is 3–4 months each time.

Even if he had completed senior high school, Wu would have attended the college entrance examination in 1979, when there was an extremely small student intake. Like most of the people of his age group, he was denied the opportunity to finish school by the disruptions of the Cultural Revolution decade. In this case, five years made a vast difference in educational, and thus employment, opportunities. People who reached college age between 1982 and 1988 capitalized on the broadening of education during the early reform era and secured their place in the ascending elevator of the Tarim Oilfield Company when it was still on the ground floor.

An oil company family background, however, got Wu into the oil company in the first place. Had he been the child of a *bingtuan* farmer (like Jia, Ren, and Jing, but born in 1959), he would have had an equally difficult life, but he would certainly not have been driving his own car or have the disposable income that he now has. The benefit of having a father who was an oil worker during the Mao era was not that Wu had a privileged upbringing: it seems that, until the 1980s, even permanent Chinese oil workers did not receive significantly higher incomes or better benefits than workers in other comparable industrial *danwei* (Wang 1966; Frolic 1980; Lim 2010). The advantage was that Wu was put in a position to later become an oil worker and continue this position into the reform era. Wu recognizes that over the past 15–20 years, Tazhi employees' "standards of living have increased more" than those of *bingtuan* or other local people and that oil workers' income is "far, far higher."

Despite the relatively elite status, it is not all parents who wish for their children to find employment in the oil company and live out their lives in the cloistered security of the Tarim compound. Midway through her daughter's final year of high school, Jing seized an opportunity to send her daughter on exchange to the United States. In 2010 Jing explained how her idea for her daughter's future was based directly on her own experience:

When I was young, I really liked to draw pictures and write. But I couldn't afford to follow these interests. At that time I thought that I was very gifted in these respects, but now I'm just the same as other people. I have received exactly the same education as others, undergone the same constrictive college entrance examination . . . so now I have lost all my creative spirit. When I went to university, I didn't have a real choice. I could only choose a major that I disliked intensely—accounting—in order to be sure of getting employed. I hope that my daughter can do something that she enjoys doing. It doesn't matter how much her pay is—it's enough that she is happy. In China, I think this is still not possible: everything depends on your college entrance examination marks. If you want to change majors—"Sorry! That's not possible." It is only overseas that there are these possibilities. I sent her overseas to allow her to live a little more as an individual.

Jing's daughter was flourishing in the United States, and by all accounts living "as an individual," but she was also following in her mother's footsteps. Six months later, at the start of her final year of college, Jing's daughter was recruited by the Kelley School of Business at Indiana University. But Jing worried how her daughter would fare as the US job market continued to shrink in the wake of the Global Financial Crisis. "My daughter chose the Kelley School so that she has a better chance of finding work, and certainly not because she likes accounting and finance." Nevertheless, by early 2013, Jing's daughter was doing an internship with a multinational accounting and legal firm, and had competing job offers from similarly elite firms. Contrary to her parents' expectations, she had decided to settle in the United States; she became a pioneer in her own right. Through being sent overseas to seek the personal freedom that Jing herself felt denied, Jing's daughter began to build the economic stability so desired by her parents and many of her peers. As seen by many Han in Xinjiang, hers was a rare "best of both worlds" story.

Among the group of early arrivals to Tazhi, education is posed as a critical factor in determining current status and thus the life chances of individuals' children. Such "educational desire" (Kipnis 2011) manifests in the pursuit of more and better education, for themselves and for their children, as well as in the expression of resentment or resignation at being prevented access to quality education, which in turn prevented them or their children from reaching their full potential. The life histories of

CHAPTER FOUR

Jia, Xie, Zhang, Ren, Jing, and Wu, and their children, show that educational opportunity can vary greatly between cohorts that are separated by only a few years, or by a relatively small distance. Micro-cohorts still matter in contemporary China, and the effects of privilege or exclusion can reverberate for generations. At the very least, however, educational attainment demands agency as well as opportunity.

Structure, Agency, and Chance in the Life Course

A comparison of the way that the oil workers in chapters 2–4 tell their stories reveals a relatively strong emphasis on individual agency by those born after 1970. The youngest (Xie, born 1970, and Zhang, born 1971) claimed to have gotten to where they are primarily through conscious planning. In contrast, the older the speaker, the more they emphasized how structures shaped their life course. This suggests the influence of a broader discursive environment in which individualism (associated with modernity) is clawing back some ground from collectivism (associated with the socialist past). In other words, a defining characteristic of modern Chinese subjects is their proactivity, so those who see themselves as modern emphasize this aspect in their narratives. In the narratives of older cohorts, personal agency was present in qualitatively different ways because the perceived space for such agency was more limited. Metastructures and national priorities were the major forces that shaped the courses of their lives, and especially those of their parents, as they described them. Wu ended by quoting a well-known Chinese doggerel that basically conforms to the CCP's own "Resolution on Party History" (Central Committee CCP 1981). Most state (and now public) discourse within China on CCP history is ultimately legitimized by this document, and traceable back to it. Wu used it to emphasize how politico-temporal structures shaped his destiny:

Born in the Great Leap Forward. . . . When we wanted to eat, it was the Three-Year Natural Disaster. . . . When I went to study, it was the Cultural Revolution. . . . When we went to work, they did "Up to the Mountains and Down to the Villages." . . . When it came time for us to have children and get married, we were only allowed one child.

Between bouts of increasingly violent coughing, he went on to muse philosophically that "it doesn't matter how you look at it, human life is short . . . but . . . at the very least, we oil workers can untiringly face hardship. This traditional attribute of the Chinese people you can still see inscribed on our bodies." For him, stoicism was agency.

In practice, all these life histories contain elements of both structure and agency. Jing's narrative is a particularly good example, because she emphasizes how she decided to pursue a career that she was not interested in so that she could be in the same place as her rather aimless husband-to-be (Ren). She traded her creative aspirations for her stability aspirations. After marriage, she used the structural norms of family unification and sociospatial hierarchy to bring Ren to work beside her in South Xinjiang—it is easier to go down in the hierarchy than up. Jing exercised agency *within* structure.

A complexity to Jia's story, which I did not relate in chapter 2, concerns the key role of chance in his retelling of how he became a Tazhi employee. As Jia tells it, his own hard work and intelligence determined that he got out of the *bingtuan*, but where he moved *to* was determined by the institutional structures of that time, and, in a small but significant way, by luck. He said, "How human life unfolds is a mystery. . . . I feel that, at decisive points in my life, I have consistently met with good fortune." In this view, chance is more than merely an opportunity for agency, or merely the product of agency or structure. Although it is all that, chance has its own life.

On Jia's graduation in mid-1988, the Jianghan Petroleum College assigned him to Xinjiang, but the specific oil field was determined at the provincial level, by the Organization Department of the Xinjiang Oil Management Bureau in Karamay. As Wu's narrative makes clear, the working conditions on Xinjiang oil fields varied greatly, so Jia's family arranged, through a distant but well-connected maternal uncle, for a letter requesting that Jia be assigned to Fukang oil field, close to Urumchi. The letter was written by a top official in Karamay. Jia considered it noteworthy that "at that time, the habit of going through connections was not as serious as it is today." In other words, he was just slightly privileged in social capital, as well as in the economic capital (his father's salary) that allowed him to attend university. Jia was to present the letter to the deputy head of the Organization Department, a close friend of the letter's author, and the request to assign Jia to Fukang would likely be granted. "I carefully stashed that letter away," said Jia.

The turning point occurred while Jia was overnighting in a cheap guesthouse in Urumchi en route to Karamay. By "happy coincidence" (*zhenghao* 正好), his roommate, a drill unit leader at the Fukang oil field, came stumbling in at 2 a.m., very drunk and vomiting uncontrollably. Jia got up and helped the man to wash and get into bed, then went back to bed himself. The next thing Jia knew, the man had sobered up

CHAPTER FOUR

somewhat and was shaking him awake, wanting to talk with him: most people staying in that guesthouse were considerably older than Jia. "You are a good young man," he said. "What are you doing here?" Jia replied that he was on the way to be assigned to Fukang and showed him the letter. The drill unit leader looked concerned and, with an air of desperation, told Jia, "On no account must you go to Fukang, [because] the oil is almost over at that place. If you go there, you will regret it. I like you, young man. . . . Don't go there, you will ruin your future." Jia had been fully prepared to use the letter of recommendation to prevent himself being assigned to an oil field far away from any big city, on which the conditions tended to be particularly arduous. But the drill unit leader had introduced another consideration—the economic demise of an entire work unit, and the people who belong to that work unit, because of a downturn in profit or outputs. Jia decided to trust in the drill unit leader. When he reported for his job assignment, he did not take out the letter of recommendation, and was assigned as anybody else without special connections would have been assigned. The Karamay officials sent Jia to what became Tazhi, then based at Da'erxian.

The elements of structure, agency, and chance in this brief anecdote are tightly woven and mutually productive, although not analytically inseparable. Jia's dispatch to Xinjiang, under the job assignment system, is clearly structure. Formally, Jia was also expected to go where the Karamay officials sent him, but an informal counterstructure of personal connections granted agency to manipulate the outcome to those graduates with the right connections. The fact that Jia met an oil worker from the very oil field that he was destined for was a coincidence, but, since the guesthouse was set up and run by the oil company to provide accommodation for out-of-town workers, the fateful meeting was not completely random. By helping the driller (exercising agency), Jia prompted the man to tell him about the decline in production at the Fukang oil field and thus give Jia a chance to choose between the structured path laid out by his family connections (which would have him assigned to Fukang) and the structure of the Oil Management Bureau job assignment system (which had him assigned to the oil field that most needed technical skills at that time, the Tarim oil field).

Jia's narrative paints a picture of a young man who was always moving forward as quickly as possible under his own steam but was never really clear whether he was moving in the right direction. His agency was in his effort, and chance and structure shaped how that effort was directed and, eventually, the outcome of that effort.

The interplay between structure and agency is an always-implicit theme of life histories and is often posed as an exclusive dyad of social scientific analysis. However, despite all the structuring structures acting on his life course, and the modern-era human's desire to claim agency, Jia points out that chance played a decisive role in leading him to where he is now. Similar patterns of interaction between these three elements surface in many of the life histories in this book, demonstrating the significant effect that chance, as well as structure and agency, can (or is perceived to) have on social and spatial migrations. Perhaps it is worth considering chance on the same conceptual level as agency and structure?

Considering chance on the same conceptual level as agency and structure entails making a distinction between retrospective and prospective aspects of chance, that is, between chance occurrences and chance-as-possibility. In Jia's story about the drunk oil worker, chance is retrospective, a previously unexpected but now fixed factor that helped to determine an outcome that is already known: he is talking about a chance occurrence. Chance occurrences are the object of emotions like relief and regret. Chance-as-possibility, by definition prospective and unresolved, is the sort of chance that is the object of hope (or fear). Many of the people quoted in this book invest hope in chance-as-possibility. For example, Jing talks about enabling possibilities for her daughter, and, since she wants these possibilities to resolve in particular ways, she inevitably invests them with hope. In chapter 6, I explore the role that hope in chance-as-possibility plays in shaping agency and structure, even as both agency and structure shape the nature of the possibilities that arise.

Individual and Institutional Aspirations

These life stories do not show only what the narrator's aspirations for themselves and for their children *are* but also, and importantly, *how* these aspirations relate back to the historical experience of the narrators and of their parents (and their respective generations). The common aspirations of individuals for themselves and their children can be grouped into three distinct (but related) types: (1) socioeconomic *stability*, (2) *freedom* to develop in their career and to be creative, and (3) social and geographic mobility—the ability to leave Xinjiang for some place higher on the spatial hierarchy while maintaining or bettering their relative social status (as a member of the elite) and thereby raising their absolute social *status*.

CHAPTER FOUR

The three primary institutional aspirations (all of which are in some sense also roles) of Tazhi parallel these individual aspirations. First, Tazhi seeks to create and maintain sociopolitical *stability* in three concentric domains: (1a) within the company through organized dependency, (1b) in the immediate surrounds of Korla and South Xinjiang by acting as a sociopolitical model, and (1c) in China generally by "contributing resources" from west to east and thereby "creating harmony" in the metropole.

Tazhi's second aspiration is the production of high and ever-increasing *profits*. However, the singular pursuit of such profit is at odds with the maintenance of stability across the three concentric domains of responsibility—profit decreases and social stability increases when (2a) within Tazhi, increased benefits are paid to employees, (2b) in Korla and surrounds, the oil company is perceived to be doing something for the region and its people (e.g., infrastructure and urban landscaping), (2c) across China, CNPC's ability to influence fuel supplies (since prices are government determined) has an effect on the lives and livelihoods of literally millions of Chinese citizens on a daily basis. Similarly, the profit-equivalent aspiration for an individual—freedom to make independent choices and follow creative desires—may jeopardize personal socioeconomic stability. For oil company offspring, Tazhi offers claustrophobic safety; those who do not choose an oil company career must possess relatively higher amounts of social and cultural capital (in the forms of *guanxi* and education, respectively) to obtain an equivalent level of material well-being (stability).

Third, Tazhi aspires to be, and to remain, the crown prince of China's domestic oil industry. Current profitability and the legend of potential (rising production, unexplored reserves) are the central, mutually productive elements of this regal *status*. The Tarim Oilfield Company's image as "the hope of CNPC," and CNPC's own powerful position, positively affects Tazhi's ability to influence relevant local and central government policy, and thus the economic condition of the company and its employees. In this way, powerful others hope in chance-as-possibility enables concrete effects to flow from the legend of potential.

The permanent employees of the Tarim Oilfield Company are privileged in not only material ways; they are privileged in that they have powerful and prefabricated large-scale stories to draw on that retain their currency even in the second decade of the 21st century. Not all residents of Xinjiang (Han or otherwise) have access to such stories. Even within Tazhi, people possess differential access to these stories. The most powerful large-scale story is the legend of potential, and Wu is an example of the type of the employee who is excluded from this story. Wu is denied full access to the legend of potential because he and his family line are not themselves imbued with potential. The same goes for other relatively low-educated Tazhi pioneers, all of whom are of his cohort, since the oil company accepted low-skilled workers and cadres from other oil companies only in the early years of the exploration campaign. Wu does his best to leverage the legend of hardship, but his protests are unheeded. Legends of hardship are common fare on the frontier.

FIVE

Lives of *Guanxi*

"One more pal is one more possibility" (*duo yi ge pengyou, duo yi tiao lu* 多一个朋友,多一条路) A BUSINESSMAN AS HE HANDED ME HIS CARD AND ASKED FOR MINE

Many Han in Korla feel that *guanxi* is crucial to shaping, if not determining, their life chances. Where "*guanxi*" means "connections" (Gold, Guthrie, et al. 2002, 3), it is the nature and strength of those connections that determines the extent to which they are useful in a given situation. When somebody says that "you need good *guanxi*" to do or obtain a certain thing, they mean that you need the right sort of relationship with the right sort of person for that particular situation. Often, the right sort of person is a government official, who will require some favor in return. As such, *guanxi* networks (*guanxi wang* 关系网) are integral to the informal governance structures of the party and state and may be conceived of as an institution in the sociological sense.[1] These networks are of course created by people and therefore infused with specific cultural practices. The protocols and practices of successful *guanxi* deployment vary in different cultural contexts, may change over time, and can be learned. In this chapter, I examine *guanxi* in the quotidian contexts that it is most often and most widely produced, discussed, deployed, and worried about by Han Chinese people living in Korla. The protagonists of the two life histories presented herein are both fortysomething state-employees-turned-entrepreneurs who grew up on *bingtuan* farms near to Korla. They belong to the same cohort—in terms of their *bingtuan* backgrounds and age—as Jia, Ren, and Jing (chapters 2–4), and, while their socioeconomic lives diverged in their 20s, all these people have shared the same urban environment (Korla) for the vast majority of their adult lives.

These stories of *guanxi* deployment show that Han *guanxi* networks in Xinjiang are an important agent in the process of normalization, as well as a symptom of that process. This is because these *guanxi* networks are embedded deep in the fabric of Han social, cultural, political, and economic life. Moreover, being intangible but with very tangible effects, *guanxi* networks are both resilient and transformative. I am not presenting an argument for the essential Han-ness of *guanxi*, or *guanxi* practice. Rather, because the most important power holders in Korla and urban Xinjiang are Han, the most useful *guanxi* networks are Han centered and state centered. While these networks are not necessarily ethnically exclusive, they are culturally exclusive, and they help to shape practices and aspirations: if you want to get things done, you have to do them with certain people, in a certain way. Such *guanxi* networks thus generalize practices that have been adopted and adapted from *neidi*.

The narratives also illustrate certain divisions within Han society in Korla. The *guanxi* networks of the in-migrants of the 1950s and '60s (and their children), known as *bendiren* (本地人), give them a slight edge over more recent in-migrants, all else being equal. *Bendiren* networks tend to be longer-standing and stretch deeper into the urban bureaucracy. This is because the individual connections in *guanxi* networks begin with a commonality, which may be achieved (shared experience such as work, school, or military service) or ascribed (such as lineage and native place). When two individuals can find, or produce, something in common, they have a "base" upon which to build "the affective component of *guanxi*," *ganqing* (感情) (Jacobs 1979, 243). The stronger this *ganqing*, the closer the two parties' *guanxi*. Since the nature of the *guanxi* base influences with whom one has *guanxi*, and one's own ability to build *ganqing* on that base influences the closeness of the *guanxi*, not all *bendiren* possess *guanxi* networks that can be leveraged for political or economic gain.

The Necessity of *Guanxi*

Guanxi is considered a practical necessity in Korla. This statement holds true even among those low-status people who would appear to possess very little of the commodity, and also among those midstatus people who deny that they themselves engage in the exchange of face and favor. A few examples serve to illustrate this point.

CHAPTER FIVE

The first example shows how *guanxi* is used to work around the contradictory local manifestations of policies that can be traced back to the central government. In early September 2009, I was riding on the motorized tricycle of a young migrant entrepreneur who sells live fish in the free market. Tensions were running particularly high that day due to rumors of attacks with hypodermic syringes in Urumchi, so when somebody coming the other way warned us that there were police up ahead, I offered to get off. A foreigner and a migrant fishmonger heading for the Uyghur part of town could only attract the wrong type of attention. The driver, however, was relaxed. He said,

It is no problem. The problem is that we don't have driver's licenses for these motorbikes. Originally, licenses were not needed, or at least not checked, but now they have started to check them. As people with *hukou* from outside Korla, we are unable to apply for three wheeled motorcycle licenses. But don't you worry about it. This is totally normal, we are used to it.

"What if you get stopped?" I asked.

If they catch us, they will want to fine us 200 *yuan* . . . but don't worry, we can sort it out, we have a person; we can just make a telephone call and it will be over.

Thus the central government's desire to promote Han settlement in Xinjiang meets a contradiction in its failure to enforce nationwide rights and standards of citizenship—in this case, nonlocal *hukou* holders obtaining driver's licenses. The migrant gets around this contradiction by cultivating a patron in the police force.

This apparent contradiction is quite deliberate. Indebted clients such as this migrant form a network through which the floating population can be monitored. The creation of illegality, and henceforth a black market, is a mechanism by which the local state promotes particularistic ties at its lowest level and thus reduces the distance between the population and local authority.

A second example shows how *guanxi* balances out the predatory behavior of the local state and effectively shifts the burden onto those who do not have access to protective *guanxi*. This example is analogous to the one directly above insofar as it shows how networks of protection from bureaucratic power operate to regulate social actors and draw them into a structured but informal engagement with bureaucratic power. A young man whom I shall call Yu Han has a brother who acts as an intermediary between the buyer and seller of secondhand housing. Officials from the city district–level Industrial and Commercial Bureau (*gongshangju* 工商局) came to check his office and found that he did not have his operating permit hung on the wall, so they issued a fine of 4,000 *yuan*. They were nitpicking because each bureau is given a target quota of fines to issue; the officials' own bonuses depend on reaching this quota. Yu Han's brother refused to pay, and they came back to harass him further. At that time, Yu Han got wind of this and rang a contact who is the leader of an Industrial and Commercial Bureau in an adjoining city district. His friend made a call and the fine was reduced to 500 *yuan*.

In a third example, a retired Third Front factory worker told me how he saved his son's career by matching *guanxi* with *guanxi*. His son scored reasonably highly in the college entrance exam and was expecting to be accepted into his first choice, the military college in Henan. However, a man high up in the prefectural Education Bureau had apparently deliberately neglected to register the industrial worker's son, with the intention of leaving a place open for his own son in the second round of offers. The retired man, habitually suspicious of foul play, asked a connection of his in another part of the bureaucracy to check that his son had been registered to apply for the military school; the omission was rectified and the retired worker's son got the position. If the worker had not used his own connections, or did not have them, then the son of the bureaucrat, despite his low marks, would have been going to the military college. The point is that his son had to have some well-placed *guanxi* as well as good marks to get into the military college.

The necessity that one has such protective relationships means that even those people who profess to disdain and repudiate the *guanxi* game must participate in it. A fourth example: two of my teacher colleagues went around to a third teacher's place for dinner on New Year's Eve and, just as they arrived at 7:45 p.m., the host's mobile telephone rang. It was a moderately rich and important man who is the father of one of the host's students, and he had called to invite her to dinner at 8 p.m. that evening with the rest of his child's teachers. She politely refused, saying that she had guests herself and was unable to make it, but the man made it clear that not turning up was not an option. To maintain her good relationship with the man, the would-be host had no choice but to ask her own guests to accompany her to the dinner, leaving the dumpling mix and the dumpling pastry spread over her kitchen table. Although she owed him nothing, more forcefully declining the invitation would have been taken as an insult by the man and would have seriously eroded the good relationship that they had built up. She "keeps him sweet" by implicitly recognizing his view of the hierarchical relationship between

CHAPTER FIVE

them; although she is not particularly ambitious, the predatory and opaque bureaucracy means that it is impossible to tell whether she may need his assistance in the future.

The above examples support Mayfair Yang's notion that the art of *guanxi* is a "shortcut around, or a coping strategy for dealing with, bureaucratic power" (1994, 15), at least at the lower levels of the social hierarchy. However, it is also true that the Chinese emphasis on relationships can be seen as a system that is produced by the bureaucracy and benefits the bureaucracy. The relationship between state formality and this informal structure of *guanxi* networks is simultaneously oppositional and cooperative. *Guanxi* networks do not only provide shelter for "a stubborn strain of resistance" to "disciplinary and normalizing techniques" that are backed up by the dominance of the state redistributive economy (Yang 1989, 35), they are also a form of discipline and normalization themselves. Kipnis writes, "I would like to suggest that the CCP co-opted, reinvented, and versioned practices of *guanxi* production as much as eliminating them altogether" (1997, 160–61). Kipnis's insight resonates in particular ways in Korla. For example, the local state does not feel the need to co-opt the entrepreneurial elite of the city-region as a group through official channels—"state corporatism" (Unger and Chan 2008)—because all the significant individuals within this group are already connected through particularistic ties to agents of the state. Their loyalty is secured informally as individuals, rather than formally as a group. A final anecdote serves to illustrate this point.

The Korla (region) Young Entrepreneurs Association (YEA, *qingnian qiyejia xiehui* 青年企业家协会) held its annual Christmas celebration and four-year anniversary on December 23, 2009. It was a big and expensive event, which the head of the association and her assistants had been planning for a number of months, and was held in the main ballroom of one of the two top hotels in town. The event began with a mini-expo of the association members' products—a sort of networking and advertising opportunity, with business cards and glossy brochures flying left, right, and center. However, there were very few people there besides the exhibitors themselves, and so even those people who were obviously window shopping were made a great fuss over. The formal program began in typical fashion, with a series of speeches by city and local party officials. The event had official support because the YEA was set up under the auspices of the Korla branch of the Communist Youth League. According to members of the YEA, the association also received some basic funding from the city government, although the head of the YEA would not confirm this.

The awards and speeches were revealing of the membership and the mandate of the YEA. All the award recipients, and all the other members that I met that evening, were local Korla entrepreneurs. This is despite there being significant contingents of people from other regions of China doing business in Korla—the Wenzhou businesspeople dominate the consumer electronics market and even have their own church; the Fujianese own almost all of the many teashops. A local jack-of-all-trades who had obtained the right to represent a popular brand of Pu'er tea received one of the awards for being an "advanced individual" (*xianjin geren* 先进个人). You could say that he was being rewarded by his local consorts for making such a direct attack on the Fujianese tea monopoly. A couple of months before, I had attended an "expert session" on the Chinese tea ceremony that he hosted and was organized by the YEA. Much of my research was conducted in the teashops of Korla and, without exception, the owners and clients of the shops that I frequented condemned him as an imposter and wrote off his chances of business success. Leaving aside the question of whether or not "you have to know tea to sell tea," it is clear that the YEA is a forum for local entrepreneurs to advance their group interests. Nonlocals (*waidiren* 外地人) are either excluded or find no benefit in joining.

A number of speakers praised the association for "solving the problems of small and medium-sized businesses"—an implicit sign that this was the association's raison d'être. When I asked a member close to the head of the association what this meant in practice, he mumbled that it was about "helping each other and dealing with the government." The first part of this clearly means establishing and strengthening business connections within the group. It is hard to know how the event went in this respect, but the lack of energy at the products expo suggests that it was not too successful. The same person later explained that "dealing with the government" meant "forging mutually beneficial links" between the association as a whole and administrative government.

The behavior of the guest of honor, the deputy party secretary of Bazhou, signaled that the four-year-old YEA had not been very successful in establishing meaningful institutional links with government. The party secretary arrived late and left almost immediately after dinner was served, having eaten very little and shown even less enthusiasm for the event or for the many people who came to toast him. He also had other places to go and, for him, the YEA Christmas party was not important enough to warrant him staying any longer than the minimum etiquette required. Apparently, the minimum etiquette was not enough for the YEA head, who thereafter proceeded to drink far too much and ended

CHAPTER FIVE

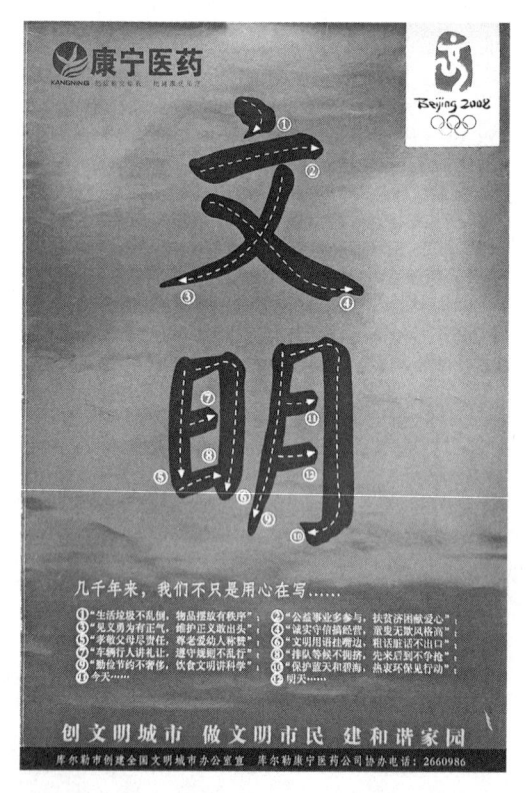

5.1 The main text in black reads "civilization," and the white text below reads "After thousands of years, we do not only use our hearts to write. . . ." Numbers 1 to 10 dictate the specifics of civilized behavior that the poster is presenting as a set of norms, and the last two points look toward the present and future: "11 today . . . 12 tomorrow. . . ." The idea here is continuity and development of "civilization."

the evening in tears. Her friends, many of them core members of the YEA (and also award recipients), tried to comfort her by assuring her that the event was a success, but nothing would convince her that the short shrift of the deputy party secretary signaled anything but an abject failure. Essentially, she was right. I noted that a few of the owners of larger and more successful private businesses in the Korla region (including the owner of the Kangning pharmacy chain) left soon after the party secretary. The failure of the event demonstrates that, in Korla, informal one-on-one particularistic ties to government remain considerably more important to private entrepreneurs than formal institutional ties through organizations like the YEA. Conversely, the key positions that agents of the local bureaucracy hold in this network help to reinforce the diffuse

LIVES OF *GUANXI*

power of the local bureaucracy with regard to both the governed population and the central state. *Guanxi* is a necessity not only for the population but also for the state in its attempts to reach down to and into the population, and thus to govern and regulate the population.

Some of the private businesspeople that do have close personal ties to local government also take it upon themselves to act as good corporate citizens (as defined by the government and therefore also in the government's interests). Figures 5.1 and 5.2, posters dating from 2007, were used to show support for Korla's bid to become an "All China Civilized City." The posters attempt to showcase the loyalty and civility of this peripheral city (to create good *guanxi* with the center) by quoting central state slogans verbatim and (mis)appropriating the Beijing Olympic logo. Since success in such a bid is a significant career achievement for the local officials who are able to claim credit for the success of the campaign, the

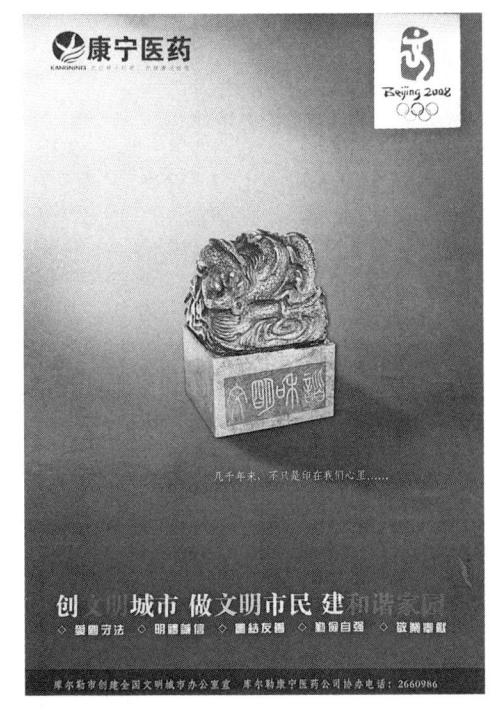

5.2 The seal reads "Civilization Harmony," and the text in white immediately below reads "After thousands of years, it is not only imprinted on our hearts. . . ." The idea here is to reinforce that "civilization" is in all of "us." The visual reference makes clear that "we" means people from the cultural core of China.

posters can also be seen as the business owner's support for particular individuals within the bureaucracy. The chain of pharmacies, Kangning, that sponsored these posters is the first-established and most successful pharmacy chain in Korla. It is very difficult to get a license to operate a pharmacy, so clearly Kangning's owner had sufficient *guanxi* within the local bureaucracy to obtain the licenses. His *guanxi wang* is even more solid now that he is one of the most prominent local entrepreneurs and taxpayers. Invoking traditional Chinese culture (the seal and calligraphy), these posters are a tangible manifestation of the confluence of private business and local government elites, of making private money and making state power, and of *guanxi* and the colonial endeavor.

It is worth comparing these informal governing mechanisms with the formal hierarchies of government and enterprise units. Elements of Walder's neotraditional image of communist political systems are useful here. Walder contrasts the neotraditional image with the "totalitarian image of impersonal mobilization and social atomization" (Walder 1986, 7). While the totalitarian image does not apply at all to contemporary Korla, different social and political spaces in Korla can be described, and distinguished, by which elements of the neotraditional image they display most strongly. In Tazhi, employees are offered "positive incentives . . . for compliance" (ibid., 6) with the system and loyalty to the party. Tazhi maintains what Walder describes as "a formally organized particularism in the distribution of goods, income, and career opportunities" (ibid., 7), so *guanxi* is important for promotion, but there is little need for employees to possess protective *guanxi*. In contrast, Korla locals outside of Tazhi are typically driven by negative incentives—socioeconomic insecurity is the default, protective *guanxi* is crucial, and party loyalty is only of value to those few with a high enough socioeconomic profile to warrant political attention. "A network of patron-client relations maintained by the Party" (ibid., 7) is evident in both places, although the party has a far more overt presence in Tazhi. Finally, "a rich subculture of instrumental-personal ties independent of the Party's control," was not apparent in Tazhi, but the necessity of *guanxi* for people outside the neo-*danwei* produces just such a subculture (ibid., 6–7).

For most people in Korla, formal regulations mean little when not supplemented by informal ties—*guanxi* resources—that can assist with either subverting or implementing the appropriate regulations. The biographical excerpts I present below demonstrate how different individuals generate *guanxi* resources and use them to move within the system and up the hierarchy. The first of these biographical excerpts was, quite consciously, framed as a process of "learning *guanxi*" (*xuehui guanxi* 学会关系).

Learning *Guanxi*

Boss Kang's father was one of the 80,000–100,000 Nationalist soldiers who defected en masse to the PLA in the September 25, 1949, "mutiny." In the early 1950s, he was demobilized and sent to settle uninhabited land some 70 kilometers northeast of Korla; this land became the *bingtuan* 24th Regiment.

In the beginning, the 1950s, on the 24th Regiment, there were basically no women. So the government took responsibility for arranging wives. . . . One government official went to Sichuan to find young women; he met my mother. Their family was so poor that they could only just feed and clothe themselves. [The official] said: "Xinjiang is very good. If you come, we will arrange work for you, but you will have to marry one of the men from that place."

My mother was a very naïve girl. She'd never met my father; she got straight on a train and came here. As soon as they met, they married.

I grew up on the *bingtuan* and went to primary school and middle school there. When I was 17, I graduated from high school. . . . I was allocated a piece of land to grow hops, under a contract system: whatever you grow, you give the regiment and they give you money, 500 *yuan* per year. In 1984 that was lot of money! A lot of money! But it really was tiring. I thought, "This work is really too hard" . . .

At school, my marks had been good, but after one year of farm work, I had learned bad habits—drinking, smoking, fighting. . . . So [at the age of 19] I bought a whole load of textbooks, and studied hard for one year: mathematics, geography . . . even English, and I attended the college entrance exam.

I swore that I would test my way out of the *bingtuan*, and I studied extremely hard. If you could test into university, you could leave the *bingtuan* and would not have to work the land; you would be allocated a job in the city, never again to wield a hoe. At that time, leaving the *bingtuan* was my motivation. No other thought—I had to test out of there.

The fearful possibility of spending one's life doing agricultural work on the *bingtuan* was a powerful motivating force for Kang and his generation to succeed academically. At the age of 20, Kang tested into Lanzhou Business College, and he studied there for four years. On graduation, he was assigned to the supply and marketing division of the Bazhou cotton mill.

At that place, I changed. Before I went there, I was very hard working and dependable . . . but I picked up bad habits—fighting, drinking, women—from the cotton mill.

All sorts of people ended up in that factory: criminals, cadres, college graduates. . . . After some time, I figured that there was no [good] future [at the cotton mill], and I used personal connections to get myself transferred to the prefectural Goods and Materials Office (*Wuziju* 物资局).

By this time, Kang had learned the importance of *guanxi*. His first lesson in how to play the game came from the ex-cons and cadres' sons at the cotton mill. It was a relatively simple lesson, as he explained with the help of a third person (Zhang San):

Guanxi is like this: I find the right person, and give them a present. For example, Zhang San is the director; I take some alcohol and cigarettes and go to see him (makes action to humbly present the gifts): "Director, I need to organize something . . ."

[Zhang San]: "I have no time!"

I wait a couple of days, and no results, then go to see him again with another box of expensive alcohol and a couple of cartons of good cigarettes: "How is my request?"

[Zhang San]: "We are still considering it."

[A couple of days later] I go there with some different presents, and inquire again. [The director replies] "OK, do it!" Then I get the transfer letter and move units—that's how it was, that simple (he laughs). . . . Human relationships in China [were] that simple.

It was not like it is these days—inviting to dinner, giving money—no. No money. At that time, it was just giving some presents. When I graduated from college, I didn't understand. I took no action [to mobilize *guanxi*], so I ended up at the cotton mill.

Kang told me that, these days, the rules of getting things done are "you get what you pay for, and everything has a known price." He emphasized that mutual trust is more important than ever because "sting operations are now carried out."

Economic structural reform, belatedly implemented in Korla, kept Kang moving along. Until the mid-1990s, the Goods and Materials Office was considered "a very good work unit." "However," he explained, describing his experience of SOE restructuring, "not long after I got there, China changed from a planned economy to a market economy." The enterprise started going downhill. By the late 1990s, the privileged ability of the Bazhou Goods and Materials Office to control essential resources had been thoroughly eroded by the emergence of multiple private entrepreneurs supplying the same materials (e.g., steel for reinforcing concrete). In 1997, after only a couple of years at the office, he took leave without pay and moved to the nearby city of Aksu. There he opened a karaoke bar and restaurant, which he operated until 2000.

In those three years, I made lots of money and [in 1999] bought an expensive car, a Lexus. . . . It cost over 600,000 *yuan*. . . . I bought that car as a status symbol. If you are doing business, you must command peoples' respect; make them willing to deal with you. A bad appearance is like saying "I am nearly dead."

In 2000, I came back [to Korla], sold the car, and squandered my money gambling and drinking. . . . Within one year, I had nothing.

Also in 2000, the Goods and Materials Office declared bankruptcy.

We all became *xiagang* (下岗) [laid-off but not completely separated from the work unit (see Gold, Hurst, et al. 2009, 1–10)]. In 2000, when I was 35, I became unemployed . . . At that time, I could do nothing. What to do? I didn't know what to do with myself.

After I was laid off, I had no income whatsoever; no money and no income; I could only . . . gamble . . . play cards for money—"King! Jack!" At that time I had already reached the time to die. I didn't feel like living.

Kang's self-destructive lifestyle took him right to the very edge, but the contacts that this lifestyle brought him were crucial to his later, spectacular, success. Some of his gambling buddies told him that there was a lot of money to be made in the construction contracting business; Kang is especially grateful for the "direction and assistance" of a current leader of Korla with whom he says he has "very good *guanxi*." On these recommendations, in 2003 he did a short course in construction supervision.

The first project I did, in 2004, was to flatten a piece of ground ready for construction. . . . The [official] project cost was 170,000 *yuan* [but the client paid 340,000] and I made a few tens of thousands out of that. . . . The second project was worth 600,000, and I made 100,000 out of it. After that, I had some capital and could become a contractor. . . . I have been successful in recent years, from the first project to now, and I have made, oh, about 70 to 80 million *yuan*.

Both the initial hint to enter the construction industry and the connections necessary to continue to secure contracts were a direct product of Kang's gambling, drinking, and whoring activities.

You get these sort of opportunities through introductions by friends—friends, and the leaders who are responsible for these projects. . . . That is, it also comes down to *guanxi*.

I know lots of people, from all walks of life (he lists a series of names and their high positions in Korla business circles). Many of those people I played cards with are in high positions in Korla business circles. Although they [were] there gambling and carrying on, they are all extremely talented people, boundless talent. I can't compare to them—I'm just a small boss; they are the heads of major local corporations. Of course, they had opportunities—Liu Si's father is one of the most well-known and influential men in Korla. My father is just a farmer.

Personal connections are a prerequisite for financial success in the construction industry in Korla. Because of the immense amount of corruption in the system and the large profits to be made, aspirant contractors need to produce the sort of iron-bound trust that shared experiences, mutually incriminating knowledge, and a web of indebtedness can generate between men. It is not new to point out the importance of being drinking buddies with your business partners in China. What this example illustrates is the precise way in which these networks are formed and operate, and the very pragmatic reasons for their existence.

There are many [contractors] like me, . . . but here in China we carry out what we call a "black box operation" (*anxiang caozuo* 暗箱操作). For example, we (gesturing to the three of us) have decided that this project goes to Zhang San. He asks us to accompany him to bid. We fake it: . . . I write 1000 *yuan*, you write 950 *yuan*, Zhang San can write 900 *yuan*—there must be three quotes—and he secures the tender, but still at an inflated price. Every construction project is like that. The next day, you two will help me. The following day, we will help you in this way. . . .

It is all worked out beforehand—this [bid] high, this [bid] low; this one is Wang Wu's, this one is Lu Xia's. Then [we] go there and pretend to bid, fake disappointment at the loss; then go together to eat and drink—it's like that. It's all like this, everything. This is the game—you know? (*Quanbu. Zhe shi quanbu de youxi, zhidao ma?* 全部。这是全部的游戏,知道吗?)

To succeed at this ubiquitous "game," Kang said you must combine three key factors:

First, you must be eager; second, you must be given opportunities; third, you need the help of other people. All three are important.

Having established himself, Boss Kang now seeks the stability that has thus far eluded him.

I plan to be careful and not to take large risks—if I went back to the situation I was in in 2000, I couldn't recover for the rest of my life. After all, I'm the son of a farmer. . . . I must conserve my gains. I must respect the law; I definitely must not break the law. I must take care of my wife, my daughter, the old folks, and my own health . . . and peacefully live out the rest of my life.

I want my daughter to have a smooth and stable life, not like me—I have seen too much of life; I have met too many villains and demons; I have been irresponsible to life. . . . When she graduates from university, she need not be a successful entrepreneur. She should enter a nice stable government job like the police or the Industrial and Commercial Bureau. . . . Ideally, I want her to stay in *neidi* and marry a peaceful man, not a man like me, regardless of whether he has little else going for him.

Guanxi as Sin and Salvation

The overarching structure of experience in Boss Kang's narrative is one of cyclical rise and fall, brought about by his own volatile reactions to the external world. In his words, his falls are a result of his own inability to resist temptation; his rises are attributed to his own eager, almost anxious, desire, and to help from others. There is something almost religious in his cyclical falls from grace and resurrections. His narrative depicts him as good but fallible—open to influence by the ever-present forces of evil (wine, women, and wager) as well as (socioeconomic) salvation by individuals who are God-like insofar as they provide him with invaluable information and assistance.

Both the immediate and broader contexts influenced Kang's retelling of his life story, and in both conscious and unconscious ways. Kang had two audiences to his story. One was me, a Westerner who he understood to be conducting research into Chinese society and politics; I had earlier done a favor for his daughter, and I attribute at least part of his frankness to the *guanxi* capital that I gained in performing that favor. The other audience was the third person in the room, Zhang San, who is a friend of Kang's and an evangelical Protestant. Zhang's presence helps in part to explain Kang's concluding appeal for moral salvation—his declaration that he accepts his responsibility as husband, father, and provider. Kang invokes a "loss of innocence," as he hints at (urban) risk taking being morally suspect and peasant risk aversion being morally upright: "After all, I'm the son of a farmer. I must conserve my gains. I must respect the

CHAPTER FIVE

law." Kang does not necessarily imply that he only engaged in corruption to save himself and his family, but he does make clear that, even as it is simultaneously a sin, illegal *guanxi* practice was, on multiple occasions, his savior. He was saving himself, and *being* saved, from ascribed disadvantageous situations (his birthplace in the *bingtuan*, his assignment to the cotton factory, and being laid off in the restructuring of the Goods and Materials Office) that caused him to sin in other ways. The story of a "bad boy," in his later years, turning to God for redemption—which is the turn from great darkness toward great light—is iterated and reiterated in monotheistic metanarratives. The trope of rise and fall in the overall narrative simultaneously references both the Christian narrative of human fallibility and salvation, and the growing obsession with stability and instability in the PRC. Kang finishes by transposing his born-again pursuit of stability onto his daughter. In his internalization of these religious and political narratives, Kang is a product of his immediate and broader discursive environments. Consequently, his biography is both unique and representative.

Kang's rollercoaster narrative stands out from those of his cohort. Most of his peers during youth, he says, are still doing agricultural work on the *bingtuan* farm where they were born. His desire to "test out of the *bingtuan*" was expressed in almost exactly the same terms as many others of his cohort. Jia, Jing, and Ren, for example, made the most of being relatively well educated among the Tarim Oilfield Company pioneers of the late 1980s and early 1990s, and rose steadily to their current positions. Kang's life and career has been characterized by uncertainty, instability, and change—jumping from place to place and job to job as work units went under or markets closed up. In contrast, Jia, Jing, and Ren have stayed in one spot and been assured of protection and privilege for their whole working lives. Thus, a comparison of these social trajectories reveals certainty/uncertainty as a key difference between life inside Tazhi and life outside. In their relative certainty, however, the lives of Tazhi people are similar to the lives of those who stayed behind on the *bingtuan*—the protective shell of state institutions limits possibility in both positive and negative ways.

Guanxi Networks' Contribution to Normalization in Xinjiang

The characterization of *guanxi* networks' production, utilization, and roles that I have presented in this chapter so far is hardly unique to Xinjiang. The popular perception that good *guanxi* is a key determinant of social and economic well-being in contemporary Korla should come as no surprise to even the most casual observer of China. Nor should the ways that *guanxi* networks are formed and utilized within Han socioeconomic circles in Korla be a surprise to China scholars; Boss Kang's story could be transplanted with little substantive change to just about anywhere in China (Yang 1994, 171; Wank 1999; Gold, Guthrie, et al. 2002; Yang 2002, 463; Osburg 2013). However, even apparently similar processes and phenomenon have different effects and different meanings in different places. In this case, the familiarity of Boss Kang's story endows it with strong comparative potential. The goal is not simply to identify distinctions but also to explain the causes and effects of difference and similarity with regard to comparable phenomena in Xinjiang and *neidi*.

It is precisely *because guanxi* networks in Korla (and, by extension, in Xinjiang) operate similarly to how they operate in *neidi* that they constitute an important assertion of Han cultural, political, and economic influence in the region. In terms of their effect on normalization and integration, Han *guanxi* networks in Xinjiang are the cultural equivalent of the transport and communications infrastructure that serves to tie peripheral regions to the core area. There are four overlapping parts to my argument: the popular perception of *guanxi* networks' ubiquity and necessity; *guanxi* networks' relationship to political/bureaucratic power and official administrative structures; Uyghurs in Han networks; and *guanxi* networks' relationship to cultural change.

First, an important element of the political and economic culture of Xinjiang is the popular perception of the necessity of *guanxi* to everyday life. This perception constitutes, in Myrdal's terms, a "folklore" of *guanxi* (1968). The circulation of *guanxi* stories is no less important than the actuality of the events being retold. The folklore is made even more powerful by its opacity to those outside the networks.

Second, there is a strong link between the CCP exercise of power and the production and exercise of *guanxi* networks that I outline in this chapter. *Guanxi* networks are the channels through which corrupt transactions take place because corrupt transactions require trust, and personal relationships can provide this trust. Although corruption is only one of the uses to which *guanxi* networks can be put, and many of the protagonists of the examples that I feature in this chapter would not think of their activities as corrupt, *guanxi* exchanges in Korla (as in China more broadly) often involve some form of corruption—defined as "abuse of public office for private gain in violation of rules" (Manion 2004, 5; in Ko and Weng 2011, 377). The level of trust that the patron has of the client (the initiator) determines, in Ling Li's words, the "exchange safety" of the transaction, and the extent to which the client can help the patron to overcome the "moral costs" and "cognitive dissonance" associated with the transaction. In the absence of a preexisting close personal relationship, a functional equivalence to trust can be produced through a particular type of "*guanxi*-practice." This practice involves the client's ritualized faking of a close personal relationship, combined with the creation of a sense of indebtedness in the patron by presenting "gifts" whose value is commensurate with the size of favor sought, all of which is conducted with respect to certain norms both legal and moral (Li L. 2011, 15–18). The *guanxi* networks formed of such practices thus become institutionalized, and these informal institutions overlap with or are integrated into the formal governing structures of the state. Ling Li argues that "the micro-level operation of corruption in China is not due to some haphazard aggregation of sporadic acts but follows certain rules and codes of conduct, which should be seen as an informal institutional mechanism facilitating the contracting process of corrupt exchange" (2011, 1). Boss Kang's descriptions of the protocols of doing (corrupt) business support this argument. These corrupt exchanges benefit CCP cadres, in terms of both social standing and economic gain, and thus contribute to making cadre positions desirable. This in turn makes the state structure reasonably stable: the governing apparatus cannot be effective if there is no incentive for cadres to follow their superiors' directives.

Third, even Uyghurs who have the capacity to engage in corrupt Han *guanxi* networks, and have significantly enriched themselves by doing so, often resent the fact that the networks exist, as well as engaging in them. Uyghurs pay a particularly high cultural/moral price for engagement in *guanxi* networks and are rarely able to reap the full benefits of the informal contracts that *guanxi* networks enable. The practice of *guanxi* play by Uyghurs in Xinjiang has increased dramatically in recent years. In certain regions, the practice is becoming so commonplace that Uyghurs now also practice Han-style *guanxi* with other Uyghurs (rather than only with Han, for instrumental purposes). This cultural transformation, which is taking place in South Xinjiang in particular, is apparently a major contributing factor to the high divorce rates in the region. Cavorting in "entertainment venues," which tends to involve large amounts of alcohol and female hostesses, directly offends religious mores and family expectations, both of which are core to Uyghur identity.

Although they made their money by learning and deploying *guanxi*, wealthy expatriate Uyghurs disparaged the operation of *guanxi* networks in Xinjiang and China. They compared China to Australia and noted that the formal legal institutions and relative respect for rules in Australia suit them much better. In *guanxi* dealings with Han Chinese, the Uyghur entrepreneurs noted that they have no feeling of safety because they cannot trust the other party to be good to their word. Uyghur entrepreneurs must "strategically" hedge against the possibility of being betrayed by their Han partners (Mei Ding, personal communication, January 29, 2015).[2] This demonstrates the importance of the network, not just the dyadic relationship between patron and client. The network is an essential element of what keeps people "honest" and the unwritten contract honored, since the trust of others in the network is the basis of the network's value to an individual. To default would be to undermine the trust of others in the network—if, but only if, the person defaulted on is part of the network. The cultural and ethnic differences, and ongoing antagonism, between Uyghur and Han people create mutual suspicion that effectively prevents Uyghurs from being fully accepted into Han networks, so a Han defaulting on a Uyghur may expect not to be penalized by other Han in the network. Defaulting on another ethnicity is made easier, and more feared, because it can be explained to co-ethnics in stereotypical and discriminatory terms which, even if untrue, ring true in this polarized society: "Uyghurs [or Han] are not trustworthy"; unspoken is "so I betrayed him." A lack of trust begets a lack of trust, and the cycle goes on.

Finally, since the cultural and geographic spread of *guanxi* networks' ubiquity (including their perceived ubiquity) is an example of how normalization proceeds and succeeds in Xinjiang, then Han cultural, political, and economic hegemony in the region (theoretically) has the capacity to outlast even the CCP. This is because normalization is based in the actual existing fact of real people adapting, reproducing, and propagating this culture on the ground in Xinjiang, not only in the administrative superstructure of the party-state. Normalization in Xinjiang is driven by change in informal socioeconomic institutions, no less than it is by change in the formal governing institutions associated with the CCP. *Guanxi* practice takes place within certain social circles that are simultaneously inclusive of some and exclusive of others, and, because it can help to gain political, economic, or symbolic benefit, *guanxi* practice creates a desire to be included. "The desire," as Prasenjit Duara observed, "is not (simply) to conquer the other, but to be desired by the other" (2001, 106). The desire of the other is sustained by their partial, but never full, inclusion—by maintaining them *as* the other. *Guanxi* practice may thus be conceived of as a form of cultural power.

CHAPTER FIVE

Normalization through cultural transformation is a conscious concern of the second of the two life histories that I present in this chapter. The narrator, Yanyan, is about Boss Kang's age and was also *bingtuan* raised. Like Kang, she lives a life of *guanxi* and frames her story with social and economic turmoil. However, she more strongly emphasizes her own agency, and refers explicitly to the position of Xinjiang people in China and her own role as a peripheral subject. Yanyan is excluded, by her gender, from the distinctively male practices of *guanxi* production deployed by Boss Kang. Kang's practices of forming homosocial bonds through bad boy behavior with the princelings of Korla's cadre body are, for obvious reasons, not open to Yanyan. Thus her peripherality is gendered and social as well as spatial, political, economic, and, as we shall see, ethnic.

The Paths and Positions of the Peripheral Subject

Yanyan was born in Xinjiang in 1968 of Zhuang parents. Yanyan's mother died giving birth to her, and her father sent her back to Guangxi to live with his older sister when she was two years old. She came back to Xinjiang at age four, to live once more with her father in Yining. However, his work as a cadre meant that he was too busy to look after her properly, and she was continually sick. Her father found a willing adoptive couple and left her with them. The adoptive father was a ranking official in the Irrigation Department and he and his family moved around a lot. Yanyan did most of her primary school in Shihezi (North Xinjiang) and then, when her adoptive father was transferred to the 29th Regiment 50 kilometers west of Korla, she went straight into the first year of middle school. She explained that in the mid-1970s

North Xinjiang and South Xinjiang enrolled students at different times of the year, so in moving from Shihezi, where they enroll in autumn, to Korla, where they enroll in spring, I skipped half a year of school. They put me straight into the next class up. When South Xinjiang changed to align enrolments with North Xinjiang, I lost another half year of schooling. And I had already started school early because I was the youngest of my family and my parents wanted me off their hands.

Hurt crept into her voice as she went on:

I'm the unluckiest. At least [my husband's generation] had decent schooling in primary school—I effectively had no primary school.

Yanyan maintains that if she were born either four years earlier or four years later, she would not have suffered the injustices that she did; she attributes this in large part to the behindness of the prevailing social, political, and economic conditions in South Xinjiang. Her adoptive parents were labeled Rightists because of her adoptive father's history as part of the Nationalist forces. Meanwhile, her birth father was "very red"—he had been on the Communist side and was a political and ideological worker in a time when "politics was above all." But she could not make her hereditary redness known because to do so would have meant that her birth father would be denounced for abandoning her. This was the mid-1970s, the last years of the Cultural Revolution decade, but Yanyan explained that the political movements associated with the Cultural Revolution revisited Xinjiang in the late 1970s, sometimes years after they had passed in *neidi*.

Many aspects are behind in South Xinjiang. . . . South Xinjiang is behind North Xinjiang and Urumchi . . . and the political climate is also behind. For example, when a certain political movement has already passed in North Xinjiang, in South Xinjiang it has not even started. When *neidi* was carrying out agrarian reform (*nongcun gaige* 农村改革), South Xinjiang was still subject to the political movements of the tail end of the Cultural Revolution. [Yanyan used "agrarian reform" to refer to the household responsibility system (*nongcun jiating lianchan chengbao zerenzhi* 农村家庭联产承包责任制), initiated in *neidi* in late 1982].

I asked what she did after completing two years of lower middle school. "I went to work in the fields. . . . Where else could I go?" she replied with a mixture of annoyance, shame, and hurt. She insisted that her assignment to rural work in 1982 at age 14 was widely referred to as a part of the "Up to the Mountains and Down to the Villages" political movement. This is despite the fact that the Cultural Revolution decade had officially been over for six years. She explained that

South Xinjiang is behind by about four years, in an overall sense . . . It doesn't matter which angle you are talking about—politics, mass movements—in every aspect of policy implementation . . . South Xinjiang is behind a full four years.

Bingtuan children being "sent down" to do agricultural work on the same *bingtuan* regiment at which they grew up and went to school was a function of the child's academic success, and of the parents' socioeconomic standing. Not all children of her age in the early 1980s on the

CHAPTER FIVE

29th Regiment were "sent down" in this way. The fact that she was channeled into agricultural labor also suggests that her adoptive parents could not, or did not, provide her any other opportunities. Again, they wanted no responsibility. From this point on, she was on her own.

Yanyan's Working Life

Yanyan worked on the land at the 29th Regiment from 1982 through 1985. At the start, she was paid only meal tickets to eat in the communal canteen. After one year or so, the *bingtuan* began to pay salaries. She got 25.36 *yuan*, which was about 70% of what a company leader on the 29th Regiment, like Jia's father, got at around the same time. "It was a pretty good salary," she said happily. "I only needed 10 *yuan* each month; I could even save 10 *yuan*." In 1986 she went to Urumchi to attend an elementary form of teachers college: "Because I had only graduated from lower middle school, I could only go to a technical secondary school."

I asked how she managed to get from being a farm laborer to being a trainee teacher—who had got her into college?

Nobody helped me. They would try to stop me. I am one of those, those . . . those sons-of-bitches. . . . I was born into a bad family. Who got me into college? Nobody would think of getting me into college! I got in because I attended the entrance exam and tested in: they had no way to stop me. If they had [still] been judging by political credentials, nobody would have let me go to study.

She began work experience at Korla's industrial satellite town of Tashidian in 1988, then stayed on to work in the same school after finishing her one-year work experience:

The school that I was at really liked me. They insisted that I stay and work there . . . so I worked there.

The school in Tashidian was where the 19-year-old Yanyan met her future husband, the 35-year-old Mr. Zhao, who at that time was also a teacher. Reflecting on the story midway through her telling of it, Yanyan emphasized,

We are the held-back generation (*bei danwu de yidai* 被耽误的一代): nobody looks after me; nobody wants me. And because I'm not properly educated, I had to learn to get things in a different way. I had to convince people [each and every time] that I was the right person for the job.

I have firsthand experience of Yanyan's persistence myself. When I chose another person as my Chinese teacher, she refused to accept it and spent 50 minutes on the telephone convincing me why she was the one I should hire. It wasn't about the money, which was minimal. It seems that she wanted to tell the story—any story that I was interested in—her way, to make it her own story.

My ideal work is as an adviser, the person who the boss of the operation listens to. . . . I am well suited to this sort of work. For example, in 1988 I recommended that Mr. Zhao get out of teaching within three years. . . . At that time he was not my husband. In 1990–91 he divorced his first wife and started working for the city government. Soon after that, Mr. Zhao was selected to be transferred to the prefectural government, but I said "stay in city government, because Korla city is developing very fast."

Korla became the capital of Bazhou in 1964. The railway line reached Korla in 1979, and Korla was made a city in the same year. In 1989 the oil company officially established its command post, stimulating rapid economic growth from the mid-1990s.

When they wanted to make him [Mr. Zhao] a cadre, I recommended that he not take up the position because I saw that he was good at doing the work but not good at CCP-style managing the workers: "You are not corrupt, so do not accept a government official position." I told him that "old doctors, old artists, old scientists, et cetera all get more valuable as they get older, but whoever hears of old cadres?"

Yanyan cultivated the most important of the connections in her *guanxi* network after leaving teaching and going into private business in the mid-1990s. Private employment did not mean that she gave up her claim to a permanent position at the school: like Kang, she took the option of leave without pay that was offered nationwide to workers in state-owned work units. The policy allowed her to retain her position, in as much as her time of service continued to accumulate and she remained eligible for a retirement pension, but have no duties at the school. First she worked as a tour guide on a semifreelance basis; following that she operated a clothing stall in the free market and, as a pioneer, was very successful for a few years. She was subsequently head-hunted by a large bank from Urumchi that was opening a high-end seafood restaurant in Korla. Her official position was assistant to the manager, but she claims that since he was never in Korla, she effectively ran the place herself. It was this hospitality role, she says, that taught her the most important things that she knows about the sociopolitical and financial aspects of doing business. Through hosting and dealing with the government and business elite of Korla on a daily basis, she learned how to talk the talk of a social circle from which she had previously been excluded. After a few years, she went back into private business.

Yanyan's Business Ventures

Yanyan is an active networker and small-scale entrepreneur. In 2008 and 2009 she was involved in a series of different business ventures and occupations, often simultaneously. The diversity of her activities and the particularities of how she approaches a given task are revealing of the everyday socioeconomic transactions that take place in Korla.

Dried fish. Long-term social connections are the primary advantage that "old Korla people" have over more recent immigrants, including oil company employees. The following example further illustrates the role of long-term networks that are built on a sense of shared experience and feeling, their importance to "old Korla people," and how they differ from the instrumental transactions that can take place between two strangers.

Yanyan planned to start a business producing dried fish from Bosten Lake. She says she has "done all the ground work and taken care of all of the finer details to establish the right conditions for starting this business." The most important part of this seems to be utilizing her connections. Yanyan was good friends with the outgoing party secretary of a nearby lakeside county. She told this man about her plans, and he said to her, "I am just about to be rotated elsewhere, but within six months somebody you know will take the position of county head." The incoming county head happened to be one of Mr. Zhao's former students and, now in position, he is apparently going out of his way to make conditions ideal for Yanyan to start this fish-drying business. Yanyan says that he regularly delegates his various departmental officials to chaperone her, answer questions, and provide documents and information. Second, he has promised to guarantee provision of a large portion of the limited catch of grass carp to Yanyan's fish-drying factory. To do this he will apparently have to reduce the amount of fresh fish sent to restaurants in Korla and completely stop selling fish to restaurants in Urumchi. Third, he will give Yanyan a monopoly by prohibiting competitors. Fourth, all the preferential policies of the national and provincial-level governments will be available to Yanyan's enterprise.

Yanyan believes that the risk to investors is very low and the potential returns very high. She believes that the product is quite good, the Ministry of Agriculture having ratified the fish in Bosten Lake to be organic. She believes that she has the correct technique and recipe for producing the fish, based on a test she did in September 2007. She produced 500 boxes and got orders for "2,000 boxes from Urumchi, and 4,000 boxes from the Tarim compound," which she could not fill. She plans to make different flavors, and different colors using plant dyes. She has aspirations to revolutionize, Xinjiang-style, the whole process of making dried fish.

The riots in Urumchi in July 2009 upset Yanyan's plans. She had a Taiwan businessman interested in putting in three million *yuan* in initial capital, followed by another three million *yuan* in the "second period" of business development, which would start after about three years. The Bosten Lake county would also put up a two-million-*yuan* interest-free loan as soon as the first three million *yuan* comes through from Taiwan. The money from Taiwan would be paid back over eight years, plus 25% of the capital (1.5 million *yuan*). The county head found this potential investor for her. However, the Taiwan businessmen's wife convinced him to pull out, ostensibly because of the 7/5 incident in Urumchi. Yanyan was sad but philosophical: "Another opportunity will come along. I just have to wait."

Knitwear. Yanyan was not deterred by the temporary setback to her fish-drying business. Since mid-2009, she has focused her energies on her knitting business, which grew over the first part of 2009 from a sporadic and home-based activity into a full-time occupation that employs piece workers and exports to neighboring Central Asian countries. Again, she used her social networking skills and existing connections to create the best possible conditions for her nascent business. She went to the street office (*jiedao banshichu* 街道办事处) in the area where her apartment is located, and they recommended that she relocate her business to a nearby neighborhood instead. The rationale was that the other neighborhood has the greatest concentration of laid-off workers, disabled people, and unemployed university graduates in the inner city of Korla, and these are the sort of people who are willing to knit clothing for some extra money. The government apparently gives between 380 and 550 *yuan* per month to these people, but the neighborhood officials will be rewarded by their superiors if they "lift these people from poverty"—for example, by teaching them to knit and get wages for their products. To encourage her business, the neighborhood office waives certain fees and taxes, and this saves her a few hundred *yuan* every month.

Yanyan has cultivated a team from among the unemployed women of the local neighborhood, simultaneously becoming an expert in technique, personnel management, and Central Asian fashions. "They like our colors," she says. "Our wool here is softer. . . . Different countries like different styles: Pakistan likes it very colorful; Kazakhstan likes it big and floppy; Russia likes it sexy." So a situation exists in which underemployed, laid-off, incapacitated, and aged Han women in an older part of inner-city Korla are being taught to knit according to certain fixed styles to fill commissions from post-Soviet Central Asia and the Indian subcontinent. Imagine these women, who rarely get out of their dusty brown concrete apartments and who live by day with the fluorescent lights turned off so as to save on electricity bills, having the opportunity for a suitable form of gainful employment. The fact that each knitter, if they are fast and work all day, might make 50 *yuan* (the slow ones may only make 20 *yuan* per day) serves simply to emphasize the value these women put on a little bit of money and a sense of feeling productive.

It would seem, from most of these examples, that *guanxi* resources are used exclusively to further or protect narrow self-interest and, more often than not, that such a system runs contrary to the public good. The prevailing discourse, both within and outside China, supports these assumptions. However, connectedness, for Yanyan, is not just about being able to do things for yourself—it is equally about being able to do things for other people, as well as being able to make a contribution to society. Certain social groups, in her view, are more predisposed to make such a contribution than others.

Constructors

Yanyan divides Korla's population into four main groups, and places them in a hierarchy of worth according to their contribution to "constructing" Korla. The four main groups are the recent in-migrants, current *bingtuan* people, ethnic minorities, and original immigrants (1950s and '60s) and their children. She explained,

> The recent in-migrants do not have a firm foothold in Korla: they do not hold high-level positions themselves, and their relationship networks do not spread deep into the administrative structures of the city and the prefecture.
>
> Most of the working-age *bingtuan* people are still on the *bingtuan* farms, and the ethnic minority population of the city is stupid and incompetent.
>
> Therefore, the most stable, the most able to sustain Korla, and those who form the backbone of Korla, are the previous generation of immigrants and their children.

The individuals who make up the other three groups lack one or other of three essential qualities that give Yanyan's highest-ranked group this key role: presence in the urban center, a broad and deep relationship network, and the ability (and the ideological standpoint) of a constructor.

According to Yanyan, the urban group that possesses a broad and deep relationship network is the earlier generation of in-migrants and their children, *bendiren*. In this context, *bendiren* can be described as people who are *of* Korla, people who belong to Korla. The ownership runs in both directions: Korla also belongs to them, since they have transferred their primary place-allegiance from the "old home" back in *neidi* to Korla. One of the most important determining factors in this transfer is the relative strength of relationship networks in each place. When the relationship network in Korla exerts a stronger pull, people are more likely to consider themselves, and to be considered, *bendiren*.

In part, these early constructors gain(ed) a sense of ownership of Korla (Xinjiang) by giving themselves to Korla (Xinjiang), that is, through sacrifice. This discourse is particularly apparent throughout chapter 1, in Wu's narrative, and in the *bingtuan* and oil company claims to constructor status. The commander of the *bingtuan*, Hua Shifei, stated in 2011, "I'm a senior farm-reclamation army man who gave my youth and dreams to Xinjiang. The spirit of our generation will be carried forward in the [*bingtuan*] to accomplish our historic mission" (*People's Daily* 2011b). The notion of sacrifice is intimately bound up with the notion of a constructor: to be a constructor *requires* sacrifice; sacrifice entitles ownership. For the central government, the sense of ownership and belonging that Han in Xinjiang feel toward Xinjiang is of the utmost importance. Troops can be moved in, buildings built, and people relocated, but these are relatively ephemeral measures, and relatively easy to dislodge, compared to a deeply felt sense of belonging. The existence of *bendiren*, not merely settlers or sojourners, helps to justify and guarantee Beijing's claims to Xinjiang.

Repositioning the Peripheral Subject

Yanyan can be considered a barometer of Han society in Korla and Xinjiang. Yanyan incorporates the metadiscourses of, or relating to, Han society in Xinjiang into her narrative and uses them as the basis for her reasoning. Some of these metadiscourses are also state discourses. Indeed, they enter popular usage because they are state discourses and even, on occasion, vice versa. Both state and nonstate actors deploy them, although often in different ways and to different ends. For example, for nonstate actors like Yanyan, the notion that certain Han are self-sacrificing constructors, making an essential contribution to nation building on the distant borderland, is an invaluable rhetorical device because it implies that the state must, in return, assume responsibility for the welfare of those people. The norm of reciprocity persists, even if it is not always honored. On the other hand, this same collection of concepts—peripherality, behindness, civilization, national unity—helps to justify heavy-handed state actions in the name of stability and development, and to put a gloss on coercive in-migration.

The discursive, spatiotemporal, and sociopolitical contexts within which all people in Korla live manifest in Yanyan's narrative, just as they manifest in other biographies in this book. For a start, peripherality and behindness inform the subjectivity of all Han in Xinjiang. Some recurrent structures of experience for urban *difang* and ex-*bingtuan* people include being "held back" or "sent down," using connections and *guanxi* networks, and leaving the employ of the state to set up a small business. These contexts and structures of experience are simultaneously a product of who Yanyan is and help to make her who she is. Yanyan's many links to, and shared experiences with, other people in Korla thus put her at the center of a network of cross-fertilization and mutual influence.

In certain respects, Yanyan's business activities parallel the projects of the central state. Her activities contribute, in small but important ways, to social stability and nation building in Xinjiang by stimulating economic activity within Xinjiang, providing employment for disadvantaged second-generation settlers, and engaging in trade with Central and South Asian businesspeople. Yanyan operates close to, but outside of, the state and almost entirely within Han social and economic circles in Xinjiang.

Yanyan's Zhuang ethnicity complicates and, simultaneously, helps determine her role in the ongoing process of normalization of the periphery. Faced with the multifaceted cultural isolation of her parents' and her own migrations and changing identities—Guangxi to Xinjiang, colonized into colonizer, ethnic majority to ethnic minority—she has learned to be "more Han than Han." Yanyan's enthusiastic adoption and promotion of Han cultural mores and ways of doing business assert the logic of normalization. She has internalized the underlying assumption of Han rule in Xinjiang: that socioeconomic inclusion is conditional upon conformity to the hegemonic culture. In this respect, Yanyan could be considered a model citizen, a model product of the relationship between peripheral individual subject and hegemonic central state in the PRC. By linking *guanxi* networks to "construction," Yanyan links self-serving to serving the people and, ultimately, corruption to nation building via normalization.

9   Teacher, laid off from Third Front factory school

10 Construction worker

11   English teacher, nonstate system

12   Housewife

13   Part-time administrator

14   Acupuncture and Chinese massage doctor

15   Retired, *bingtuan*

16   Retail businessman

Local Han Divided

The examples and narratives in this chapter have highlighted the role of *guanxi*-as-necessity for some and *guanxi*-as-resource for others. This is a symptom of certain socioeconomic divides within the Han people of Korla. First, urbanized *bendiren* are best positioned, relative to economic status, to utilize their networks for personal gain and protection. This is because people in these urban *bendiren* groups ("old Korla people" and ex-*bingtuan* people) have long-term networks that tend to be characterized by mutual trust, and because they tend to occupy most of the positions of administrative power in the city and prefectural governments. Ethnic minorities and recent in-migrants, for obvious reasons, are on the outside of these local Han networks. Ordinary Tazhi people have relatively weak ties with local government, in part because many of them are relatively recent in-migrants and in part because it is most important for them to build up ties *within* the neo-*danwei*.

Second, the narratives and examples in this chapter have outlined certain socioeconomic divides within the *bendiren*. In contrast to the necessity of *guanxi* for the lower (but aspirant) sectors of Han society in Korla, *guanxi* is perceived and deployed as an enabling device by networked individuals like Yanyan and Kang. The narratives of Yanyan and Kang point to a number of internal and external factors that help determine why some people are networked and others are not (or are not able to use their networks for personal socioeconomic gain). Unspoken, but loud and clear in both of these narratives and in the implicit and explicit statements of many other of my interlocutors, is the necessity of learning *guanxi*.

Within *bendiren*, ways of learning *guanxi* are gendered. Whereas Kang's story highlights the importance of male homosocial bonds, Yanyan's first significant step in establishing her *guanxi* networks was to marry Mr. Xi, the son of local cadres.[3] Being relatively young and female, and thus unthreatening, Yanyan was able to observe *guanxi* practice in operation from close quarters, both in her husband's social circles and in her role as the manager of the seafood restaurant where Korla's business and political elite regularly dined. What she was watching was predominantly men producing and deploying *guanxi* with other men but, crucially, what she learned was how she, as a woman, could fit into and make use of the same system.

Common to both Yanyan and Boss Kang, the key external factor in learning *guanxi* is generational, which is linked to work history. In Korla, long-term connections exist between a relatively small group of people who share or have shared the same or similar experiences. Long-term connections and shared experiences help to generate and support a sense of mutual trust. For both Yanyan and Kang, the state-owned work unit was an important site for "learning *guanxi*" and making connections that would lead to later opportunities. Although they themselves did not enter the local bureaucracy, they are both connected to peers in these positions.

In contrast, the rapid growth of Korla and the expansion of the population has meant that the younger generations of locals (those born in the 1980s, for example) are much less connected to useful *guanxi* networks. For a start, society in Korla is far more atomized. Second, the younger generation's education and work histories exist largely outside the state *danwei* (including the *bingtuan*), limiting interactions and shared experience. Third, they are more intermixed with other, more recent migrants. Fourth, their peers do not hold decision-making positions in the local state bureaucracy because those are mostly still held by the older generation (born 1950s and '60s). Those of the younger generation who are in the state bureaucracy are rarely close associates of those outside it. A state/nonstate employee division exists, exacerbated by the fact that many younger state employees are not Korla locals, or are children of high-up cadres, which automatically puts them at a distance from ex-*bingtuan* children. Thus, the system of *guanxi* is also experienced as constraining, excluding, and repressive. For some, the system demands much more than it provides in return. Such people are among the subjects of the next chapter.

SIX

Married to the Structure

> Certain structures, in their long life, become the stable elements of an infinity of generations. They encumber history and restrict it, and hence control its flow. Other structures crumble more quickly. But all structures are simultaneously pillars and obstacles. . . . Mental frameworks are also prisons of the *longue durée*.
> FERNAND BRAUDEL, *HISTORY AND THE SOCIAL SCIENCES* ([1958] 2009, 178–79)

Among the assumptions of life for many Han in Korla are, first, that industry and employment in Korla is dominated by state enterprises and, second, that cadres in redistributive positions have the power to make arbitrary decisions that directly affect the success of *private* enterprises. Consequently, life chances for those with links to the state—permanent state employment in a viable work unit ("inside the system" *tizhi nei* 体制内) or particularistic ties to state agents—are assumed to be distinctly better than for those who are both "outside the system" (*tizhi wai* 体制外) and lacking economically valuable connections. While such state domination of the industrial structure is not unique to Xinjiang, it is particularly strong in Xinjiang and helps to mark out Xinjiang as "behind" the core area of China. People in Korla characterize this state stranglehold over economic life in the city-region as a "structural problem" (*tizhi wenti* 体制问题). Elite and nonelite people agree on what the "structural problem" is, but present very different versions of what the negative social consequences are.

Nonelite people complain that the SOE-dominated industrial structure of Korla (see chapter 2), and the necessity of *guanxi* with state officials (see chapter 5) restricts their social mobility, and thus marriage prospects. The two nonelite

CHAPTER SIX

people portrayed in this chapter were both born on the *bingtuan* in the early 1980s and moved to the urban area of Korla soon afterward. They have neither permanent state employment nor solid personal links to the state. These people perceive themselves as being in a permanent state of economic insecurity, so they seek certainty while attempting to sustain possibility—and thus hope. Hope is the psychological counterweight to their assumption that the formal and informal structures of their lives are immutable. The certainty that they seek is socioeconomic proximity to the state, its institutions, or its agents because proximity to the state is seen to guarantee social reproduction. The state's magnetism underpins a society-wide "organized dependence" that is analogous to that which Andrew Walder (1986) found in the socialist-era Chinese factory. Held together by nostalgia and residual expectation as much as by formal state structures, organized dependence is the essence of Korla's micropolitical economy.

The elite maintain that this very same structural problem creates a low-quality, dependent population, who expect to be spoon-fed by the state and are unwilling to branch out into entrepreneurial pursuits. The elite are represented by an oil company cadre born on a nearby *bingtuan* farm in the 1960s, and a retired *bingtuan* cadre who is a generation older than him. For these two cadres and other people with employment connections to the state, the "iron rice bowl mentality" of (the rest of) the population contributes to the "behindness" of Xinjiang. And so the cycle goes on: a lack of reform creates a backward mindset, and backward mindset is an obstacle to reform. An important point here is that the objects of elite anxiety are not predominantly the ethnic other—the cadres are talking about Han people. For the nonelite, this structural problem is a livelihood problem, but for the elite, it is a problem of governance.

Despite differences in how they perceive the structural problem, both elite and nonelite pose market liberalization as the solution. Echoing state discourse, they say that Xinjiang should "catch up" to *neidi*. The inherent promise of the market economy in this discourse is that, in exchange for the secure paternalism of the centralized economy, it will enable all people to reach their full potential. Political and economic elites are attracted by the neoliberal potentials that the market holds for governing the broader populace "at a distance" (Rose 1998, 165). Yet, inexorably, the elite critique of others' organized dependence leads to a self-referential critique of systemic embeddedness. The oil company cadre's ruminations on the connections between political and economic reform, his recognition of the inherent contradictions of the path that he argues the CCP must take, and his own implied role in sustaining and justifying permanent postponement demonstrate that elite individuals and powerful institutions within the system are also "married to the structure."

This chapter begins with a story that brings together the key hopes and worries of the Han population of Korla, with a focus on the marriage economy. As demonstrated in chapter 4, marriage is the culmination of a series of status aspirations, and nobody, man or woman, can be deemed successful, or at least complete, until they have married. Marriage is seen to enable childbirth, and thus continuity of the family line and possibility for the future. As the hope for a successful marriage and reproduction is fulfilled, a new hope is (literally) born.[1] The discourses, rituals, expectations, and deviations of marriage are central to the everyday political economy of Korla.

The Marriage Economy

"I've broken up with my girlfriend," said Rhys, in English, as he settled into his chair in Dicos on a Sunday afternoon. They had been together just one month. "Why'd you do that?" I protested. "She seemed pretty nice." He looked at me with a somewhat pained expression.

That girl was really selfish. . . . Every evening I would pick her up after work and go to my house where my mother had cooked dinner for us three. Unless I ordered her to wash the dishes, she would not do anything, just sit there and watch TV.

My mother talked to her three times—about things to do with running a family, but she didn't say anything, just sat there. [The way she acted] shows that she does not really love me from the bottom of her heart . . . and shows that she does not love my mother. If you love me, you have to love my mother. But she just wants to live alone with me in a separate house and go to my mother's house to eat.

The girl was a nurse, and Rhys explained that his uncle says that nurses have a bad reputation:

They meet so many men and have been with so many men, and they have a lot of experience.

"Experience is good." I said. Rhys replied,

Yes, experience is good, (pause) but I am not experienced, I have not been with lots of girls, so it's not good for me. . . . Her experience is of men using her, and girls like her

CHAPTER SIX

learn how to get as much out of men as possible. . . . It is hard to change this habit . . . so I broke up with her.

Last Tuesday, my mother cooked some very nice dishes—prawns . . . and she was very happy that night, the girl, because the food was very nice and it was a special atmosphere . . . and afterward I took her home and dropped her at the door of her apartment and broke up with her. I said, "You are not the right girl from me to marry," and I explained to her it was because she was too selfish, and only thinking about what she can get from the situation. I asked her if she was considering marrying me because of my apartment, and she said yes.

Some months later, while we were waiting for another potential bride (who never showed up), another of Rhys's early-30s bachelor friends explained the economics of marriage in Korla as he saw it:

Men of our age cannot hope to marry a girl who is 25 or 26, we must look for the ones who are 28–30 because they are already well into marriageable age and are getting desperate. They have lower standards and will marry just about anyone who is reasonably financially secure and not too bad looking. But the younger ones are still idealistic and demand both money and looks—though money is more important. If [Rhys] was wealthy, he wouldn't have to look for girls, they'd find him—he'd have an entire group of girls surrounding him wherever he went.

Time and youth, especially for women, are key commodities in the marriage economy. A few days after Rhys broke it off with the nurse and was away in Urumchi, the mother invited the nurse around for dinner and had another talk to her. Rhys's mother said, "You are not the right girl for my son to marry," and gave her 1,000 *yuan*. The girl had given Rhys's mother a few presents during the time they've been together, amounting to about 600 *yuan* altogether according to Rhys, and they did not want the girl to be out of pocket. Rhys assured me that the breakup gift was standard practice:

Some girls in Korla are very rich from breaking up with guys. . . . [The girls] say, "You have taken my youth, and you should pay me for it now that you are going to break up with me." Youth is a type of capital—if they lose their youth it is very difficult for them to get married to a good person.

The lament "today's girls are too mercenary" (*xianshi* 现实) has become such a truism that even the young women themselves go around saying it. Rhys said that he and the nurse had already talked about the

162

amount of financial input to a new apartment or the redecoration of the old apartment that each of them should put in. He thought he should only put 30% in and she should put 70% in, because he already owns an apartment and is putting that in also. But she didn't agree, arguing that he should put everything in. Sharing the nurse's views, a 19-year-old recent high-school graduate stated, "I will only marry a man whose family can afford to provide, at the very least, the apartment in which we will live. This is the absolute minimum, and it is perfectly justified that the man's family should buy the apartment." The same applies to other girls looking for marriage partners in Korla: young men in Korla bitterly relate stories of girls interviewing them about their assets, employment, and prospects, whether they would have a car, and even the exact division of housework labor.

Parents are the primary drivers of pragmatism in marriage negotiations. Rhys's "ex-girlfriend," a Ms. Deng, broke off their relationship at the behest of her family. Ms. Deng's family had not allowed her to marry Rhys because of his mediocre status as a temporary teacher and had arranged for her to marry a moderately well-off businessman. Similarly, Rhys's mother constantly pushed him to marry, while imposing certain nonnegotiable conditions on the process and outcome. She had no house of her own, was divorced with no partner or other children, and was about to retire from a low-paying job with minimal pension benefits. In other words, Rhys's mother relied on him emotionally and financially—and increasingly. Rhys was extremely loyal to her, regularly suffering her scolding for still being single. In Dicos, Rhys rocked back and forth on his chair: "I just want to find a girl to get married to, to stop my mum worrying. She says that if I don't get married before I am 30, it will be hard to find somebody good to get married to—there will only be divorced women left."

Rhys was torn between the unceasing pressure to marry, his apparently decreasing options and economic limitations, and his romantic ideals. As a result, he approached marriage transactions half-heartedly, almost completely disassociating marriage and emotional loyalty. Rhys and his ex-girlfriend regularly spent time together, both as a couple and with groups of Rhys's friends. They even went on overnight trips together. The nurse had reservations about this, but Rhys denied that his ex-girlfriend was a factor that should be taken into consideration. He kept emphasizing that he had taken the nurse home to meet his mother and that this was already a big step in establishing a stable relationship. He explained that he gave her the key to his house so she could go there if need be: "This requires a lot of trust, but she did not think that either of these actions signified that we had a stable relationship; she still did not think that I was loyal because of my ex-girlfriend."

Although he never said it aloud, all his friends knew that Rhys continued to hope that he would one day be well-off enough for his ex-girlfriend (and her family) to accept, and that she would be freed up by a breakdown of her own marriage. His hope was sustained by the apparently distant relationship that Ms. Deng had with her husband: as of 2012, they had no children, despite being married since 2006; the husband was often away on "business trips," suggesting that he had a mistress and freeing her to spend time with Rhys. At the same time, it was only by playing out the courtship game with other potential brides that Rhys could assuage his impatient mother, meet his spoken and unspoken social obligations, and retain his sense of personal dignity. Although Rhys insisted that he played the courtship game with a genuine intention to marry, the odds of finding a suitable match were not good because his standard of a woman was based on Ms. Deng. His marriage-market maneuvers also balanced out his relationship with his ex-girlfriend, since he did not appear to be waiting for her. This toned down mutual obligations and expectations—not least important, in the eyes of society—and helped them to maintain a sustainable level of emotional intensity. In this scene, all the actors were "married" to the structured rituals of courtship, in preparation for a union that is also an economic transaction.

Gendered Structures of Exchange

Men and women possess and exchange different "commodities" on the marriage market in Korla. Men need to create an impression of economic security to compete successfully, but judgments of economic security do not only take income level into account: self-employment is heavily discounted in comparison to state employment. For example, a moderately successful private businessman called Liu split up with his girlfriend of five years because the girl's mother opposed their marriage. Despite Liu having good business connections, a high income by Korla standards, and a reasonable amount of capital, the mother insisted that his work was "unstable." Liu talked with his girlfriend about it, saying to her, "It's up to you, it's your decision whether you choose to listen to your mother." "I'm not about to force her to marry me," he explained to us. She chose to marry an army man, prompting other young men drinking tea with us to comment, "What's so good about being in the army? . . . The most you will get is a few thousand a month, and that is only just enough to get

MARRIED TO THE STRUCTURE

6.1   Television advertisement for breast enlargement pills and topical cream, purportedly a French product "Beaute-buxom." Xinjiang Television, December 9, 2009. The vertical text above reads "[If] a woman has good breasts, her husband won't run away."

your own house when you get out. As if somebody in the army has a better income than a good businessman!" This mother wanted her daughter to be provided for by the state—she wanted her daughter to "eat state rice" (*chi guojia de fan* 吃国家的饭). Korla locals insist that, especially for men, *whose* rice you are eating significantly affects your marriageability.

Women are primarily marketing their own bodies, loyalties, and youth for a once-only transaction. For many men, a woman's value decreases sharply after she has been married once or has passed a certain age. This means that a woman is only willing to "sell" at what she considers to be a fairly good "price"—the combination of looks, affect, and economic security possessed or promised by her suitor—but cannot afford to wait too long. The increased pressure to marry as one gets older forces down the price, especially for women, and renders the individual increasingly pragmatic.

A middle-aged small-business owner explained that divorced women find it hard to get married again because "Chinese men don't want 'used goods,' especially if that woman has a child, and even more so if it is a boy child.... This means that women marry one man and stay married

165

for their whole life; they try very hard to keep the family together." Her husband added, "This is a good thing. The women are very loyal because they know that they don't have a good chance at a second marriage. So this tradition means that women are very forgiving of their menfolk, and it creates a more stable society." His wife suggested that this also gives rise to a situation in which men are less faithful, and many do not treat their women with respect, but he did not respond.

Infidelity as a Luxury Good

Zhou Yu is one of many young women who have internalized the idea of marriage as a one-way gate. Like Rhys, she comes from a family with little money and very few connections in the right places. Zhou Yu is an example of a young woman for whom, like both Rhys's and Liu's ex-girlfriends, marriage was first and foremost an economic strategy; feeling was secondary. She is married to a slightly pudgy noncombat army officer and spends her time raising their son, taking care of the housework, and lunching with her girlfriends (or sometimes me) at midrange establishments. After one such lunch in late 2009, she stated as if factually, and without a hint of regret, "I married too early. . . . I could have still had my choice of men even now [at 28]." Although she says that her husband is faithful to her, she obviously finds him boring. "Chinese men have a special characteristic—when they are courting you they will help you to food, buy you presents and flowers, and be extremely gracious toward you, but as soon as you marry them the romance disappears." She made a grabbing motion on the table and quickly followed through to shove the imaginary object deep into her pocket. "[They feel that] you are already in their pocket, you already belong to them, so there is no need for any more pleasantries." If the assumption is of a single chance at marriage, which will almost invariably result in routine and gendered role-playing, if not male infidelity, then for young women entering the marriage market there is all the more need to secure the best possible *economic* deal the first time around. Unmarried or divorced Tazhi men are thus primary targets for young women looking to marry.

As well as an object of economic aspiration, Tazhi is simultaneously an object of moral critique and immoral desire for those outside its walls. Tazhi people are widely and vocally criticized for their supposed adulterous practices, yet at the same time envied for their capacity to engage in those practices. A legend (and male fantasy) that circulates in Korla goes something like this:

There are bars across the road from the Tarim compound which are well known as pickup joints for people whose spouses are out of town. If a woman walks up to you and offers you a single cigarette, that means that she is alone, that her husband is out of town. If she offers you two cigarettes, that means that her husband is around. A taxi driver told me this. He delivered a woman to that bar one evening, and then only half an hour later she came out with a man and went directly back to her apartment in Tazhi.

Adultery becomes attractive for its connection to economic status—a matter of style—as well as for the illicit excitement of the act itself.

Zhou Yu's brief affair, described below, can thus be read as a reaction to the social, cultural, and economic constraints that she lives within, and the lifestyle models (Tazhi, Beijing, the West) that she experiences through rumor and the mass media. Not long after the lunch date described above, Zhou Yu rang me up and asked if I had time in the afternoon; she said she was feeling bad and really needed to talk to somebody. We met at a secluded coffee shop. She started by asking me what I think of women who have sex outside marriage: "Everyone has a right to love, don't they, Tom? I have a right to love, even if I am married. If there is not that love in my marriage, surely I have a right to find it elsewhere." Then she told me a story of a man she has met a couple of times:

He's a smooth operator. He set up the initial meeting with me by predicting where I would park my electric bicycle, then striking up a conversation. It worked out even better than he expected. . . .

He is a typical "big man"—he doesn't listen to suggestions from women, he just organizes it all and expects you to go along for the ride. Anyway, he set up dinner with a whole load of friends and invited me along. The first time I refused, then I accepted the second invitation. After dinner we went to karaoke and he drank a lot. He is that sort of man, a big drinker. There were little hire-girls there—really little! (She made a gesture indicating that the girls were only just over 1 meter tall.)

After a while he sat down beside me and said "I want" (*wo yao* 我要). "What do you want?" I asked. I wanted to give him an excuse, a way to back out and save face, so I offered him tea and alcohol: "You want some tea? Do you want some more alcohol? Wait, I will get you some . . ." "I don't want that," he said, and told me directly that he wanted sex with me. At that time I had some contradictory feelings. On the one hand I really wanted it, and on the other I felt guilty for being there. . . .

But Tom, I look at my future life, and I can predict what is going to happen every day. It's like a long straight corridor, and I can see all the way to the end. My husband says that's how it should be—each day watch the sun rise, each evening watch the moon rise, and pass each day uneventfully.

What should I do now, Tom? I have a feeling of guilt, of having done wrong. At the same time, I feel excited and enlivened—my life has something more to it now.

We discussed affair-strategy, given that the risk she was taking by engaging in an affair was far greater than the risk he, although also married, was taking.

If my husband found out, it would mean the end of our marriage, but if his [the big man's] wife found out, it would not affect his life greatly. So, for all the talk of male-female equality in China, real equality is still a long way off.... It's not like that in the West, is it? These double-standards are normal in China. Most people, both men and women, would look down on me if they knew what I've done.

I don't want to lose my family—the most important thing to me is still my family. And not only that, my husband is my only form of income. Without my family, I am destitute and penniless.

Zhou Yu made the pragmatic decision not to sleep with the man again. She may well have made different decisions, both in marriage and in cases like this, had she been financially independent. On the other side of the bargaining table, Rhys would have solved his "marriage problem" and put his mother at ease long ago if he commanded enough economic power to provide for both a prospective wife and for his own mother. Both Zhou Yu and Rhys, and thousands of other young people in Korla alone, are subject to very direct economic constraints in their choice of marriage partner.

Formal and Informal Structures of Control

The formal and informal structures of Korla create a society-wide "organized dependence." The recognition that one's life is constrained by *guanxi* networks and a state-dominated industrial structure provokes, in people "outside the system," a nostalgia for the *danwei* and a simultaneous longing for market liberalization that they believe (or at least hope) will help level the playing field. Looking at the same social scene, cadres and other people "inside the system" foreground the decline of morality in their nostalgia, while the primary aim of market liberalization and structural reform is, for them, efficiency.

Guanxi and State Employment

Both Zhou Yu and Rhys attribute their low socioeconomic status and thus their marriage woes and dilemmas to their lack of *guanxi*. Zhou Yu:

My classmates and I all graduated from the same college at the same time, but we were all assigned to very different places to teach. Two of my classmates with well-off families and good connections were assigned to [good urban schools], and got full-time jobs very quickly. Others were assigned to the country, to very very small schools in tiny villages . . . and their lives would be many times more difficult than those who were assigned to good schools in the city. It's really unfair. . . . Once you go down to work in the country, you may wait a lifetime to return and never get back.

Rhys made a similar critique, explicitly coupling a man's marriage prospects to his work unit's status.

The government controls the place very tightly, so a husband who works for the government is desired by young women looking to marry. There are three top work units: number one, the Tarim Oilfield Company; number two, the National Tax Office; number three, local government—including city and prefectural government—and other state-owned enterprises like the banks and the railway. . . . Much further down the list are [permanent] teachers, who are only attractive because of the stability of the job.

Just as with the workers in Tazhi, there is a significant difference between being a temporary teacher and being a permanent teacher in one of Korla's government schools. Individual schools are responsible for temporary teachers' salaries, whereas the Education Bureau at one or other level of government (city, prefecture, province) is responsible for the salaries of permanent teachers; the higher the bureaucratic rank of the bureau responsible for a given teaching position, the higher the regard in which that teaching position is held. At the bottom of this system, temporary teachers have no job security and very little negotiating power: in June 2009 all the temporary teachers in Rhys's prefectural government middle school had their pay cut by 400 *yuan* per month. The ostensible reason was the Global Financial Crisis, an excuse which the school leaders obviously put very little thought into, since the crisis had barely had any impact on Korla's economy—and certainly not on the running of a government-funded school. The point is that the leaders did not care whether their employees believed their rationale or not. Rhys explained,

CHAPTER SIX

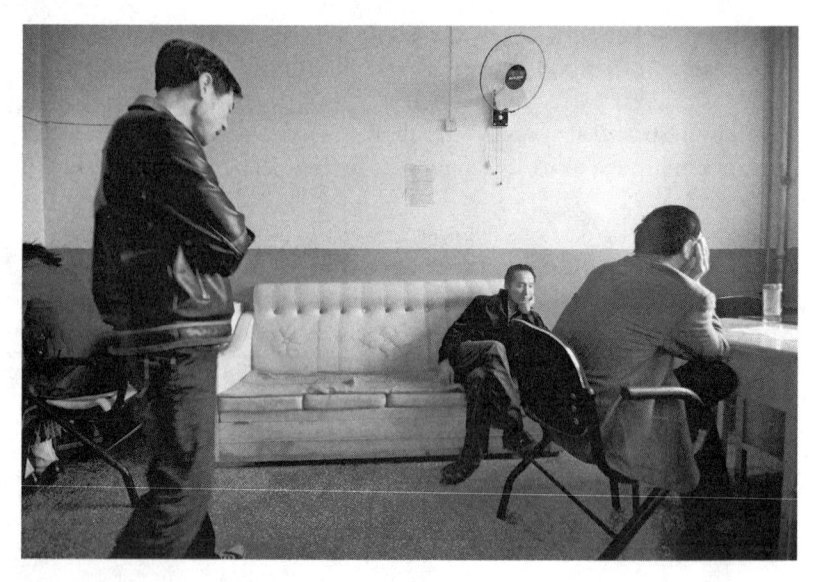

6.2 Teachers awaiting a negotiation

"The school leaders just say, 'Do you want to work or not?' If you ask for your equal rights, OK, you lose your job. You just have to accept the money that they will give you; they set the price."

Figure 6.2 shows temporary teachers in the headmaster's office of a private, tuition-based boarding school for students who are repeating the final year of high school. All of these teachers have been laid-off from permanent jobs in government schools or have quit temporary positions in those schools. They are awaiting the arrival of the headmaster, and yet another negotiation about the constant changes in their pay and conditions. Already, they have no insurance, no pension, and no job security at all. The terms of their contract are arbitrarily changed by their employer, the entrepreneur, almost every month. One month they may have to be present or on-call at the small private boarding school 24 hours a day, every second day; the next month it is back to 12 hours a day, six days a week. They don't like it, but teachers are common and they have little chance of permanent employment in a government school.

Everyone applying for a permanent position in a school or in the government bureaucracy must sit for some sort of examination, but most people in Korla agree that these examinations are far from free and fair. The lower the level of administration conducting the examination, the more corrupted the process is likely to be. One strategy is to set a very easy exam, which results in a cohort of high-scoring applicants and justifies the leaders' basing their decision on other factors that are less tangible. Foremost among these factors is the leaders' relationship to the applicants, so "if you have a good relationship with the leaders, you will get the job."

The perception that severe limitations are placed on opportunity for people without links to the state creates a desire for the market liberalization of Xinjiang's industrial structure among Rhys and his cohort. This "market desire" exists alongside their desire for state employment—they are interested in personal financial security and life chances, not economic governance per se. Rhys argued that where there are more private companies, "the government does not have such complete control." In "open" places, he said, getting a good job does not depend so much on connections within the government because private companies pay relatively more attention to merit-based selection. Rhys described a hierarchy of "openness" in China's government-enterprise structure—with eastern metropolitan China at the top, Urumchi a good deal less "open," and Korla at the bottom. This structural-conceptual model, with its embedded premise of regional marginalization, is one of the baseline assumptions of people in Korla. On and around this model, Korla people build their understanding of their place, and their personal potential, in the world.

Organized Dependence

The state domination of Xinjiang's industrial structure and the related assumption of the region's behindness also frame elite and bureaucratic views of Xinjiang and its people. In September 2011, the official in charge of the Ministry of Commerce's research project on Xinjiang's 12th five-year plan laid out the three major obstacles to Xinjiang's development as he saw them. They were "people's mind-set, . . . the lack of [local] talent, . . . and Xinjiang's industrial structure" (*Global Times* 2011c). In much the same way as articulated above by Rhys and others, market liberalization —"opening up"—and development is the solution put forward in state discourses (see, e.g., Yili Govt. 1999; Yili SASAC 2011). Two county-level cadres with whom I spoke in January 2010 made much the same points. Similarly, they were concerned with the effect that such "structural problems" could have on the productive capacity (rather than the life chances) of people "outside the system." The two cadres spoke with experience: Shen was a retired *bingtuan* political commissar (*tuan zhengwei* 团政委) of over 70; Wei, in his late 40s, was an oil company manager (*chuzhang* 处长) at the height of his career.

Shen and Wei posed Xinjang's industrial structure as the first "core problem" (*hexin wenti* 核心问题) and causally related it to other social and structural problems. Shen said, "To use Xinjiang people's words, the level of reform and opening up in Xinjiang is unfavorable compared to *neidi*. For example, some time ago most of the enterprises in *neidi* changed into private companies or joint ventures, but Xinjiang still has mostly SOEs." This means, he asserted, that Xinjiang people's "attitude toward reform and opening up is different from *neidi*." He said that there is a slower pace of life in Xinjiang due to the assumption of state care and lack of market competition—an "iron rice bowl mentality."

Shen's critique, that Xinjiang people lack economic initiative, was made repeatedly by people in Korla. A local teacher who helped me to do a survey (*N*=105) of the migration patterns of stallholders in the market commented:

From the survey we did this morning, you can see that of all the people doing small business in the market, there is only one Xinjiang person, and he comes from somewhere else [not Korla]. This testifies that Xinjiang people do not have the entrepreneurial spirit—on our own doorstep, all the people doing business are from somewhere else.

Most Korla people blamed institutions for this perceived ideological and structural behindness. A former state enterprise employee said, "My company pays us based on results, so people are motivated to work hard; government employees just go to work and sit there for eight hours, and their job is done." Although the structure was seen to be the original cause of this lethargy, its embodiment in the working population mitigates against its own reform.

Hung and Chiu's research with laid-off (*xiagang* 下岗) workers in northeast China provides a partial explanation for why many Xinjiang people apparently maintain an iron rice bowl mentality. Laid-off workers' nostalgia for the feeling of belonging to a unit—apparently no less powerful than their nostalgia for the cradle-to-grave social security and other entitlements—led Hung and Chiu to the conclusion that the "system of 'organized dependence' is . . . not just economic and political in nature but also social and psychological" (2009, 103). Taking this one step further, my findings suggest that an iron rice bowl mentality can exist independent of current or former state employment.

The informal *guanxi* networks and formal institutional structures explored in this and previous chapters are of primary importance in understanding the generalized phenomenon of organized dependence that, I argue, defines socioeconomic life in contemporary Korla. Such structures produce experiences and discourses, that, iterated repeatedly, become "mental frameworks" in the Braudelian sense, shaping nostalgia, aspiration, and collective perception, and hence the practice of everyday life (Braudel [1958] 2009, 179, see chapter epigraph). Inspired also by Hirokazu Miyazaki, I am here describing the *longue durée* "trajectory of how prevalent economic ideas generate concrete effects" (2006, 151).

"Organized dependence" is inherently structural but, in Xinjiang at least, it is much bigger than the individual *danwei*, or even personal memory of the state's somatic embrace. Xinjiang has long received hefty subventions from the central government (Millward 1998, 44ff; Becquelin 2004, 362) and, as well as being pumped into state institutions and invested in public infrastructure, this money has been disbursed to individuals through "border posting" subsidies (*dicha butie* 地差补贴) and the like. Mr. Wu (chapter 4) noted that border subsidies once constituted 32% of his net salary. The incremental reduction of these subsidies to individuals is a major cause of discontent among Xinjiang Han—including those who are no longer, or have never been, state employees. Children of laid-off state employees take up their parents' indignation or, like Mr. Wu, incumbent state workers expect the same social security guarantees for their children. More broadly, employees in the now far-healthier state sector become aspirational models for those increasingly marginalized people whose iron rice bowl, if they ever had one, has already been broken. Thus, the expectation of or desire for state care—the iron rice bowl mentality—extends beyond the institutional boundaries of the *danwei* through newly produced and reproduced memories, inheritance, and a sense of relative deprivation.

Korla peoples' iron rice bowl mentality is, I suggest, the result of a deliberate strategy to link the psychology and desires of people in Xinjiang to the center—to create a desire to be included by the center, and to be incorporated into the center. It is symptomatic of a structure of loyalty and expectations, a society-wide organized dependence, not simply an artifact of behindness. This organized dependence extends, in a distinct but recognizable form, into the ranks of the political and economic elite. The fortysomething oil company cadre, Director Wei, turned Shen's connection between politico-economic structures and the ideological "behindness" of the masses on its head, to implicate those who govern:

As Uncle Shen explained this morning, control of Xinjiang's resources—including natural resources, social resources, and interest resources (*liyi ziyuan* 利益资源)—is concentrated in the hands of the government. Right? The government exercises distribution rights [over these resources]—of course they are going to take care of their own needs first.

CHAPTER SIX

In referring to "interest resources," Director Wei sought to highlight how economic structures are one of the tools of control and social management used by the core in the periphery. He and Shen had explained earlier that the most significant "interest resources" are the embedded interests of the politico-economic elite because they shape political culture, alliances, and behaviors on an everyday level (see especially chapters 3 and 5). Noting the inefficiencies and conflict inherent in the many levels of government and excessive administrative overlap of the Chinese bureaucracy (further complicated in Xinjiang by the *bingtuan*), Wei and Shen advocated "structural reform." They noted resignedly, however, that attempts at structural reform inevitably meet another problem: "China is too big, and the structure of the CCP is not so flexible. Because any change would impact on many different people's interests, such an attack on vested interests has the possibility of upsetting the stability of CCP rule." By the same logic, the fostering of those vested interests through official patronage helps to shore up CCP rule. Vested interests throughout the structure constitute an impediment to change—be it reform or revolution—and as such, can be seen as a resource (i.e., a *liyi ziyuan*) of a centralized bureaucracy on constant alert for deviations from the party line. Indeed, in his assessment of the effectiveness of the Great Western Development Plan (GWD)[2] in reducing regional disparities, Victor Shih finds that "the GWD campaign was intentionally an enormous exercise of rent distribution. Politicized bureaucrats used the campaign as a means to consolidate their hold on the Party and to increase the power of the central bureaucracy" (2004, 427). "Rent distribution" in the form of developmental funding is an example of how formal and informal networks are intertwined, and together help to tie the interests of cadres at all levels to the interests of the state. Since developmental funding flows to areas that are rhetorically positioned as behind, the discourse of behindness can itself be seen as a tool of governance.

Married to Authoritarian Rule

The second "core problem" identified by Director Wei was China's party-state structure and its interactions with capitalism. Wei made it clear that this overarching "structural problem" gave rise to specific structural problems such as those raised above—industrial and administrative problems—as well as social and systemic problems like corruption, moral decline, and the widening gap between rich and poor. The discussion began when the older and more conservative cadre, Shen, lamented that

China has developed a lot, but a new phenomenon has arisen in the age of reform and opening up: society is not fair, short of justice, short of correctness. . . . Everybody just chases money, lives for money. There is no moral bottom line. This is our country's big problem at the moment—including cadres. According to the CCP's own words, cadres are The People's servants, but today's cadres . . . exercise special rights, take public money, and eat and drink excessively. . . . When the public sees this, their hearts are not at ease; they feel resentful. This is a big problem. But the CCP is now fixing this problem.

Director Wei waited respectfully for two beats, then spoke up:

Actually, it is not possible to solve the root problem. . . . I think that this is also a structural problem. Think about it, what is more important, the back of your hand or the palm of your hand? Of course, both are important. This structure, because it is mutually dependent, has no checks and balances. Is the palm to supervise the back of the hand or the other way around? Neither is possible—if the back discovers the palm has a problem, is it likely to cut that part off, to fix the problem? It cannot do this. This is the core of the problem.

Articulated in January 2010—following a year of CCP self-congratulation for 60 years of uninterrupted rule, and after a series of events in Xinjiang which, although not seriously threatening to CCP control over the region, comprehensively shook the regime all the way to the top—Director Wei's comments were perhaps indicative of a deeper insecurity, and even some soul-searching, in the ranks of the Xinjiang CCP. Director Wei next reeled off the "national conditions" that determined China's need for one-party rule by the CCP: very large country with an ignorant and diverse population; the CCP's monopoly on resources; the absence of a viable alternative; and the priority of economic development over political reform (cf. Liu 2011 [2006], 158–59). At the very least, this show of support functioned as discursive cover for the critique that followed:

The West now says that the CCP is autocratic and, actually, I agree. . . . [But] China, at this time, needs a strong leader—to govern with an iron fist, to first delineate and promulgate a standard: Here! You must be above this line; below is wrong.

CHAPTER SIX

First, by way of autocratic rule, establish democratic value standards. Then, when everybody accords to these universal standards, begin to implement democracy. That is, first tight, then loose.

[To do this], China needs the world, especially the advanced Western cultures, to help. Help does not mean give money or goods, it means help in a structural and ideological sense. The West's criticism is not a bad thing—it is also a form of help—but the West should look at it from another angle. That is, how to help the CCP maintain and stabilize their political power.

Now, what is the CCP most concerned about, above all other things? The maintenance of their power. Why is corruption getting worse and worse, why are social divisions getting wider and wider? Because the CCP is focused on holding on to power. If they change, they will come crashing down; if they don't change, the country will come crashing down. These are both extreme outcomes, and neither is acceptable—so now we walk a middle road, take it slowly.

Out of a choice of losing the party and losing the country, the CCP is most concerned about losing the party. If you lose the country, you can still try to get it back. If you lose the party, you lose everything; if you keep the party, at least you still have something.

Director Wei based his neo-authoritarian prescription on this understanding—that the CCP would sooner destroy "China" than relinquish its claim to sovereignty over "China." He argued that political, as well as economic and structural, reform is necessary for the stability of both the party and the country. But he also argued that the CCP itself was (and is) the biggest obstacle to such reform. Having created institutions—both formal and informal—to perpetuate their rule, the CCP is now bound up in these institutions. The CCP itself is married to the structure.

Wei's pragmatic approach was to guarantee the nonnegotiable criterion of continued CCP rule before moving toward any given future ideal. Perhaps because he too is married to the structure, he saw no alternative but to work within the structure. But Wei was not happy with the Hu-Wen approach of the time. With a disparaging reference to Hu Jintao's "eight honors and eight disgraces" (*ba rong ba chi* 八荣八耻), Wei called for a period of moral reshaping under an authoritarian strongman. (Note the resonances with Zhou Yu's desire for a "big man.") Outwardly, Wei asserted that market reform and some unspecified help from the West would enable China to hold itself together through a glacially slow top-down process of political reform. Inwardly, since he had no way of influencing these things, he must have hoped.

Pragmatic Hoping: Hope as Sustenance, Hope Manifest

Many Korla people view the world through these twin frames: on one hand, an earthbound pragmatism, and on the other, a flighty, potentialized hope. Korla people deploy, often simultaneously, the mental technologies of hope and pragmatism to navigate the world that they live in. Uncertainty (and therefore the risk that things will not turn out the way that one would like) is a condition of hope—as a possibility resolves one way or the other, hope must evaporate, or reorient toward a new end (Miyazaki 2004, 9). In distinction, pure pragmatism seeks to shore up (perceived) certainty in some area of life—in other words, closing off particular possibilities. While pragmatism seeks stability, hope seeks possibility. They tug in different directions but are complementary rather than mutually exclusive. Being risk averse yet aspirational (with respect to marriage, livelihood, and politics, for example), Korla people seek stability while attempting to maintain possibility.

The mental lives of Rhys, Zhou Yu, Director Wei, and many others are reinvigorated and sustained by the perceived existence of possibility. Zhou Yu's desire for excitement is the antithesis of the stability and predictability that she chose in marriage and (pragmatically) chose to return to. She returned, however, to a changed situation. Zhou Yu's affair opened up a possibility that she was not convinced existed before. The assurance that she was still attractive to other men was an assurance that she did not expend all her resources in the act of marriage; that she could still inspire doors along her "long straight corridor" to open. Her affair was one such door—it opened for her and she stood momentarily in the doorway, savoring her newly re-acquired and dangerous agency. Although she shut the door and continued along the corridor (ending the affair), the recent historical fact of the affair meant that the doors ahead now held possibility. She could, therefore, hope.

Zhou Yu's structure of experience began with a sense of doomed certainty, and a subsequent lack of hope. She reinvigorated her hope through a transgressive act in the material world. In contrast, Rhys began with hope. In a sense, he clung to uncertainty, in the face of the apparently certain loss of the woman he loved. This hope against hope shaped his actions (and the actions of significant others), and was eventually realized in the material world. In 2012 Ms. Deng divorced her businessman husband and set up house with Rhys. In 2014, after deferring many times for financial and family reasons, they married, and she gave birth late that year.

CHAPTER SIX

Rhys got to "where he is now" (time of writing, 2015) by sustaining the hope that Ms. Deng and her first husband would divorce. It was not a vain hope. As well as precluding Rhys from marrying his "ex-girlfriend" first, the structures of the marriage economy also encouraged the serial infidelity of her first husband by effectively nullifying any social or economic penalty for male infidelity. The businessman's infidelity broke down or prevented the formation of binding ties within his marriage to Ms. Deng. Their eventual divorce was driven in part by this situation, and also by the fact that Rhys's ex-girlfriend did not bear any children during the six or seven years of their marriage. In not having children, she sustained Rhys's hope (which may also have been her own). At the same time, Rhys's unwavering hope, which manifested in his demonstrated loyalty to her and his strategic lack of enthusiasm with dating or marrying anybody else, doubtless also influenced her actions with regard to both childbirth and her eventual divorce. Hope, in this case, led to its own realization.

It is going too far to suggest that Director Wei's January 2010 hope for an authoritarian strongman who would clean out the CCP was realized in Xi Jinping's ascension to power in November 2012. But it is notable that Wei's words echoed in Xi's early description of himself—this description was articulated through Xi's influence over mainstream discourse within China, and was iterated and reiterated in both domestic and foreign reports and analyses. The period from mid-2009 to early 2010 that is the psychological-temporal context of this book was, one might say, the right time for a discourse like that to emerge (or re-emerge). Events in Xinjiang during this period were certainly significant enough to influence thinking at the center over the longer term. And no doubt it also worked the other way around. In my experience of that era of "posts"—after the glory of the Beijing Olympics, the onset of the GFC, and the shock of the 2009 Urumqi riots—Wei was not alone among the Korla elite in hoping this hope.

The state of mind of people in Korla is associated with the transition in which Minxin Pei has argued that China is "trapped" (2006). Hope, too, exists only in a state of transition: it is oriented prospectively, but shaped by past experience, and can only continue to exist as long as it remains unrealized. The terms denoting the key landmarks of transition—that which is ahead and that which is behind—resonate particularly strongly in Xinjiang, iteratively defining the mental geography of the here and now. Many Korla people consequently feel permanently in between. Developmentally, they are between the "behindness" of Xinjiang and the non-Han ethnic groups, and the modernity of the (eastern

Chinese) metropole. They are always being told that they are "modern" but are constantly aware that it is only a relative modernity. Historically, they are also in a sort of limbo—for them, as for many Chinese, much of the past remains unspeakable, if not unknown, the present is uncertain, and the future is untrustworthy. If a worldview is how people "see the world, live in the world, and wear the world" (Berger and Mohr [1982] 1995, 287), then theirs is a "transition worldview."

State discourses maintain that stability is so important precisely because China is in a period of transition. Transition is thus a useful justification for unpopular state actions, from the violent eviction of farmers from their land to the sudden shift, or the inertia, of the reform process itself. Permanent postponement, historically associated with imperialism and elemental to a state of transition, seeks rhetorical support in the possibilities of the future.

The state of "not-yet" (Bloch 1986), in which Xinjiang seems permanently to exist, is complicated by various human temporalities of imperialism's own making. The iron rice bowl mentality of the "old Xinjiang people" is seen, by cadres in particular, as an obstacle to economic reform. Furthermore, since many Han people confront the new in the act of moving to Xinjiang, since they are less bound by tradition through the act of leaving their native-place, and since a large proportion of them are small-scale entrepreneurs, the "new Xinjiang people" (recent migrants) are arguably ideal subjects of a new economic era. The changing population makeup—from "old" to "new" Xinjiang people—is diluting the expectation of and the nostalgia for organized dependence: claims of entitlement by the newcomers carry less weight and, being mostly rural people, their historical ties with state enterprises are often weaker. However, the intimate connection between Xinjiang Han people's loyalty to the central state and the physical and psychological structures of organized dependence implies that a weakening of organized dependence in Xinjiang will see a commensurate weakening of loyalty to the center. This puts the state in a double bind: the sociopolitical status quo in Xinjiang is in some way sustained by a lack of structural reform, while at the same time, structural reform is seen as necessary for the colonial endeavor to move into its next phase.

SEVEN

The Partnership of Stability in Xinjiang

Once in every generation, without fail, there is an episode of hysteria about the Barbarians. There is no woman living along the frontier who has not dreamt of a dark barbarian hand coming from under the bed to grip her ankle, no man who has not frightened himself with visions of the Barbarians carousing in his home, breaking the plates, setting fire to the curtains, raping his daughters.
J.M. COETZEE, *WAITING FOR THE BARBARIANS* (1999, 8)

For many Han people, the illegally circulated closed-circuit television footage of an Urumchi street on the evening of July 5, 2009, confirms their deeply held beliefs about the uncontrollable, unpredictable, and violent nature inherent in every Uyghur man, woman, and child. A Xinjiang-born Han businessman told me the story of "a little Uyghur girl whose role was to pick up a brick and smash the skulls of Han people lying beaten on the ground—to make sure that their brains were splattered." He continued, his voice breaking with anger and disgust, "What do you say? A little 13-year-old girl! This whole ethnicity is animal! They're animals." Stories of children involved as both perpetrators and victims of violence were deployed by all sides, but all the stories remain unconfirmed.

The casual nature of the violence on that day (known as the 7/5 incident, or 7/5) in Urumchi at first shocked and stunned Han people in Xinjiang. Following the same response pattern as 9/11 in the Anglo world, the shock quickly turned to indignation, anger, and fear. Han anger with the Uyghur perpetrators was soon eclipsed by anger with what

7.1 CCTV footage, Urumchi, 8:38 p.m., July 5, 2009. Uyghurs (young man, left, and middle-aged woman, right) beating a Han.

7.2 CCTV footage, 8:51 p.m., July 5, 2009. The same Han man as in figure 7.1 is circled (left). The young woman bottom right of frame in figure 7.1 is circled (right) kicking a different Han man.

CHAPTER SEVEN

many Xinjiang Han saw as the languid response of the security forces,[1] and in particular with Xinjiang's first-in-command, secretary of the Xinjiang CPC, Wang Lequan.

Less than two months later, on September 3, following reports of (assumed Uyghur) assailants using infected hypodermic needles to attack Han women, children, and the elderly, crowds of Han people gathered outside the offices of the Xinjiang government to demand Wang Lequan's resignation. The Han protesters' basic complaint was that he had failed to protect them and their property; failed to "maintain stability" (*baochi wending* 保持稳定). The Han protestors were on the same piece of politically sensitive ground—Urumchi People's Square—where state security forces had first cracked down on the initially peaceful Uyghur protests on July 5.[2] In contrast, however, there was no police action to disperse the Han protesters of September 3, despite their direct challenge to the Chinese Communist Party's top representative in Xinjiang. Moreover, they appeared to get their way. By September 5, the Urumchi party secretary, Li Zhi, and the Urumchi police chief Liu Yaohua had been removed from their positions (*Ku'erle Wanbao* 2009g, 1, 11); in late April 2010, Wang Lequan was reassigned to serve as vice-secretary to Zhou Yongkang in the Central Politics and Law Commission (Xinhua 2010). The incoming party secretary, Zhang Chunxian, brought with him a raft of state capital investment, subsidies, and preferential policies that were clearly aimed at integrating Xinjiang and placating the Han population by benefiting them. As described in chapter 6, the extension of organized dependence across society is believed to help preserve social stability.

These events raise important questions about the interplay of interests between various levels of the state (including both party and government) and the various social groups that they claim to represent. Why were the direct criticisms of Wang Lequan tolerated? Was the replacement of Wang Lequan a tacit acknowledgment of these criticisms as legitimate and thus a symbolic rectification by the central party? Does the role and position of Xinjiang within China somehow modify the authoritarian state-society relations prevalent in (most of) the rest of the PRC? As these questions imply, I broaden the sociospatial scope of this chapter from "Han individuals and social groups in Korla" to "Han social groups in Xinjiang" and their collective and specific relationships with the central government.

I propose that the above questions are best addressed by attention to a particular "mass frame" that helps to structure social life in contemporary Xinjiang. Mass frames are defined by William Hurst as "coherent worldviews shaped in large part by the *structurally rooted* collective life experience of social groups" (2008, 71). Hurst distinguishes mass frames from other forms of collective action frames—for example, of the type deployed by "rightful resisters" (O'Brien and Li 2006) or "moral economy" protesters (Perry 2008, 44–45)—by noting that the latter emphasize the *agency* of individuals and social groups involved. While consciously produced frames are episodic and strategic, mass frames are ever present and structural. These types of frames can coexist—indeed, social actors that engage in strategic framing often draw upon the discourses, practices, and assumptions of a mass frame. The social group outlined by the mass frame that I concentrate on here is a subset of the Han in Xinjiang, which I term the Han mainstream.

The Han Problem

The argument of this chapter is that the Han mainstream in Xinjiang view their relationship, including their mutual obligations, with the central party and government through a mass frame that I term "the partnership of stability." Central to the production and reinforcement of this mass frame are the psychology of organized dependence and state discourses, past and present. State discourses portray Han in Xinjiang as "constructors" supporting the physically and culturally barren border region (see chapter 1). Key structural elements of this mass frame include historical and continuing dependence on preferential policies and subsidies from central coffers; an urban industrial economy that remains heavily state dominated, helping to create a culture of organized dependence that extends beyond the work unit; and the existence of a significant other in the Uyghurs (see chapters 2–6). The partnership of stability holds that the Han mainstream do their part by occupying the border region and by accepting the party as the best solution for a multiethnic, increasingly stratified China and the government as the party's administrators. In return they expect protection and that what is being built in Xinjiang is first and foremost for their benefit, regardless of the official policies granting special privileges to minorities.

In post-7/5 Xinjiang, the Han mainstream acted in accordance with their understanding of the partnership of stability, as well as in response to more immediate information—including leaks from within the state, media reports, and rumors. As of mid-2015, the flow-on effects of the

CHAPTER SEVEN

turmoil in Xinjiang in 2009 have been consistent with the most important assumptions of the partnership of stability. This mass frame—shaped as it is by state discourse and the structural context of Xinjiang, then embodied and mobilized by a particular section of the population—can *in return* also shape state actions in Xinjiang. I am thus describing a feedback loop that can be traced to the unifying imperatives of the central state.

The rising proportion of Han in South Xinjiang is helping to drive the region's progression from a "frontier of control" (military occupation) toward a "frontier of settlement" (Han civilian occupation). Long-term occupation is the basis of Uyghur claims to Xinjiang. Demographic change toward a Han majority in Xinjiang weakens such claims through a fait accompli. Employing the language of a democracy that does not exist in Xinjiang, a number of Han people have confidently stated (in my presence, and in part, but not always entirely, for my consumption) words to the effect that "separatism is not an issue, because we [Han] outnumber them [Uyghurs], so if it came to a vote, we would win." The subtext, of course, is "if it comes to a fight, we will win."

CCP policy adviser Ma Dazheng voiced a common view among the leadership when he wrote that "Hans are the most reliable force for stability in Xinjiang" (quoted in Bovingdon 2004, 27). Especially at times of Uyghur unrest, one Han person on the ground in Xinjiang has a higher political value to the central government than a Han person of equivalent economic worth and cultural level who lives in central or eastern China because the Han person in Xinjiang also, by the simple fact of their existence, performs a vital function: occupying Xinjiang.

The logical extension of this view—that there is a positive correlation between a high Han population and sociopolitical stability in Xinjiang—is that stability *among* these Han is of paramount importance. As the Han population of Xinjiang grows in both relative and absolute terms, and simultaneously becomes increasingly stratified, both the difficulty and the imperative of maintaining sociopolitical stability among the Han also grows. In making these statements, I am challenging the widely held assumption among scholars and observers that the central government perceives "the Uyghur problem"[3] as the primary threat to social and political stability in Xinjiang, and thus to the center's ability to achieve its sociocultural, political, and economic objectives in the region. I claim that the "Han problem" is more central. Understanding how socioeconomic differences among Han in Xinjiang influence their political potential is crucial to understanding this logic.

Han Social Groups in Xinjiang

I divide Han in Xinjiang into three conceptual categories—the Han elite, the Han mainstream, and the Han subaltern. There are not hard boundaries between these groups. The three factors which most clearly define them are (1) socioeconomically valuable *links to the state*—these include both informal personal relationships with power-holding individuals within the state and formal employment relationships with viable urban work units, (2) independent economic influence combined with relative *spatial mobility*, and (3) *time of migration*.

Time of migration has a strong influence on the strength and extent of local networks, including connections with lower levels of the state. "Early" migration—pre-1990s—is also an important factor in itself, because of the implied entitlement due to "border supporters." Earlier migrants, however, tend to be less spatially mobile because they are more likely to be lifetime state employees and to have fewer connections with *neidi*. As a result, they are less likely to be economically independent outside of Xinjiang. The potential mobility of a given group acts as an incentive for the authorities to create favorable conditions for members of that group, in order to get them to stay in Xinjiang. The social categories that I present here are thus network based but not entirely network dependent.

The Han elite are a relatively small and economically powerful group. They always have close formal or informal links with the state, but time of migration varies. To a large extent, their high-level connections with the state obviate the need for a broader network of lower-level local connections. Tazhi employees—including Directors Jia, Xie, Ren, and Wei, Section Chief Jing, Party Secretary Zhang, and Mr. Wu—are the Han elite who feature most prominently in this book. The Han elite also includes the permanent employees of other central SOEs, and large-scale business owners or investors. The latter, and their capital, are highly mobile, while the employees of elite central SOEs tend to be tied to their work units for much of their career. The Han elite play important roles in Xinjiang—they may attract in-migration by stimulating economic activity or act as role models for the rest of the Xinjiang population. Although they are culturally and economically influential, they are not disruptive because it is against their interests to be so.

The Han mainstream can be split into two groups—those with ongoing state employment (regardless of migration status) or strong informal links to the state, and those with *only* early migration status or *only* economic influence combined with spatial mobility. In other words, the significant division is between those "inside the system" and those "outside the system." The Han mainstream includes people who identify as "old Xinjiang people," along with small-scale entrepreneurs and other settlers from *neidi*. For an individual to be considered a part of the Han mainstream, at least one adult member of their immediate family must hold a Xinjiang-based *hukou*. Yanyan, Boss Kang, and the YEA businesspeople (all in chapter 5) are examples of the "inner" mainstream, and TCM doctor Zhang Yonglei (introduction and chapter 1), Zhou Yu, and Rhys and his friends (chapter 6) are examples of the "outer" mainstream. Both "old Xinjiang people" and more recent in-migrants can be either inside or outside the system, depending on the nature of their employment. When Han elsewhere in China are reminded (through leaders' statements and television dramas, for example) of the pioneers and constructors, past and present, who have helped and are helping to secure Xinjiang's place in the PRC, they are reminded of the Han mainstream. This rhetorical positioning, along with the size, diversity and local social networks of the Han mainstream means that, as a group, they are both influential and potentially disruptive.

The Han subaltern in contemporary Xinjiang are recent in-migrants without any valuable links to the state, and for whom the move to Xinjiang has failed to raise their relative socioeconomic status substantively. The Han subaltern includes sojourning seasonal migrant workers from *neidi*, such as the Jiangsu boys in chapter 1, and the *bingtuan* underclass. The former are highly mobile, but the latter are effectively immobilized by their *bingtuan hukou*. Unlike full *bingtuan* members (who, like political commissar Shen, are "old Xinjiang people" and members of the Han mainstream) and rural people elsewhere in China, the *bingtuan* underclass are effectively tenant farmers locked into a debt cycle. If they default by leaving the *bingtuan*, they have nowhere to go back to. Although essential as an occupying and labor force, the Han subaltern groups have little influence over others in Xinjiang. They are the most potentially disruptive group among the Han because they have so little to lose and because, as rural people from *neidi*, they have a far weaker set of expectations and loyalties toward the state.

Relative stability among the Han mainstream is seen as a prerequisite for stability in Xinjiang more broadly because some disaffected Uyghur or Han subaltern groups may take advantage of unrest among the Han mainstream to create their own commotion. Although subaltern Han groups have little or nothing in common with Uyghurs, demonstrations and uprisings are contagious. This would put the authorities in the unenviable position of trying to contain instability among multiple interest groups, all with different, or even competing, demands and different rules of engagement. The mere threat of Uyghur unrest makes the maintenance of stability among the Han mainstream that much more important.

The Need for Instability

The perceived threat of Uyghur unrest—instability—allows for, and is produced by, a discourse of what Buzan, Wæver, and de Wilde term "securitization." They write, "In security discourse, an issue is dramatized and presented as an issue of supreme priority; thus by labeling it as *security* an agent claims a need for and a right to treat it by extraordinary means" (1998, 26). Securitization has both economic and political aims and consequences. Many examples of exception in Xinjiang are justified by way of this discourse.

Economically, the "instability declaration" aims to attract funds from higher levels of government. Certain government and public security institutions within Xinjiang have long been dependent on the perception of instability for their livelihood—or even for their continued existence. In Xinjiang, the *bingtuan* needs instability to secure continued funding from the center. James Seymour offered his interpretation of a Xinhua report that called for the whole nation's "support and understanding" for the *bingtuan* mission: "If you want us to defend China against the forces of central Asian nationalism, you should be willing to pay for the service" (2000, 185). Xinjiang Han people, and institutions of government and administration, leverage the discourse of instability in similar ways, and the 7/5 incident helped to drastically increase the politico-economic value of the "instability card." Within days, many "old Xinjiang people" were confidently proclaiming that "this is a good thing for Xinjiang—the central government will sit up and take notice." Politically, securitization grants an excuse to have troops on the streets and to curtail normal freedoms with the acquiescence of the Han population. The perception of a destabilizing "other" in the Uyghurs also produces ethnic solidarity among the Han and promotes Han political loyalty to, and dependence on, the center. In these ways, the perception of instability is a resource.

On the other hand, state actors may at times choose to downplay instability. State actors make declarations about stability to attract people and investment back to Xinjiang and to stop them from leaving, to create a feel-good factor within Xinjiang and thus stimulate consumption (including, especially, real estate consumption), and to make leaders appear to be successful in producing (or enforcing) and maintaining stability. Thus, in Xinjiang, stability as a concept and an aspiration is inextricable from the perceived threat of instability. The threat of instability and its counterpoint, the assurance of stability, are such valuable tools in Xinjiang not because ethnic violence is necessarily around the next corner but, *rather*, because in the Han imaginary that possibility is ever-present.

Han Discontent

The outpouring of popular anger directed publicly against Wang Lequan in the aftermath of 7/5 was an unprecedented event in reform-era Xinjiang. Provincial-level leaders across China are very rarely considered allowable targets of criticism (Sun 2010). Wang Lequan had been in the top position in Xinjiang for 15 years—a contravention of the standard CCP practice of regularly rotating high-level cadres to prevent them from building up local networks. However, the cadre exchange system did not apply to Xinjiang because, for as long as Wang Lequan maintained stability in Xinjiang, he was the right man in the view of Beijing. Backed by Zhou Yongkang, Wang Lequan's implementation of continuous "Strike Hard" (*yanda* 严打) campaigns in the early 2000s made his political career. In the highly securitized political atmosphere of Xinjiang there was no space for open criticism, despite extensive Han dissatisfaction with Wang Lequan and the provincial-level government of Xinjiang since well before the summer of 2009.

Wang Lequan was infamous for his cronyism. Popular perception among Han people in Xinjiang prior to Wang Lequan's removal was that a "Shandong clique" dominated the politics of the Autonomous Region and that Shandong-based businesses were provided with lucrative contracts—most hurtfully, for projects that could easily have been done by Xinjiang-based businesses. One story concerns compressed-earth pavers: "Why do we need to bring dirt from Shandong?" was the rhetorical ending to this story when first told to me by a third-generation *bingtuan* person. "Hasn't Xinjiang got any dirt of its own? We have heaps of dirt. Look around you—*there is dirt everywhere in Xinjiang*." The hurt pride in the speaker's voice, and specifically the reference to Xinjiang as dirty, highlights the inferiority that many Xinjiang Han feel with respect to the developed regions and people on China's eastern seaboard.

In April 2009 an anonymous post made to a web forum by a government employee from northwest Xinjiang expressed a feeling of resentment, common among people in Xinjiang, at being left behind the economic advances of the eastern seaboard cities. The post referred to the comparative salaries of government workers across China as proof that Xinjiang was being neglected by the central authorities and exploited by its corrupt and ineffectual leadership: "They're an interest group, concerned only with their own 'stability'" (Baidu Tieba chatroom 2008). The writer put stability in quotation marks as a mocking reference to the most commonly heard political aphorism in relation to Xinjiang: "Social stability is a prerequisite and guarantee of Xinjiang's development" (State Council Information Office 2009). The government employee went on, "There's no way they'll look after [us here at] ground level, only if it affects their own stability will they give us an increase [in wages], and even then that won't keep up with costs [of living]" (Baidu Tieba chatroom 2008).

Immediately after 7/5, the savvy Third Front factory worker who matched *guanxi* with *guanxi* to get his son into military college (chapter 5) used the widespread discourses of corruption and salary discrimination against Xinjiang government employees to help explain his predictions for transition politics in Xinjiang:

It is possible that the central government will move to slowly change Wang Lequan for somebody else, but not until things have become calmer and more stable in Xinjiang. A new leader at the moment would be at a loss and make the situation even worse.

Replacing Wang Lequan immediately after 7/5 would also, I suggest, have been seen by people in Xinjiang as a tacit admission of CCP failure. The worker surmised hopefully that 7/5 may provide the opportunity for the center to "punish [Wang Lequan] for his crimes" and gave two reasons for a change of leadership:

One: In China, there is a policy to change leaders often to avoid than building up a network of cronies and entrenching corruption; he is long overdue. Two: Xinjiang people are disappointed with Wang Lequan because before he came our salaries used to be one of the highest in China, but now we are among the lowest, and our extra benefits have also shrunk in comparison.

The retired worker's nostalgia for a bygone era of relative privilege—not simply because he was a state employee, but because he was a state employee *in Xinjiang*—has its basis in official wage figures. The average wages of state employees in Xinjiang fell from 17% above the national average (sixth highest) in 1978 to 21% below (fourth lowest) by 2008. The steepest decline was between 2004 and 2008 (a fall of 11 percentage points relative to the national average), which meant that the sense of relative deprivation was at a high point in 2009.[4]

This man was not alone in his nostalgia, nor was he alone in the accuracy of his predictions. Indeed, the general feeling among the many Han whom I spoke to in the second half of 2009 was not only that Wang Lequan *should* go, but that, sooner rather than later, he *would* go. Xinjiang Han became increasingly confident of the strength of their case against Wang Lequan as the events and aftermath of 7/5 temporarily, but radically, altered the discursive space of Xinjiang.

With 7/5, Wang Lequan failed on his principal pledge (stability) and could thus be held to account for his other transgressions—whether real or imagined. Yanyan, the ethnically Zhuang but culturally Han protagonist of chapter 5, explained:

Wang Zhen had a high-pressure policy toward Uyghurs. But Wang Lequan's policies, over the years, have caused Uyghurs to become insufferably arrogant, and to be impolite and disrespectful toward Han people.... So this has given rise to the Han people's slogan of July 7: "If the government won't take action, we will take action ourselves" (*Zhengfu bu zuowei, women lai zuowei!* 政府不作为,我们来作为!). For a long time, the leaders of Xinjiang have not educated or conditioned the Uyghurs [to the Han way of life and social norms].

The Han in Xinjiang are not like Shanghai people—"wa wa" wimpy crybabies. If you hit me, I'm not going to just sit and take it, I am going to hit you back.... And it was not until the Han took to the streets [on July 7] that the government realized that the situation was serious.

Until that time, they were just sitting on their backsides thinking that it wasn't a problem: "We have it under control; we can suppress the Uyghurs any time." So now all Xinjiang people are criticizing Wang Lequan—every day on TV speaking bullshit....

That's not to say it's only Wang Lequan who is to blame, but it's mainly him. Why? Because in China the party secretary is the top leader—he has the power to move troops into action, so he should take 90% of the blame! He can say what he likes, it's high time he stepped down.

Wang Lequan's stability guarantee failed on two related fronts. On the first front, Wang Lequan failed to guarantee to Han settlers and to the center that the Uyghur "natives" would not rise up and threaten the settlers' lives or livelihoods, or the economic functioning of Xinjiang as a whole. On the second front, Wang Lequan failed to guarantee to the center that the Xinjiang Han would not leave Xinjiang in droves, or protest and act in destabilizing ways—either of which threaten central power in Xinjiang, far more so than Uyghur rioting in and of itself.

The Fall of Wang Lequan

Wang Lequan's removal in late April 2010 was seen by many Han in Xinjiang as a sign that the central government really did care about their opinions and their livelihood. The political capital that the center gained in Xinjiang by removing Wang Lequan also gave the incoming Zhang Chunxian an immediate public relations advantage, since he was seen as a representative of the party center. However, such opportunistic sympathy is by no means a given. In the PRC, even nonviolently expressed popular discontent with official actions has not necessarily led to higher levels of government intervening on behalf of the protesters and has on occasion led to a brutal crackdown. Unrest in Xinjiang has generally been treated even more harshly. Gardner Bovingdon shows that, even in the more forgiving period from 1980 to 1997, protesters' demands were partly or fully met in only four instances, two of which can be considered of relatively little significance. The atmosphere became increasingly intolerant during the 1990s and into the 2000s, as Wang Lequan's hardline approach dominated (2010, 105–34 and appendix).

Framing and Perception

In July and August 2009, the Han public came to perceive open criticism of Wang Lequan as permissible and created a "political opportunity" with ongoing significance to the political economy of Xinjiang. Cai Yongshun writes, "Political opportunities are not necessarily predetermined in popular resistance; they may be created or even perceived rather than real" (2010, 87). Perceptions about the safety of open protest were shaped by Han peoples' preexisting understandings of the partnership of stability, by social networks both horizontal and vertical, and by the media.

Several China scholars have pointed to frames as important influences on the outcomes of popular resistance (O'Brien and Li 2006; Mertha 2008; Perry 2008; Hung and Chiu 2009). Stability is one of the most powerful frames in the contemporary PRC, since in CCP rhetoric, stability is a necessary condition of development, development ensures stability, and both are seen as essential to maintaining the party's hold on power (CPPCC News Online 2005; Li Q. 2011). A shift in emphasis from one to the other can indicate a shift from a hard-line approach (stability first) to a more moderate approach (development first), or vice versa. The stability frame is both more complex and more powerful in peripheral regions of China that have high non-Han populations that are perceived to have separatist tendencies. In Xinjiang, Wang Lequan made "stability overrides all" (*wending yadao yiqie* 稳定压倒一切) his governing maxim (ChinaNews.com 2008) and, by doing so, made stability the standard on which his administration was judged.

Mertha writes that, in contemporary China, "activists of all stripes have managed to wriggle their way into the policy-making process and even help shape policy outcomes. They have succeeded in part because they have understood and accepted the general rules of the game of policy making under the rubric of 'fragmented authoritarianism'" (2009, 996). Han people in post-7/5 Xinjiang, in particular the protesters of September 3, 2009, can be considered activists in that they sought to influence high-level political decisions that they perceived to directly affect their lives, but over which they had (and have) no formal influence. They understand and accept that the rules of the game were based on stability as the "number one responsibility" for cadres at all levels (CPPCC News Online 2005) and that they themselves are seen by the center as the key agents of stability in Xinjiang. That is to say, the rules of the game in Xinjiang, although (like elsewhere in China) flexible within a range, are delineated by the partnership of stability. Video that I obtained of the anti–Wang Lequan protests on September 3 is notable for the casual attitude of the demonstrators, implying that they felt secure there would be no crackdown by the security forces.

Social networks were an important factor in creating a sense of political safety among the protesters. Cai Yongshun shows that social networks are a "political asset" in China. Horizontal social networks (among social peers) increase the likelihood of collective resistance and promote group solidarity; vertical social networks (between resisters and agents of the state) increase the chances that the resistance will be successful by helping resisters exploit any fractures within the state, by signaling the likely response of the security forces, and by leveraging state agents' "moral responsibility to help the people with whom they are connected" (2010, 88). A former classmate who is now a bureaucrat, police officer, or news editor is the ideal type of "vertical" connection. As chapter 5 has shown, the "old Xinjiang people" who make up the bulk of the Han mainstream have the most thorough and deep-reaching *guanxi* networks. Cai concludes that such relationships "blur the boundaries between the state and society in China and make political participation, or the way citizens exercise political influence, more subtle and perhaps more effective" (ibid., 109). Yanyan's expression of dissatisfaction with Wang Lequan's government is an expression of dissatisfaction from Xinjiang Han more broadly, including within the government apparatus itself.

The Role of the Media in Creating Political Opportunity

Immediately after the July 5 violence, the government attempted to isolate Xinjiang by cutting off the Internet, text messaging services, and international calls. A Xinjiang-wide intranet was set up, which initially had only one web address available—the government-run Tianshannet. The severing of interprovincial lines of communication was extremely disruptive to business and social life, causing unknown millions of *yuan* of lost revenue for Xinjiang-based businesses both large and small (Grammaticas 2010) and creating widespread resentment among the population. These disruptions were framed within the discourse of securitization as a sacrifice that was necessary to prevent "law breakers," understood to mean Uyghurs, from organizing "further instances of violent criminal activity" (news.china.com.cn 2010; Tianshannet 2010).

However, the main reason for the Internet blackout in Xinjiang was government fear of Han criticism and rumor mongering—more than fear of Uyghur violence. Very soon after the July 5 riot, a concerted antirumor campaign was launched with the slogan "Don't Believe Rumors; Don't Spread Rumors; Don't Start Rumors; Trust in the Party" (*bu xin yan; bu chuan yan; bu gen yan: xiangxin dang* 不信谣; 不传谣; 不跟谣: 相信党), and it was also made clear to the public that the punishment for spreading rumors was 5–10 days in jail (*Ku'erle Wanbao* 2009h, 6). In late July, the vice minister of the Central Propaganda Department visited Xinjiang and, at a meeting with provincial leaders and media personnel, emphasized the media's important role in "guiding public opinion" by "transmitting the just voice (*zhengyi zhi sheng* 正义之声) of the party, government and the masses" (Li 2009, 1).

The state's attempts to stifle popular discourse were not entirely successful. First, information and rumor from other parts of China still got through to people in Xinjiang, and a feeling among Xinjiang people that they were being kept in the dark lent an aura of truth to information from outside the firewall that it did not always deserve. Information that apparently originated with "a friend" in the security services or government was treated with the same hushed reverence. Second, some Han people read it as a confirmation of instability in Xinjiang. Oilfield worker Mr. Wu said, "After 7/5, everybody was without the Internet, and they all realized [Xinjiang] is not stable, still not stable." In this way, measures supposed to combat instability actually ended up creating greater instability by fueling a sense of instability in the population (cf. Social Development Research Group 2010). In this repressive context, small signals took on great significance. The Xinjiang public's perception of the degree and nature of support for Wang Lequan at the party center was negatively affected by media reports through July and August 2009. Seen from ground level in Xinjiang, the center appeared to be opening a space for public criticism of Wang Lequan.

The anti-Uyghur riots that occurred on July 7 were both a response to and further evidence of the increasingly popular perception that "the government is useless" (Branigan 2009). The immediate publication (the morning of July 6) on Tianshannet of pictures of murdered Han helped to consolidate popular Han support for the anti-Uyghur vigilantes. An informant telephoned me late in the evening on July 7, and without greeting me, he declared, "The Han people have stood up!" It was a conscious reference to Mao Zedong's well-known declaration that "the Chinese people have stood up," understood to mean throwing off the tyranny of oppression both from within the country (the Kuomintang) and from outside (the imperialist powers of Japan, Europe, and the United States). My informant similarly implied that the Han of Xinjiang will suffer oppression (by Wang Lequan and his allegedly pro-Uyghur policies) and humiliation no longer. This sense of collective agency—"if the government won't take action, we will take action ourselves"—was later to act against Wang Lequan.

Also a double-edged sword was the evidence cited in support of the widely reported assertion that the 7/5 riots were a premeditated act of violence designed to sabotage ethnic unity. Intelligence that was apparently gathered in the 10 days prior to July 5 undermined the Xinjiang-based authorities. The official central line, released by Xinhua in both Chinese (Sina.com 2009) and English on the morning of July 6 read,

According to the government, the World Uyghur Congress has recently been instigating an unrest [sic] via the Internet, calling on supporters "to be braver" and "to do something big." On Saturday evening, information began to spread on the Internet, calling for demonstration in the People's Square and South Gate in the Urumchi city. On Sunday, Rebiya called her accomplices in China for further instigation, according to the government statement. (Xinhua 2009a)

This attempt to prove the involvement of "separatist elements" outside of China (to avoid the 7/5 riots being framed as a domestic problem) was read by Chinese people in Xinjiang as evidence of the incompetence of Xinjiang cadres and security services. The video images shown at the beginning of this chapter, which came from surveillance cameras operated by the Urumchi security forces, also emphasized the poor response time of the police on the day. These videos circulated illegally in Xinjiang through late 2009 and later became available on YouTube (2009). Stories and rumors, already rampant, were bolstered by this sort of evidence. The information that was reported in the media was thus interpreted in the context of the information that was not officially reported. A young English teacher explained,

10 days ago, on June 28, all the evidence that something was going on and about to happen in Urumchi was available—lots of discussions on the Internet; the police even listened in on Rebiya calling her brother to arrange this. . . . This was reported in the *Bayinguoleng Daily* on or about the 11th or 12th of July. So everybody in Xinjiang has the right to call Wang Lequan and the government to account over what they were not doing, and should have been doing to prevent this. . . . [The security forces] didn't realize it was this serious. . . . This was their mistake; they were caught off-guard.

A cartoon in the *Korla Evening News* (*Ku'erle Wanbao* 库尔勒晚报) on July 29, 2009, expressed these feelings in a satirical form. The rhyme was titled "Carrying out duties in this manner." It was accompanied by a picture showing two cats watching a group of mice feasting and playing right under their noses, but on the boundary between their two districts. Both cats are saying, "It is your jurisdiction" (2009c, 4).

The retired Third Front factory worker, quoted earlier, lamented,

In the past we had one very strong point, as Mao Zedong said, "The people you call will come; those who come will fight; those who fight will win." At present, the fighting spirit of the militia and the armed police is greatly lacking. They say "I haven't received any orders to move, so I don't move." The great generals of the past were great generals because they did not wait for orders from above—they made war when the opportunity to make war successfully arose. Not like today.

CHAPTER SEVEN

On July 13, the central government announced a series of 24 "Provisional measures concerning the accountability of high-level party and government cadres," effective immediately. Item seven stated that high-level cadres would be "held accountable" by "instructing them to make a public apology, suspending them from work while their case is investigated, or having them voluntarily taking the blame and resigning, ordering them to take the blame and resign, or [unilaterally] removing them from their post" (*Renmin Ribao* 2009a). The announcement was seen in Xinjiang as a direct response to the governance failures exposed by the riots of July 5 and July 7, and policy positioning for the eventual removal of Wang Lequan. A former local government employee said, "Altogether, there were eight items focused on cadres at county level and above. We counted that Wang Lequan is guilty of five of them."

Despite the best efforts of the center, criticism began inevitably to slip sideways, from Wang Lequan and the Xinjiang authorities to the Communist Party and system more broadly. A common story held that Wang Lequan was drunk on that day, and he was not answering his mobile telephone. Since nobody lower down in the hierarchy was game for making the decision to suppress the rioting Uyghurs, it was well into the evening by the time the order was given. My Han interviewees criticized what they saw as a system that rewarded only obedience, not initiative, where the population had no right to choose their leaders, and where those with power or powerful connections can get away with anything. Some compared China unfavorably to America or Australia in these respects. Many made the point that this system impacted directly on their daily lives because it extended into the workplace and into the microeconomic functioning of society. With large numbers of officials sent to investigate the situation in Xinjiang, and informants hypersensitive to any signs of unrest, the center could not but have been well aware of this growing discontent.

Hu Jintao's visit to Xinjiang between August 22 and August 25 emphasized the distance that the party center was attempting to put between itself and the besieged Wang Lequan. China Central Television images of Hu's visit, which monopolized the prime-time national news for two consecutive days following Hu's safe return to Beijing, did not feature a single handshake between the two men. Their meeting—at the airport on Hu's arrival—was dealt with in one sentence and Wang Lequan's absence from the rest of the hour-long TV reports was noticeable.

Only days after Hu left Xinjiang, the first reports of stabbing attacks with hypodermic needles appeared. The ensuing rumor-mill caused a near-hysterical reaction among the Han people in Xinjiang. By early

September in Urumchi, increasing numbers of people were reporting to hospitals with physical ailments that they attributed to unseen Uyghurs who lurked in public places with poisoned syringes. Han vigilantes took to the streets once again and had to be forcibly prevented from marching on the Uyghur area of town. Up to 10,000 people (overwhelmingly Han) gathered to demand security guarantees (ChinaView 2009) and Wang Lequan's resignation. One protester said, "We are here in People's Square peacefully. We are just giving the government some advice." Others threw plastic bottles and called for his execution (Branigan 2009). The advice to get rid of Wang Lequan was clearly meant to be heard by the central government.

The unrest in Xinjiang and the continued perception of instability prompted capital flight and Han emigration, and hit the regional economy very hard. Tourism, one of Xinjiang's most important industries, shut down almost completely just at the onset of the summer high season. Over 98% of all tourists canceled their trips by mid-July, causing immediate losses of an estimated one billion *yuan* (Xinhua 2009b). Small business suffered badly from the lack of tourists, the communications blackout, and the negative economic mood. Many Han people to whom I spoke in the second half of 2009 expressed their desire to leave Xinjiang, often making bitter comments like "I love Xinjiang, but this business, 7/5, has made me want to leave. One can't live a peaceful life here." Prospective buyers of new apartments began to look elsewhere in China, and although the listed prices did not drop much, sales volumes in both Urumchi and Korla dropped sharply (*Ku'erle Wanbao* 2009e; 2009f; 2009a). Construction work slowed or stopped. A real estate executive told me that some work units had been ordered by the city government to buy up multiple floors of new apartment buildings and offer them to employees at a discount. These work units apparently included ex-state enterprises that would not usually offer such benefits. By keeping advertized housing prices stable, the intervention helped to maintain a façade of economic confidence in Xinjiang and protect the interests of people who already owned new apartments—both important factors in attracting and keeping population. Similarly, the local purchasers of these apartments made a de facto commitment to staying in Korla because they were not permitted to sell their apartments within three (sometimes five) years, and the oversupply of similar new apartments kept rents down. According to a well-connected informant in the

Industrial and Commercial Bureau, many Han entrepreneurs in Urumchi held fire sales and fled back to the east coast within weeks of July 5. Xinjiang's economy, he claimed, "has been put back at least five years by this [riot]—even if the central government works really hard to direct investment into Xinjiang and restore investor confidence."

These events and interactions show that party center's concern about levels of satisfaction and social stability among ordinary Han people in Xinjiang, already at a premium to *neidi*, was heightened in post-7/5 Xinjiang. Internalizing the state discourse that Xinjiang is a "special region" and that they played a nationally important role in its integration, these Han people demanded "special" treatment. The shifts in central policy toward Xinjiang—most noticeably those subsequent to the replacement of Wang Lequan—demonstrate how these calls were answered.

Zhang Chunxian's "New Era"

April 26, 2010: Immediately on being appointed secretary of the Xinjiang CPC, Zhang Chunxian drove his car to Shaoshan [Mao Zedong's birthplace] and stood looking up quietly and in reverence at the statue of Mao Zedong. Thus, he bade farewell to Hunan and, shortly afterwards, flew over 3200 kilometers [2000 miles] to Urumchi to begin his journey of governing Xinjiang.
HE ZHANJUN (2011)

By the time Wang Lequan was replaced by Zhang Chunxian in late April 2010, the party and state machinery were already working on the first stage of a renewed drive toward the integration of Xinjiang. "More than 500 officials from 64 departments ha[d] been sent to towns, villages, schools and companies in Xinjiang to inspect social situations and collect people's suggestions, amid efforts to study how to improve the livelihoods of residents and promote ethnic equality and unity" (Xinhua 2010). A leading edge of Zhang's "new approach" to governing Xinjiang was (and is) the *dui kou* (对口), or "counterpart assistance," scheme under which provincial-level administrative units in eastern China provide specific regions in Xinjiang with massive injections of cash and in-kind support, particularly technical and administrative assistance (China Government Administration of Economic Growth 2010). The idea of *dui kou* was not new in itself, having been part of an earlier (1997) "Assist Xinjiang" (*yuanjiang* 援疆) plan, but it was expanded and intensified in 2010 (Liu 2011). The *dui kou* money was reportedly to be invested in agriculture, industry and mining, construction of large-scale infrastructure projects, improving "people's livelihoods" and social welfare, and improving housing in rural and *bingtuan* areas (Hu Yue 2010).

Although fixed assets accounted for the vast majority of *dui kou* financial investment from 2010 to 2012 inclusive (All China Data Centre 2013), the dissemination of *neidi* techniques of governance is equally significant. Each year since 2013, 70,000 urban officials have been sent to spend one year in rural areas of Xinjiang (Xinhua 2015), and the central government has directed Xinjiang administrators to "train ethnic cadres" in order to "increase their recognition of the Chinese nation, Chinese culture and socialism with Chinese characteristics" (Xinhua 2014b). With its explicit purpose to transform administrative culture and social relations, the *dui kou* scheme epitomizes the logic of normalization.

Internet and Media

One of the first (and most significant) things that Zhang Chunxian did when he took office was to reconnect Xinjiang with the same level of Internet service as the rest of China. "Re-opening" the Internet had to be Zhang's privilege—it served to distinguish him from his disliked predecessor and was meant to show that he is: (1) in control; (2) putting Xinjiang on the path to real stability; and (3) not scared of opening lines of communication. On the first anniversary of 7/5, he made an "unceremonious" tour of Xinjiang—going down to "ground level" and talking to ordinary people—to reinforce that signal (He Zhanjun 2011). His own microblog on qq.com (*People's Daily* 2011c), although only open for two weeks, helped to reinforce his image as a receptive "people's man" and position him as a new generation of modern CCP leaders who are in tune with social trends and the needs and desires of the population. Zhang Chunxian used the publicity generated by his microblogging to "urge [the] timely handling of people's appeals" by local officials (CRIEnglish.com 2011), implying an acceptance of the public consensus that Xinjiang officials, especially local officials, had been slow to respond to the needs of the population. Thus, the "Internet card" was one of the first of a series of tools that aimed to help Zhang establish his claim to be a moral and competent leader who has the support of the center and the best interests of the people—and the nation—at heart. Regular positive write-ups in the local and national media continued to drive this point home to the Han public of Xinjiang (Women of China 2012; Xie 2012).

The Post-7/5 Support Package for Xinjiang, 2010–14

A massive amount of resources were put at Zhang's disposal and, in his first year of office, he apparently announced "an average of one policy to benefit the people [of Xinjiang] for each less-than-three-day period." The initial objectives of these policies were to "improve the government's image" in the eyes of the people, and to push forward "leapfrog development," which together are seen as the only way to assure the CCP's overriding objective: "maintenance of [CCP] rule through stability" (*changzhijiu'an* 长治久安).

The positive tone of the Xinhua report assessing Zhang Chunxian's first year in office signaled that the brief period, post-7/5, of allowable overt dissatisfaction in Xinjiang ended with Wang Lequan's reassignment. The report on Zhang stated, among other things, that his "political intelligence" causes him to realize the necessity of sweeping out the old "lazy government" (inescapably associated with Wang Lequan) and bringing in a "new wind" of "effective" and "industrious government." Responding directly to the widespread public criticism that the government "cherishes acting according to ritual . . . drinking, feasting and dancing," the report drew a line between Zhang Chunxian's administration and that of Wang Lequan: "no colorful ribbons fluttering in the breeze, no drums and gongs making a clamor, no long and tedious speeches . . . just a few cadres, a few workunit representatives, very few media, and a brief 15-minute ceremony" (He Zhanjun 2011).

Zhang had begun his "cleanup" immediately upon assuming office. On May 27, 2010, the *People's Daily* proclaimed, "Xinjiang Government Structural Reforms See Early Results." The report can be read as a populist swipe at Wang Lequan's style: the Government Responsibility System emphasized "government by the law, responsible government, service-oriented government, and clean government." It declared that the government would "do its utmost to solve the problems of most concern to the population" (*Xinjiang Ribao* 2010).

The policies that the CCP effected in Xinjiang in the first years of Zhang Chunxian's tenure had two main goals: to placate the population of Xinjiang and to integrate Xinjiang with the rest of China. Economic development and sociocultural normalization are seen as conditions of integration, and these efforts are directed at both Han and Uyghur people.

Specifically, placating or "livelihood" (*minsheng* 民生) policies fell into two key sets:

1. *Ownership of resources*. In June 2010 tax on extracted natural resources changed from a fixed, volume-based calculation to a variable, and much higher, price-based calculation. The reform significantly raised the amount that local governments in Xinjiang receive in taxation rev-

enue (*Global Times* 2011a). The new policy was seen as addressing the widespread complaint that Xinjiang's natural resources were being exploited for the benefit of eastern China but with precious little benefit to the people (Han or Uyghur) of Xinjiang (see, e.g., Tewpiq 2008). In November 2011 the new resources tax was implemented nationwide on oil and gas (Reuters 2011).

2. *Income and economic opportunities.* First, training and re-employment programs for Xinjiang college graduates—both Han and Uyghur—were expanded (Shao Wei and Mao Weihua 2011). Second, agencies at the Autonomous Region level assumed responsibility for the financing of subsidies, basic income guarantees, and performance bonuses to "grassroots" employees in administrative government and redistributive agencies, rather than leaving these benefits to the whims of often chronically underfunded local areas. The beneficiaries included teachers, sanitation workers, and local paramilitary leaders, but the focus was on local-level cadres (fabang.com 2010; Zhang 2011).

Integration or "leapfrog development" (*kuayueshi fazhan* 跨越试发展) policies fell into four key sets:

1. *Special Economic Zones.* Two new Special Economic Zones (SEZs) were declared in Xinjiang in 2010, and Korla's Economic Technology Development Zone was elevated to national level the following year (Lu 2011). The first of the new SEZs is at the port of Korgas on the China-Kazakhstan border, and the second, optimistically dubbed "the Shenzhen of the west," is in the iconic Uyghur-heartland city of Kashgar (news.163.com 2010).

2. *Infrastructure.* Starting in early 2010, the central government massively increased fixed capital investment in Xinjiang. The focus was on transportation infrastructure—including roads, bridges, railways, airports, oil and gas pipelines, and irrigation and drinking water networks—along with the SEZs and urban redevelopment mentioned above. Fixed capital investment accounted for 82% of Xinjiang's GDP in 2012. In a comparative view, while Beijing registered a 32% increase in fixed capital investment between the beginning of 2010 and the end of 2012, fixed capital investment in Xinjiang increased 126%, almost four times the rate, to surpass Beijing in 2012 (All China Data Centre 2013).[5] This upgraded transportation infrastructure is positioned to affirm Kashgar, Korgas, and Korla as the key logistics hubs of South Xinjiang.

3. *Preferential policies and opening.* Preferential policies, including tax exemptions, rent waivers, and business subsidies, were also set to attract investment from *neidi* and abroad (China Government Administration of Economic Growth 2010; *Global Times* 2011b; *People's Daily* 2011a).

The American security and surveillance equipment supplier Honeywell was one of the foreign companies to take advantage of this new openness and the heightened perception of social unrest in Xinjiang (Asia Today 2011). Honeywell established an outlet in Urumchi around the same time as the government and security forces were installing tens of thousands of surveillance cameras in public areas throughout the city and the region (*Guardian* 2011).

Even in the dominant oil and gas industry—petrochemical companies accounted for 50.8% of the total industrial output of Xinjiang in 2010 (China Knowledge 2012)—a limited diversification of ownership structures began. Initially, private and listed companies were allowed to make investments in natural gas distribution, as well as the exploitation of smaller fields as joint-venture partners (EIN News 2011; Platts 2011a; Brightoil Petroleum 2012). In March 2015 the Tarim Oilfield Company announced plans to sell a 49% stake in its oil fields to domestic state and private investors. The move was framed as a "pilot project" of the nationwide reform of state-owned energy companies (*China Daily* 2015), continuing the pattern of testing new policies on the frontier (such as with the resources tax reform in 2010) and emphasizing CNPC's will to promote Tazhi as the model for other SOEs to follow.

4. *Central SOEs and the new industrial form.* "Leapfrog development" is said to depend on the construction of a "new industrial form" (*xinxing gongye* 新型工业) for Xinjiang (XJASS 2012). Central SOEs in Xinjiang were instructed in late 2011 by then SASAC director Wang Yong to help bring about this new industrial form by acting as its "backbone" and as "models" for other enterprises to follow (Wang 2011b). Official statements connecting the "Assist Xinjiang" project with central SOEs became frequent, clear, and increasingly prescriptive following the "First Central SOEs Assist Xinjiang Meeting" on August 20, 2011. Central SOEs were to "build capacity," not only by injecting "abundant capital" into the system (that role now to be augmented by private capital) but most importantly by bringing "core technologies, advanced managerial concepts, and a highly-skilled management team" (MOFCOM 2012). The stated aim was, and is, systemic transformation.

The task of constructing a new industrial structure in Xinjiang, and thus transforming the social structure of the region, implies both continued privileges and certain "political responsibilities" for central SOEs. While checking on central SOEs' "Assist Xinjiang" projects in April 2012, a SASAC vice director emphasized that Xinjiang-based SOEs can draw on SASAC, the Xinjiang government, and relevant departments of the central government to "resolve any problems" (Xinhua 2012b). The audience of Autonomous Region government officials, SASAC officials, and high-ranking representatives of central SOEs did not need to be reminded that private enterprises are not guaranteed such bureaucratic assistance. Speaking in Beijing a few months earlier, Wang Yong had clearly laid out the guidelines and the benefits of party-government-enterprise integration: "build the party [inside] the enterprise, [and thus] make political advantage your competitive advantage" (SASAC 2011). Wang's guiding philosophy was that state control of key industries helps to consolidate "the CCP's ruling party status" (2010).

The exercise of metropolitan power through the enterprise in addition to formal channels of government is a phenomenon reminiscent of earlier colonial endeavors in Asia. Take, for example, the British and Dutch East Indies Companies (Stern 2011; van Roosmalen 2011) or the "Railway Imperialism" of early 20th-century Japanese and Russian occupation in Manchuria (Davis 1991, 155). More recently, Vladimir Putin attempted to set up a state corporation, answerable directly to the president, to handle the exploitation of eastern Russia/Siberia (Fushita 2012). In Xinjiang, the *bingtuan* and the oil company are model examples of this long-running imperial tradition.

Normalization

On the sociocultural front, Zhang Chunxian's "new era" (Xinjiang Wenhua Bu 2011) had by 2015 become, by most metrics, even more restrictive for Uyghurs than Wang Lequan's era. Potentially beneficial policies toward Uyghurs were overshadowed by the ongoing project to dilute and reshape Uyghur culture so that it accords with the CCP's vision of the role of ethnic minority culture in a unified and harmonious China. Unpopular policies continued from Wang's time included the demolition of old city areas of Kashgar, the unilateral enforcement of Mandarin-medium education, and coercive Uyghur labor migration to factories in eastern China. Zhang's forceful normalization of all areas of life in Xinjiang meant that (what the state saw as) problems in the region were treated in the same way as (what the state saw as) similar problems in *neidi*.

Most disruptively, normalization has entailed birth control policies being more rigorously enforced among the Uyghur population (Radio Free Asia 2013b), mainly Uyghur-occupied rural land being appropriated for development (Radio Free Asia 2014), and any religious activity without official state sanction being suppressed (CECC 2011; Reuters 2012a). In

July 2014 Zhang Chunxian wrote in *Qiushi* that all ethnic groups in Xinjiang should be subject to the same family planning policies. The rationale given was "to decrease and stabilize moderate birthrates" (2014) in Xinjiang, but continuing official incentives for Han in-migration to Xinjiang (*Global Times* 2014) and a gradual relaxation of the family planning policy everywhere in China except Xinjiang and Tibet (*China Daily* 2014) signal more specific objectives. It is plausible to suggest that changes in the birth control regime in Xinjiang aim to change the ethnic composition of the region and subject those Uyghurs who are already born to the same disciplinary norms that Han everywhere in China have been subjected to for over three decades—thus, in one stroke bolstering the frontier of settlement, responding to Han cries of unequal treatment, and normalizing Uyghur society in rural Xinjiang.

The years 2012–14 saw a dramatic upsurge in violent incidents that appear to have been sparked by either the appropriation of land for development projects (Radio Free Asia 2012; 2013a) or the prosecution of constraints on religious practice (*Global Times* 2012; Turdush 2013; Radio Free Asia 2015). The former is related to how "leapfrog development" is being carried out: Han developers and *neidi* capital implementing get-rich-quick projects without local residents' consultation, and more than likely in collusion with government officials in key positions. Uyghur farmers are relocated to apartment complexes that fracture the social structure of rural life and provide them with no income opportunities. Given that such phenomena is widespread in *neidi*, we can think of leapfrog development as *economic* normalization (see Cliff 2016). For their part, enforced secularization and other constraints on religious practice and childbirth are directly related to the project of *cultural* normalization. The policing of these constraints appeared increasingly to be conducted by Uyghurs in low-level official positions and, as a result, Uyghur casualties were high on both sides of this state-society conflict. All of this hit the Uyghur villages and townships of southwest Xinjiang most hard, since that is where the development is focused, and the people there maintain strong traditional and Islamic values. In no way are they "normal" by the standards of the Chinese metropole.

It was not only non-Sinified Uyghurs who found life tough in the first years of Xinjiang's "new era." Rapid inflation, especially of essential items like food and housing, stretched household budgets, balanced only partly by wage increases for low-end service jobs as many migrant workers chose other destinations. As posited at the beginning of this chapter, even the Han mainstream are a privileged group *only as long as* they continue to perform their role of occupying Xinjiang. Outside Xinjiang, people holding a Xinjiang *hukou* feel like an underclass. While there are preferential policies for people to move to Xinjiang, there are many social and structural restrictions on the spatial mobility of Xinjiang people, both within China and internationally. First, it can be quite difficult for Xinjiang people to get a Chinese passport, even as it is fast becoming a mere formality for residents of metropolitan eastern China. Second, there is discrimination against Xinjiang people in *neidi*. For example, Xinjiang Han people are often tarred with the same brush as Uyghurs by being restricted—by government regulation—to only certain hotels in a given city or, even in the absence of this regulation, being refused occupancy once the hotel receptionist sees their Xinjiang *hukou*. That is in addition to their status as "outsiders" and consequent wage and social discrimination, including undesirability as a marriage partner. Xinjiang Han thus possess what we might call a spatially mutable value—a value that decreases sharply as they move east. New central policies toward Xinjiang aim to raise the attractiveness of the periphery and, in conjunction with the disincentives to moving east, thereby both attract new settlers from the core region and retain the old ones.

Conclusion: Partners in (In)Stability

Most studies of Xinjiang touch on social and political stability in the region, and almost all of these studies presume that, in this respect, the central government is focused on dealing with "the Uyghur problem." Liu Yong, for example, critiques the central government's response to 7/5 as "an economic band aid," saying that the measures will not be effective in addressing Uyghur discontent and quelling dissent (2010). I contend that the central state conceives of the problems in a different way. Policies implemented in Xinjiang from 2010 to 2014 did not focus on winning over the Uyghur population on Uyghur terms. Rather, the massive injection of funds into Xinjiang and the *dui kou* program were intended to make the region attractive to Han and accelerate cultural change in Xinjiang. That means privileging Han people and ways of doing things.

Ethnic conflicts are not just about ethnicity: Han actors in post-7/5 Xinjiang expended at least as much energy on *intra*-ethnic maneuvering. The Han focus was on how the central and province-level authorities would handle their demands; for them, the Uyghurs' primary and continuing role in the drama was as providers of instability. This intra-ethnic focus is evident in a late 2010 comment made by Yanyan, who had been highly critical of the CCP a year earlier:

Since [early 2010] there have been many changes, the party has been providing many good things for the people. . . . This is a direct result of 7/5. The CCP cares about the people. The CCP is good—it is the new secretary, he is good. The new secretary is good.

The new secretary, Zhang Chunxian, presented himself as a cultural warrior from the outset. He proposed to bring to Xinjiang a broadly defined and transformative "modern culture." This "modern culture" is aesthetic, aspirational, and secular, and closely mirrors the "exemplary society" (Bakken 2000) being built around Tazhi in Korla: it aims to transform the psychologies of Han as well as non-Han people, and its primary goals (*Xinjiang Ribao* 2012) are defined exclusively by 21st-century metropolitan Chinese standards. The absence of any positive mention of Islam aligns the first of these goals—"modern rationality"—with a secular and homogenizing imperial rationality. The idea of teaching Uyghurs to adopt Han "social norms and ways of life" would be comforting to Yanyan and the extensive network of "old Xinjiang people" whose views she articulates. Han in Xinjiang are often disdainful, if not fearful, of Islam, and their centralizing entreaties to Beijing were cultural as well as political and economic. The second goal—"national identity"—outlaws any identity that does not fit within the notion of the *Zhonghua minzu*. The third goal—"civil rights"—is population specific and could exist only in the absence of a discourse of instability. As Liu Xiaobo points out, any right is retractable at any time by the authorities, and the recipient is expected to be grateful for any temporary concession (2011 [2006], 158–59). Director Wei and most of the "inner" Han mainstream actively defend the "need" for such centralized authoritarian power: they maintain that Chinese people are accustomed to it and unprepared for political liberalization. For many Xinjiang Han, the total institution of the SOE is preferable to the vulnerability of the partial market economy. Zhang's "modern culture" seeks to harness this nostalgia for organized dependence in the service of social control.

The intensification of state capital investment reflects the belief that Xinjiang's economy needs greater direct central involvement and guidance. A guiding slogan of Xinjiang's party committee articulates the motives of this recentralization from the perspective of frontier governance: "If the grassroots are stable, then the whole of Xinjiang is stable; if the whole of Xinjiang is stable, then the whole country is stable"

(Zhang 2011). Xi Jinping reiterated this position in September 2014 (Xinhua 2014a). Standardizing and increasing the bonuses of grassroots cadres and controlling these funds from the provincial level in Xinjiang is one aspect of this program. These ideological-economic measures aim to strengthen both formal and informal governance structures by recentralizing loyalties in Xinjiang. In the imperial worldview that is held by the Chinese core and by the Han on the frontier, culture moves from the center toward the periphery, and instability moves from the periphery toward the center.

Conclusion

The Han in Xinjiang are a socially, economically, and culturally diverse group of people. Their experiences of life are similarly diverse. However, internal socioeconomic and experiential heterogeneity notwithstanding, there is much that experientially unites Han in Xinjiang. Common elements of the subjectivity of Han in Xinjiang relate directly to the three major themes of migration, empire, and time. First, with the experience of migration prominent in their family history, old Xinjiang Han maintain a sense of belonging and ownership vis-à-vis both Xinjiang and *neidi*, but this sense tends to be less firm than that of a person who *knows* that they only come from one place. While they straddle two places (as they almost always do), the settler is always in limbo and can never fully and constantly belong to either one. In both places, there is always something that unsettles their sense of belonging (being a Xinjiang person in *neidi*, or being a Han in Xinjiang, both somehow out of place). To be sustained, the Han sense of belonging in Xinjiang needs to be actively maintained. Second, and relevant to the theme of empire, is the Han's unspoken sense of dependence on the core region, but also of their own indispensability to that core. Third, and related most closely to the themes of empire and time, is a sense of peripherality and behindness. This sense produces, and is produced by, state and popular discourses emphasizing Xinjiang's distance from and difference from the political and cultural core of China, as well as the empirical fact of that distance and difference. The metacontext of Han experience in Xinjiang is their role as agents and objects of a colonial endeavor on a cultural and political periphery. The politico-economic and temporal particularities of the frontier loom large in their everyday lives, distinguishing their perspectives and experiences from those of Han people in the core region of China, despite all that they share.

The Time of the Frontier

The Han view from Xinjiang contributes to an understanding of contemporary core-periphery relations and postimperial frontier processes in China. The frontier perspective provides both critical distance from and a reverse angle on the policies and practices of the metropole, revealing a certain fragility. To rephrase Anaïs Nin's famous line, the metropole lives on its reflections in the eyes of others.

From the center to the borderlands, discourses emphasizing the behindness and instability of Xinjiang, and its need for civilization, coexist with the notion of the frontier as a laboratory and a site of national renewal. As a result, the Han of Xinjiang themselves embody spatial and cultural peripherality, and, simultaneously, impending civilization. In this context, prospective orientations flourish. Prospective orientations include the legend of potential, "promissory notes of transformation" (Stoler and McGranahan 2007, 8), the turn to hope, and the acceptance of constant deferral. These not-yets manifest in frontier lives like reflections on the surface of a lake: they are constantly changing and sometimes imperceptible, but they always reappear. In the visual (images and aesthetics), the prospective (imagination and aspiration), and the historical, we can see the time of the frontier.

Imperial Thinking

Imperial pasts echo in Xinjiang, and in the center's imagination and treatment of the periphery. Harald Bøckman contends that the CCP inherited "a fair portion of [the] implied thinking" (1998, 310) of the Manchu Qing empire, and Mark Elliott makes the more direct point that "China still thinks like an empire" (2012). Imperial thinking is a function of the PRC being "the last consequential regime in the world which has not given up the vision of a polity that is a vast multiethnic empire in content, albeit one that is a constitutional republic in form" (Horner and Brown 2011).[1] A couple of examples from the recent past serve to underscore these claims.

The popular Han depiction of the hypodermic needle scare in Xinjiang

CONCLUSION

8.1 Waiting. Bus station on the highway north of Karamay, North Xinjiang, 2007

in September 2009 parallels the English response to and representation of the 1857 Indian Mutiny. The facts that in Xinjiang no one was ever confirmed to have been stuck deliberately with an infected needle and that early reports of deaths were later shown to be false, demonstrates the motivational power of popular anxieties (*Ku'erle Wanbao* 2009b; Xinhua 2009c). In the case of the Indian Mutiny, Jenny Sharpe recounts the hyperbolic reports in English-language newspapers in both the Indian colony and the British metropole. Sharpe notes that "the general tenor of the editorials and letters . . . exhibits a desire to transform rumor and hearsay into fact and information" (1993, 229), giving this example from a London newspaper:

A large number of women and children, fell into the hands of the infuriate crew, thirsting for the blood of the infidel. . . . We know little of the exact scenes which transpired, and imagination hesitates to lift the veil from them. We hear, however, that the whole [were] murdered in cold blood. (*News of the World*, July 19, 1857, quoted in Sharpe 1993, 229)

As Sharpe points out, the British colonial press reserved the most horrific fates for women and children, often sexualizing their alleged murders—for "once an English man has been struck down, then anything is

210

possible; in death his mortality is revealed and sovereign status brought low" (ibid., 230–31). Similarly, in Xinjiang the apparent victims of the hypodermic needle attacks were "defenseless" women, children, and the elderly, and the assumed perpetrators were "cowardly" and licentious Uyghur men. To adapt and paraphrase Sharpe, the (Uyghur) savages penetrating the bodies of the Chinese women, children, and elderly was a symbolic penetration of the home and a sexualized defilement of the virtuous Chinese woman; the Chinese man, symbol of colonial power in Xinjiang, must not be seen to be so defenseless, especially at a time when the full might of the Chinese state security apparatus had apparently failed, for the second time in two months, to guarantee personal physical security to its population. Barely subcutaneous Han male anxieties were wrapped up in and virtually indistinguishable from state anxieties about colonial power.

Speaking in Urumchi two months earlier (July 2009), Zhou Yongkang drew a causal chain of stability—and thus, by implication, instability—from the provincial capital to the nation:

Resolutely implement various measures to guarantee the state of affairs does not get worse or spread; use the stability of [Urumchi] to guarantee the stability of the whole of Xinjiang; use the stability of Xinjiang to guarantee the stability of the entire nation. (Xinhua 2009d)

In doing so, Zhou most likely spawned the clone that the Xinjiang party committee voiced in late 2011, and I quoted in the conclusion to chapter 7: "If the grassroots are stable, then the whole of Xinjiang is stable; if the whole of Xinjiang is stable, then the whole country is stable" (Zhang 2011).

Zhou himself was following in the discursive footsteps of hardline "Han warriors" (*Han jun* 汉军) past—notably Wang Zhen and Zuo Zongtang (左宗棠), who are both seen as heroes by many Han in Xinjiang. Popular legend in Xinjiang has it that Wang Zhen's proposal (carried out in some places in Xinjiang) to comprehensively wipe out the Uyghur population on the basis that they "were a troublemaking minority who would cause problems for the party in the future" shocked even Mao Zedong, who immediately promoted Wang to the Ministry of Agriculture and Reclamation (*nongkenbu* 农垦部), where he would be less able to stir up ethnic conflict. But it was Zuo Zongtang, the commander who reconquered Xinjiang in the 1870s and proposed its formal incorporation as a province (Millward 2007, 132), who apparently came up with the idea that "if Xinjiang became unstable, the Mongols would be disturbed; and if the Mongols became restless, then, in a chain

CONCLUSION

8.2 Wang Zhen statue in Korla. Retired *bingtuan* pioneers bring their grandchildren here to (in their words) "educate them about the great man—old uncle Wang."

reaction, the political center itself would be jeopardized." Woodside suggests that this "has to be one of the most extravagant domino theories ever conceived" and points out that Zuo's "triumphant conquest of Xinjiang [also reflects] . . . a much older, more pessimistic theme: that of the vulnerability of the imperial center" (2007, 22). In the minds of the leadership in Beijing and Urumchi, and of the Han settlers in Xinjiang, it is clear that the borderlands are central to the idea of the nation. The maintenance of this position relies, at least in part, on the borderlands' apparently contradictory temporal status.

Asynchronicity

Xinjiang is discursively asynchronous: simultaneously imagined as "behind" and "ahead." Xinjiang people experience this as a sense of delay—

212

waiting to be civilized. Delay can be seen in images throughout this book; figure 6.2, plates 9 to 16, and figure 8.1 make this sense particularly explicit. Perhaps this is what Chinese modernity is all about, and it is not unique to the frontier. But on the frontier relativity is laid bare; extremes predominate. Certain policies and institutions that are past their day in the core region are central elements of Xinjiang's cultural and political economy, yet the same cultural and political economy gives rise to new institutional and policy forms.

The *bingtuan* is perhaps the paramount example of institutional behindness in China, but this lingering past seems also to be an important element of Xinjiang's future. Xinjiang's dry climate and extreme temperatures helped to contain the expansion of the agrarian practices of the core region, and thus the frontier of settlement, until the middle of the 20th century. Although recent migrants still view the landscape with disdain and disappointment, it has been more than 60 years since the organizational capacity and high modernist ethos of the CCP-led state made the exploitation of Xinjiang's flat and "empty" land both viable and desirable. Xinjiang was one of the first places in China to practice mechanized agriculture on a large scale (*China Daily* 2012). Consider also the *bingtuan*'s direct ownership of large, contiguous tracts of this land, virtually uninhibited access to the headwaters of Xinjiang's key irrigation rivers, and unmatched degree of coercive control over its population, as well as a demonstrated willingness to wield these powers in support of high-level goals. Disputes over labor, land, and environmental resources have been the catalyst for the vast majority of "mass incidents" in China in recent years; control over these resources is without doubt something that the stability-addicted central state is most nostalgic for. The perceived—or discursively constructed—emptiness is cultural and historical, as well as physical. In addition to superficially legitimizing occupation and aggressive schemes of cultural transformation, this presumed emptiness enables new urban forms that are designed from on high to be drawn on the landscape with the moral ease that they are drawn on paper.

Urbanizing the *bingtuan*, thus attracting Han in-migration, is an important facet of normalization (Cliff 2013). The urbanization of the Korla region entered a new stage with the May 2012 announcement that the *bingtuan*'s 29th Regiment would be elevated to the status of a city and developed accordingly (Bingtuannet 2012b). By January 2013, when I revisited with Jing and Ren, the new city of Tiemenguan had been established. Such development is an attempt to consolidate the frontier of settlement: the *bingtuan* is now being directed to "build cities," rather than "open wasteland," as a way of "garrisoning the frontier" (Bingtuannet

2012a). Change, here, takes place *within* continuity: a new tool for a long-standing job.

Consistent with metropolitan imaginings of the frontier, Xinjiang retains its role as a policy laboratory. The society-wide organized dependence—negatively portrayed as an "iron rice bowl" mentality by Wei and Shen—is associated with the disproportionately high value put on state employment by many people in Korla. The increased involvement of central SOEs in Xinjiang's economy since early 2010, and their active and high-profile employment programs that are targeted exclusively at Xinjiang locals (MOFCOM 2012; Xinhua 2012a), would suggest that organized dependence is on the return in Xinjiang. From the perspective of SASAC, Xinjiang seems to be a test case for central SOEs' capacity to sustain party power in a diffuse but resilient way. Xinjiang appears, in this respect, to be ahead of the core.

Problematizing Integration

There is an essential contradiction between the core region's goal of integrating the borderlands and the way that the center perceives itself. Bøckman presents a historical reading of the view from the core:

The aim of all local pretenders was always to restore the imperial order. This is not only abundantly documented in Chinese historical records, but is also in popular sayings like "strive to gain the political power of the Central realm" (*zhulu zhongyuan*). Looking outward, the aim was to seek congruence between the imperial order and the cultural realm, even if that was rarely feasible. (1998, 312)

There are two potential mismatches to the idea of "congruence between the imperial order and the cultural realm." The first is a situation in which the cultural realm is bigger than the imperial order—as is the case in the contemporary period with Taiwan. The stated objective here is to expand the imperial order (territory), by diplomacy if possible and by force if necessary. The second, and most relevant to this discussion, is a situation in which the imperial order is bigger than the cultural realm—as is the case with Xinjiang or Tibet. In such cases, the apparent aim is to expand the cultural realm through normalization (making Xinjiang more like *neidi*, and especially people in Xinjiang more like people in *neidi*).

China's northwest frontiers have traditionally presented an obstacle to such congruence—and hence to the ideal expressed in the dynastic era's "grand unity" (*da yitong* 大一统) or the PRC's "unified, multi-ethnic nation" (*tongyi de duominzu guojia* 统一的多民族国家) (Lary 2007, 9; *Renmin Ribao* 2009b; Elliott 2011, 406–7). Elliott distinguishes between these two conceptions of unity and implies that the PRC-era conception is more difficult to attain.

> Empires [like the Qing] are fine with being uneven, asymmetrical, hierarchical, but nation-states [like, in principle, the PRC] are supposed to be regular, symmetrical, and smooth. Additionally, the demands upon the modern state to tell a consistent story are far greater than they were upon the pre-modern state. If there was slippage between different conceptions of "China" and "the Chinese" in Qing-style grand unity, no one was much bothered by it. But because modernity presupposes precision, transparency, and finite boundaries . . . the notion of unity in China today is understood much more literally than in the Qing. (2011, 411)

On the face of it, both Qing and PRC conceptualizations assume that the unity which they respectively seek is possible—an assumption that I question. As I argued in the introduction, complete integration of the frontier is impossible as long as the core defines a frontier as that which is culturally distinct from the core. This is because the context of the periphery produces a culture on the periphery which, to a greater or lesser degree, differs from the core. The unifying ambitions of the metropole are thwarted by its own vanity.

The integration of the persistent frontiers of China's northwest is not only impossible, it is undesirable to the imperial-thinking core. My assertion would seem to fly in the face of recent evidence—the immense amount of diplomatic, military, cultural, economic, and human resources that the CCP center has put into the project of integration since the establishment of New China. While there is little doubt that many individual and institutional actors in this great drama, right up to and including the highest organs of state, honestly believe in and have committed their entire existence to the project of integration, such integration necessarily implies raising the cultural level of the periphery to that of the core, and thus the end of the core's self-attributed status as a center of light and culture in relation to the dark and distant frontier. The abundance of references to "the center" (*zhongyang* 中央) or "the kernel" (*hexin* 核心) in PRC political discourse is testimony to the continuing importance of the notion of the core as distinct from and superior to the noncore. The existence of the periphery sustains and enables such a conceit. Integration is undesirable as long as the core continues to want to be seen as a core.

CONCLUSION

The ethnographies I have presented in this book demonstrate that this "paradox of integration" manifests strongly in the lives and psychologies of Han people living on the frontier. First, Han in Xinjiang define themselves in relation to a core that is elsewhere, and teleologically "ahead" of Xinjiang, reproducing in mirror-image the imperial thinking that I have attributed to the core. Second, it is increasingly the case that most Han have little to do with Uyghurs. Han energies are focused intra-ethnically: other Han present the greatest threat to any given Han individual's aspirations, and provide the greatest opportunities. Uyghur activities and actions that cannot be ignored, such as the July 5, 2009, riots in Urumchi, provoke intense indignation and disdain on the part of the Han. Third, Han in Xinjiang are used to being peripheral. Being peripheral has become part of their identity and is a major source of income for Xinjiang and for Han in Xinjiang. Being peripheral, unstable, and behind is a politico-cultural performance and an economic activity for Han people and institutions in Xinjiang. A state of exception is the desired state. Officially integrating Xinjiang would remove it from the national stage, it would entail a recategorization of the region and its people from "peripheral" to merely "provincial," and it would be experienced as a demotion.

For these reasons, the frontier must be—and must be maintained as—both ahead and behind, both burden and salvation.

Notes

INTRODUCTION

1. The organization's full name is the *Xinjiang shengchan jianshe bingtuan* (新疆生产建设兵团). For more on the *bingtuan,* see chapters 1 and 2 of this book, Seymour (2000), Becquelin (2000), and Cliff (2009).
2. *Bayinguoleng Mengguzu zizhizhou* (巴音郭楞蒙古族自治州).
3. *Talimu youtian gongsi zhihuibu* (塔里木油田公司指挥部).
4. The Xinjiang Han have never been the subject of an ethnographically based book-length study in English, regardless of theme or scope. Scholars working ethnographically in Xinjiang have tended to study the Uyghur and, to a lesser extent, the other minorities of Xinjiang (Rudelson 1997; Bovingdon 2002; Harris 2004; Bellér Hann 2008; Dautcher 2009; Harris 2009; Smith-Finley 2013). Hansen's study of Han settlers in Yunnan and Gansu touches on similar themes and is perhaps the closest equivalent to this book in terms of framing and approach. However, Yunnan and Gansu are far more integrated into the Chinese core area. Hansen explains that she wanted to research in Xinjiang but could not get permission—the area and the topic of Han in-migration were deemed too sensitive (2005, 3).
5. Becquelin conservatively estimated that, in the early 2000s, people without a Xinjiang *hukou*, including many sojourning migrant workers and the prison population, amounted to 790,000 people, or almost 4% of Xinjiang's population (2004).

CHAPTER ONE

1. See Leibold (2011) for a discussion of the early 20th-century debate surrounding the definition of *Zhonghua minzu* and

related terms, including Han; Mullaney (2004a) for the creation of subsidiary ethnicities in the early 1950s Ethnic Classification Project; and Gladney (1998a) for examples of the contradictions within and the flexibility of these ethnic categories.
2. All Han-identified people outside the PRC geobody are implicitly included in the notion because they remain the "sons of the yellow Emperor," but it seems unlikely that a non-Han person (such as a Uyghur or Mongol) living outside the PRC could be included in the *Zhonghua minzu*.
3. *Jiashugong* are often referred to as synonymous with *wu-qi gong* (五·七工), "May 7 workers," because both groups are entirely made up of women who worked in state or collective enterprises but were afforded none of the pension and housing rights normally associated with these positions in the Mao era. See, for example, *Zhongguo Shehui Baozhang* (2009), *Bingtuan Jianshe* (2010).
4. *Zhongyang zhengfa weiyuanhui* (中央政法委员会).
5. See the extensive literature on rural people in the city, and urbanites' view of the "quality" (*suzhi* 素质) of country people, among others (Kipnis 2001; Jacka 2006).

CHAPTER THREE

1. The phrase comes from a report authored by the Social Development Research Group at Tsinghua University (2010), which suggests that "making a fuss" has become one of the negotiating tools of people and groups denied legitimate institutionalized expression of interests.
2. Mooncakes are *materially insignificant* entitlements because nobody in the Tarim Oilfield Company is short of food or money, because most people would be thoroughly sick of mooncakes by the end of the mid-autumn festival period, and because these mooncakes would be all but valueless as a gift. The oil company mooncakes would be valueless as a gift because they would be instantly recognizable as those given out by the work unit, implying that the giver holds the receiver in low esteem.
3. CNPC as a whole employed over 1.5 million people at the time of going to market in the year 2000, and even after recurrent layoffs through the early 2000s, over one million people were employed in the extraction of petroleum and natural gas in China by the end of 2008; see ZGLDTJNJ (2009, sec. 3-1). In 2014, CNPC had about 540,000 permanent employees; see *Renmin Ribao* (2014b). The total number of people employed by the Tarim Oilfield Company, including contractor employees, was close to 30,000. Of the Tarim Oilfield Company's 12,000 permanent employees, only 4,000 worked directly under the auspices of the Tarim headquarters. A further 2,000 employees worked at the petrochemical facility in Korla's industrial park, and 6,000 at a small, old oil field in southwest Xinjiang.

4. The deep and difficult to drill angled wells that are the norm in the Tarim Basin apparently cost 1.4 times as much as a standard straight well, but their yield is 3.5 times as much, according to the CNPC website (2009b). Using official statistics of yearly crude oil and natural gas outputs and the labor force of the oil and gas extraction industry for China as a whole, along with Tarim-specific statistics reported by Reuters, I calculate that Tazhi produced about 7.4% of China's oil equivalent in 2010, with only about 1.2% of the permanent workforce (ZGLDTJNJ 2009, sec. 3–1; ZGNYTJNJ 2010 secs. 3–4, 3–9; Reuters 2011; China Data Online 2012a; 2012b).
5. The CNPC website uses the following terms: permanent (*guding* 固定); contractor (*jiepin* 借聘); temporary (*linshi* 临时)—a "3-in-1 employment system" (*san wei yi ti yonggong zhidu* "三位一体"用工制度). See CNPC 2009b. In the parlance of the Tarim Oilfield Company, permanent employees are also referred to as "contracted" employees (*hetonggong* 合同工). In practice, contract renewal for permanent employees is assumed; none of my interlocutors could think of an example to the contrary. My use of the term "contractor employee' as the English translation of *jiepin* denotes that they are employees of contractors.
6. One square meter is equivalent to 10.7 square feet.
7. Most of those who thought that the transfer was "not all bad" were the decision makers and teachers who had no employment relationship with the oil company itself. In contrast, all the permanent oil company employee-teachers with whom I spoke strongly opposed trading their comfortable positions for the status of an ordinary teacher in the prefectural system. These two categories of school employee arose because both leaders and ordinary teachers who were employed at the Tarim school before 2002 were, or were made, permanent oil company employees at the time of employment. Many of them had been transferred from other positions within the oil company.
8. It is apparently rare for the company to take on a new permanent employee who is already married. There may be no single overriding reason for this, but one factor is that if they were married, the company would be obliged to provide an apartment for them to purchase and also to provide employment for their spouse. For young people looking for employment with the Tarim Oilfield Company, it is strategically astute to remain unmarried.
9. My interviews in Xinjiang and Heilongjiang show that "spontaneous" (non-state-organized) marriage migration by women from the inner lands of China was also a common phenomenon during and after the famine of 1958–61. Whether spontaneous or state organized, a large proportion of these women became workers in collective enterprises that were attached to the large work-unit systems but were not eligible for the full range of benefits (such as pensions and health care) that their husbands

NOTES TO PAGES 86-157

enjoyed. Thus, the positions of state worker and collective worker during the Mao era parallel the positions of permanent employee and temporary employee in the present day.

10. The wives are paid about 1,500 *yuan* per month, and at the end of the year they get between 15,000 and 20,000 *yuan* as a bonus. This is still 25–30% higher than the average fully employed person in Korla city, particularly as most of these women do not have any skills and only the most basic education. The ones who do have skills and education are fostered by the company and put into positions of more importance and responsibility. In this way, they may become permanent employees. The unskilled wives do light gardening work around the compound, teach kindergarten, or work as manual labor in an oil company factory.

11. According to Downs (2008, 127), only 30 out of 60 (10 per year for six years) of these young stars returned to work in China.

CHAPTER FOUR

1. These stories are exactly the same except for the reason that Wu's father came to Xinjiang, and it is possible that the two reasons coexisted. Why not get away from stifling tradition and parasitic family members at the same time as doing something for New China? And perhaps there were other reasons that we can only speculate about—by 1956, Wu's father had been in the military for 18 years, probably all of his adult life. Now he was a soldier without a war. Xinjiang had only just shifted from a military administration to a civilian one (1954); most people were ex-army; and the grand projects to develop the oil fields or open up the wasteland were all couched in military terms and conducted in a military fashion. It was, to borrow Judith Shapiro's words, "war against nature" (2001).

2. Until late 2007, when he retired, Zeng was the fifth-ranked member of the Politburo Standing Committee and a vice president of the PRC (Downs 2008, 133; Miller 2008, 72).

CHAPTER FIVE

1. Sociological theorist Jonathan Turner defines social institutions as "a complex of positions, roles, norms and values lodged in particular types of social structures and organizing relatively stable patterns of human activity with respect to fundamental problems in producing life-sustaining resources, in reproducing individuals, and in sustaining viable societal structures within a given environment" (1997, 6).

2. I thank Mei Ding for sharing these findings of her PhD research (2014) into expatriate Uyghurs.

3. In an ironic twist of history, Mr. Zhao had married his first wife largely as a result of his own family's inverted social status during the Cultural

Revolution. His first wife came from a good class background, from which he had hoped to get some "reflected redness."

CHAPTER SIX

1. Vanessa Fong made this point in a book-length study of how only children grow up in late 20th-century China (2004).
2. The GWD (*Xibu da kaifa* 西部大开发) was a massive program of investment and in-kind support that was launched in 2000, ostensibly to level out socioeconomic and developmental differences between "western" China and the developed coastal provinces.

CHAPTER SEVEN

1. Uyghurs were not the only perpetrators of violence on July 5, 2009. Eyewitnesses report that state security forces used lethal force against Uyghurs through the night of July 5 (Millward 2009, 352–54; Radio Free Asia 2009a; 2009b).
2. The demonstration on July 5 began as a peaceful affair, demanding a thorough and transparent government investigation into the Shaoguan incident on June 26, in which two Uyghurs were killed by Han mobs (ChinaNews.com 2009; Harris and Isa 2011, 28; Smith Finley 2011, 75–76).
3. The most comprehensive single volume on contemporary Xinjiang, S. Frederick Starr's *Xinjiang: China's Muslim Borderland* (2004), was accompanied by a policy paper called *The Xinjiang Problem* that posed (incorrectly, in my view) "the Uyghurs and the Chinese State" as "the key players in Xinjiang" (Starr and Fuller 2004, 16, 74, 75).
4. Data compiled from China Labour Statistical Yearbook (1990, 87; 2009, sec. 4–3.) and Xinjiang 50 Years (2005, 394–95).
5. See "Total Investment in Fixed Assets" and "Gross Domestic Products" for Beijing and Xinjiang.

CONCLUSION

1. See also Elliott (2011, 408, note 8). Evelyn Rawski's (1996) response to an article written almost 30 years before by Ping-ti Ho (1967) apparently instigated the discussion over the significance of the Qing period in contemporary China and gave rise to what is now known as the New Qing History.

Bibliography

All China Data Centre. 2013. "Total Investment in Fixed Assets." Retrieved July 10, 2013, http://chinadataonline.org.rp.nla.gov.au/member/macroyr/macroyrtshow.asp.

Amnesty International. 2001. "China: 'Striking Harder' Than Ever Before." July 6. Retrieved May 13, 2004, http://web.amnesty.org/library/Index/engASA170222001!Open.

———. 2002. "China's Antiterrorism Legislation and Repression in the Xinjiang Uighur Autonomous Region." March 22. Retrieved March 8, 2005, http://web.amnesty.org/library/index/engASA170102002?open&of=eng-CHN.

Asia Today. 2011. "Honeywell Opens New Office in Xinjiang, China." *PRNewswire-Asia*, April 26. Retrieved May 15, 2011, http://asiatoday.com/pressrelease/honeywell-opens-new-office-xinjiang-china.

Bachman, David M. 1991. *Bureaucracy, Economy, and Leadership in China: The Institutional Origins of the Great Leap Forward*. Cambridge: Cambridge University Press.

Baidu Tieba chatroom. 2008. "Xinjiang gongwuyuan zhang gongzi xiaoxi [Xinjiang Public Servants' Salary Raise Information]." Retrieved May 4, 2011, http://tieba.baidu.com/f?z=312919295&ct=335544320&lm=0&sc=0&rn=30&tn=baiduPostBrowser&word=%B8%B7%BF%B5&pn=30.

Bakken, Borge. 2000. *The Exemplary Society: Human Improvement, Social Control, and the Dangers of Modernity in China*. Oxford: Oxford University Press.

Bazhou Government. 2007. "Zizhizhou jianggu nashui dahu [Autonomous Prefecture Rewards Biggest Taxpayers]." February 13. Retrieved May 28, 2012, http://www.xjbz.gov.cn/html/news/bttpxw/2007-2/13/10_33_11_190.html.

Bazhou Government Net. 2004. "Bayinguoleng Menggu zizhizhou lishi yange [Bayinguoleng Mongol Autonomous Prefecture

Historical Evolution]." June 23. Retrieved November 24, 2008, http://www.tianshannet.com/GB/channel59/401/403/200406/23/94774.html.

BBC News. 2014. "China Arrests Ex-Security Chief Zhou Yongkang." December 6. Retrieved January 18, 2015, http://www.bbc.com/news/world-asia-china-30352458.

Becquelin, Nicolas. 2000. "Xinjiang in the Nineties." *China Journal* 44: 65–90.

———. 2004. "Staged Development in Xinjiang." *China Quarterly* 178: 358–78.

Bellér Hann, Ildikó. 2008. *Community Matters in Xinjiang, 1880–1949: Towards a Historical Anthropology of the Uyghur*. Leiden, The Netherlands: Brill.

Benjamin, Walter. [1936] 1969. "The Work of Art in the Age of Mechanical Reproduction." In *Illuminations*, edited by H. Arendt, 217–51. London: Fontana.

Berger, John, and Jean Mohr. [1982] 1995. *Another Way of Telling*. New York: Vintage.

Bernstein, Thomas P. 1977. *Up to the Mountains and Down to the Villages: The Transfer of Youth from Urban to Rural China*. New Haven, CT: Yale University Press.

Bian, Yanjie. 2002. "Chinese Social Stratification and Social Mobility." *Annual Review of Sociology* 28: 91–116.

Bingtuan Jianshe (Bingtuan Construction). 2010. "'Wuqigong,' 'jiashugong' ke canbao [May 7 Workers and Housewife-workers Eligible for Social Insurance]." 5 (2): 31.

Bingtuan Second Agricultural Division. 2006. "Er shi gai kuang [The General Situation of the Second Agricultural Division]." Retrieved January 25, 2010, http://www.nes.gov.cn.

Bingtuannet. 2012a. "Hebei sheng dali bangzhu nong er shi jian xin cheng [Hebei Province to Make a Great Effort to Help The Second Agricultural Division Build a New City]." July 17. Retrieved August 13, 2012, http://epaper.bingtuannet.com/index.asp?id=63117.

———. 2012b. "Nong er shi wu wan yuan da jiang mianxiang shehui zhengji shiming [Second Agricultural Division Offers 50,000 Yuan Prize, Turns to Public for City Name]." *Bingtuan xinwen (Bingtuan News)*, May 19. Retrieved July 18, 2012, http://bt.xinhuanet.com/2012-05/19/content_25266411.htm.

Bloch, Ernst. 1986. *Prinzip Hoffnung (The Principle of Hope)*. Oxford: Blackwell.

Bøckman, Harald. 1998. "China Deconstructs? The Future of the Chinese Empire-State in a Historical Perspective." In *Reconstructing Twentieth-Century China: State Control, Civil Society, and National Identity*, edited by K. E. Brødsgaard and D. Strand. Oxford: Clarendon.

Bovingdon, Gardner. 2002. "The Not-So-Silent Majority: Uyghur Resistance to Han Rule in Xinjiang." *Modern China* 28 (1): 39–78.

———. 2004. "Autonomy in Xinjiang: Han Nationalist Imperatives and Uyghur Discontent." *Policy Studies* 11.

———. 2010. *The Uyghurs: Strangers in Their Own Land*. New York: Columbia University Press.

Branigan, Tania. 2009. "New Mass Protests and Violence Break out in Urumqi, Witnesses Claim." *Guardian*, September 3. Retrieved November 29, 2011, http://www.guardian.co.uk/world/2009/sep/03/urumqi-china-new-violence-new-claims.

Braudel, Fernand. [1958] 2009. "History and the Social Sciences: The *Longue Durée.*" *Review* XXXII (2: Commemorating the *Longue Durée*): 171–203.

Bray, David. 2005. *Social Space and Governance in Urban China: The Danwei System from Origins to Reform.* Stanford, CA: Stanford University Press.

Brightoil Petroleum. 2012. "Brightoil Petroleum Announces 2012 Interim Results.", February 27. Company Press Releases. Retrieved May 10, 2012, http://www.todayir.com/e/ownnews_showdetails.php?itemid=91610—0.

Bruner, Edward M. 1986. "Experience and Its Expressions." In *The Anthropology of Experience*, edited by V. Turner and E. M. Bruner. Urbana: University of Illinois Press.

Buzan, Barry, Ole Wæver, and Jaap de Wilde. 1998. *Security: A New Framework for Analysis.* Boulder, CO: Lynne Rienner.

Cai, Yongshun. 2010. *Collective Resistance in China: Why Popular Protests Succeed or Fail.* Stanford, CA: Stanford University Press.

Cannon, Terry. 1990. "Colonialism from Within." *China Now* 135 (Winter): 6–9.

Castets, Rémi. 2003 "The Uyghurs in Xinjiang—The Malaise Grows." *China Perspectives* (September–October 2003): 34–48.

CECC (Congressional-Executive Commission on China). 2011. "Local Officials in Xinjiang Continue Curbs Over Religious Practice." December 16. Retrieved August 28, 2012, http://www.cecc.gov/publications/commission-analysis/local-officials-in-xinjiang-continue-curbs-over-religious-practice.

Central Committee CCP. 1981. "Resolution on Certain Questions in the History of Our Party since the Founding of the People's Republic of China." Adopted by the Sixth Plenary Session of the Eleventh Central Committee of the Communist Party of China on June 27, 1981. Retrieved March 20, 2011, http://www.marxists.org/subject/china/documents/cpc/history/01.htm.

Chan, Anita, and Jonathan Unger. 2009. "A Chinese State Enterprise under the Reforms: What Model of Capitalism?" *China Journal* 62: 1–26.

Chan, Kam Wing. 2008. Internal Labor Migration in China: Trends, Geographical Distribution and Policies. *Proceedings of the United Nations Expert Group Meeting on Population Distribution, Urbanization, Internal Migration and Development.* United Nations: 93–122.

Chatterjee, Partha. 1993. *The Nation and Its Fragments: Colonial and Postcolonial Histories.* Princeton, NJ: Princeton University Press.

Chen, Tian. 2014. "Industrial Worry." *Global Times*, May 19. Retrieved June 4, 2014, http://www.globaltimes.cn/content/861137.shtml.

China Daily. 2011. "CNPC Plans Steady Overseas Expansion." Economy. October 21. Retrieved September 4, 2012, http://www.chinadaily.com.cn/china/2011-10/21/content_13945825.htm.

———. 2012. "Farm Machine Maker Looks to Greener Pastures." Business, Companies. July 14. Retrieved July 18, 2012, http://usa.chinadaily.com.cn/business/2012-07/14/content_15580946.htm.

———. 2014. "Fewer Couples Want Second Child." October 30. Retrieved March 30, 2015, http://www.chinadaily.com.cn/china/2014-10/30/content_18825388.htm.

———. 2015. "Xinjiang to be at the Heart of Reforms of Major State-Owned Energy Firms." March 17. Retrieved March 29, 2015, http://usa.chinadaily.com.cn/epaper/2015-03/17/content_19833360.htm.

China Data Online. 2012a. "Natural Crude Oil Production and Output." *Petroleum and Natural Gas Extraction*. Retrieved May 21, 2012, http://chinadataonline.org.rp.nla.gov.au/member/hyn/hyntshowpd.asp?hy=07&code=00413.

———. 2012b. "Natural Gas Production and Output." *Petroleum and Natural Gas Extraction*. Retrieved May 21, 2012, http://chinadataonline.org.rp.nla.gov.au/member/hyn/hyntshowpd.asp?hy=07&code=00420.

China Government Administration of Economic Growth. 2010. "Zhili Xinjiang: Kaipi xin silu [Governing Xinjiang: A New Approach]." *Lingdao Zhengce Xinxi (Leadership and Policy Information)* 21 (May 31): 24–25.

China Knowledge. 2012. "Xinjiang to Become China's Largest Oil and Gas Base." January 4. Retrieved May 10, 2012, http://www.steelguru.com/chinese_news/Xinjiang_to_become_Chinas_largest_oil_and_gas_base/244006.html.

China Reconstructs. 1956. "Karamai—Newest and Biggest Oilfield." *China Reconstructs* 5 (11): 7–9. Beijing: China Welfare Institute.

———. 1964. "China Mainly Self-Sufficient in Petroleum." *China Reconstructs* 13 (3): 11. Beijing: China Welfare Institute.

———. 1968. "Notes on the Taching Oilfield." *China Reconstructs* 17 (12): 38–43. Beijing: China Welfare Institute.

China Social Security. 2009. "Heilongjiang 'wuqigong,' 'jiashugong' can lao wuyou ("Heilongjiang May 7 Workers and 'Housewife-workers' No Worries Getting Old Age Pension]." *Zhongguo Shehui Baozhang* 9: 44.

ChinaNews.com. 2008. "Wang Lequan jiangshu Xinjiang 90 niandai fenlie douzheng: ceng bei lie ansha mingdan [Wang Lequan Tells of the Fight against Separatism in the 1990s: A List of Violent Incidents in the Past]." February 2. Retrieved November 20, 2011, http://www.chinanews.com/gn/news/2008/02-20/1167713.shtml.

———. 2009. "Xinjiang pilu da-za-qiang-shao-sha baoli fanzui shijian dangri fazhan shi-mo [Xinjiang Announces How the Illegal Beating, Smashing, Looting, Burning, and Killing Incident Developed]." July 6. Retrieved November 27, 2011, http://www.chinanews.com/gn/news/2009/07-06/1762907.shtml.

ChinaView. 2009. "Crowds Demand Security Guarantees in Urumqi after Hypodermic Syringe Attacks." September 4. Retrieved November 27, 2011, http://news.xinhuanet.com/video/2009-09/04/content_12000507.htm.

Clarke, Michael. 2008. "China's 'War on Terror' in Xinjiang: Human Security and the Causes of Violent Uighur Separatism." *Terrorism and Political Violence* 20 (2): 271–301.

Cliff, Thomas. 2005. NeoOasis: The Story of the Xinjiang Bingtuan. MA diss. Canberra, The Australian National University, Asian Studies.

———. 2009. "Neo Oasis: The Xinjiang Bingtuan in the Twenty-First Century." *Asian Studies Review* 33 (1): 83–106.

———. 2013. "Peripheral Urbanism: Making History on China's Northwest Frontier." *China Perspectives* (3): 13–23.

———. 2016. "Lucrative Chaos: Inter-Ethnic Conflict as a Function of Economic 'Normalization.'" In *Ethnic Conflict and Protest in Tibet and Xinjiang: Unrest in China's West*, edited by B. Hillman and G. Tuttle. New York: Columbia.

CNPC. 2006. "Zhongguo shiyou talimu youtian gongsi: qiye yuanjing [PetroChina Tarim Oilfield Company: Corporate Outlook]." Retrieved February 21, 2011, http://www.cnpc.com.cn/tlmyt/qywh.htm.

———. 2008. "Xiqidongshu erxian gongcheng kaigong jianshe Hu Jintao fa hexin Wen Jiabao zuo pishi [The Second East-to-West Gas Pipeline Project Begins Construction: Hu Jintao Sends a Letter of Congratulations, Wen Jiabao Writes a Memorial]." Retrieved February 4, 2012, http://www.cnpc.com.cn/CNPC/zt/xqdsexgc.htm.

———. 2009a. CNPC Annual Review, 1–15. Beijing: China National Petroleum Corporation.

———. 2009b. "Talimu moshi—xie zai Talimu shiyou huizhan 20 zhou nian zhi ji [The Tarim Model—Inscribed on the 20th Anniversary of the Tarim Petroleum Exploration Campaign]." April 8. Retrieved May 18, 2012, http://news.cnpc.com.cn/system/2009/04/08/001232150.shtml.

———. 2010a. "Gongxian nengyuan chuangzao hexie: Zhongguo shiyou Talimu youtian gongsi jianjie ['Contribute Resources, Create Harmony': A Brief Introduction to the Tarim Oil Company of CNPC]." August. Retrieved September 24, 2010, http://www.cnpc.com.cn/tlmyt/gsgk/tlmjj.

———. 2010b. "Talimu youtian jianshezhe zhi ge: yu zeren tong zai [The Song of the Tarim Oilfield Constructors: An Ever-Present Responsibility]." *Talimu shiyou bao (Tarim Oil News)*, September 8. Retrieved May 29, 2012, http://www.cnpc.com.cn/tlmyt.htm.

Coetzee, J. M. 1999. *Waiting for the Barbarians*. New York: Penguin Books.

Cox, Robert W. 2002. "Civilizations and the Twenty-First Century: Some Theoretical Considerations." In *Globalization and Civilizations*, edited by M. Mozaffari, 1–23. New York: Routledge.

CPPCC News Online. 2005. "Fazhan shi diyi yaowu, wending shi diyi zeren [Development Is the Number One Task, Stability Is the Number One Responsibility]." July 8. Retrieved November 15, 2011, http://cppcc.people.com.cn/GB/34952/3528323.html.

CRIEnglish.com. 2011. "Xinjiang Party Chief Urges Timely Handling of People's Appeals." March 18. Retrieved May 12, 2011, http://english.cri.cn/6909/2011/03/18/1461s626951.htm.

Current Background. 1968. Hong Kong, American Consulate General. January 15.

Dāmalā, Abd al-Shakūr. 2011. "Statement on the Occasion of the Military Operations in the Prefectures of 'Hūtan' and 'Kāshghar' in East Turkestān." Translated by David Brophy. *Jihadology*, August 25. Retrieved July 12, 2012, http://jihadology.net/2011/08/25/new-statement-from-the-amir-of-the-turkistan-islamic-party-shaykh-abd-al-shakur-damala-statement-on-the-occasion-of-the-military-operations-in-the-prefecture-of-hutan-and-kashghar-in-east.

Dautcher, Jay. 2009. *Down a Narrow Road: Identity and Masculinity in a Uyghur Community in Xinjiang China*. Cambridge: Harvard University Asia Center.

Davis, Clarence B. 1991. "Railway Imperialism in China, 1895–1939." In *Railway Imperialism*, edited by C. B. Davis, K. E. Wilburn Jr, and R. E. Robinson, 155–73. New York: Greenwood.

Davis, Deborah. 1992a. "Job Mobility in Post-Mao Cities: Increases on the Margins." *China Quarterly* 132: 1062–85.

———. 1992b. "'Skidding': Downward Mobility among Children of the Maoist Middle Class." *Modern China* 18 (4): 410–37.

Ding, Mei. 2014. "The Travelling Minzu: Uyghur Migration and the Negotiation of Identities in China and Australia." PhD diss., Anthropology and Archaeology, University of Otago.

Dirks, Nicholas B., ed. 1992. *Colonialism and Culture*. Ann Arbor, MI: University of Michigan Press.

Downs, Erica S. 2008 "Business Interest Groups in Chinese Politics: The Case of the Oil Companies." In *China's Changing Political Landscape: Prospects for Democracy*, edited by C. Li, 121–41. Washington, DC: Brookings Institution Press.

Duara, Prasenjit. 2001. "The Discourse of Civilization and Pan-Asianism." *Journal of World History* 12 (1): 99–130.

———. 2006. "The New Imperialism and the Post-Colonial Developmental State: Manchukuo in Comparative Perspective." *Asia-Pacific Journal: Japan Focus* 1715 (January 30). Retrieved August 22, 2012, http://www.japanfocus.org/-Prasenjit-Duara/1715.

EIN News. 2011. "Brightoil Acquires Xinjiang Tarim Basin Dina 1 Gas Field." *EIN Presswire*, November 11. Retrieved May 10, 2012, http://world.einnews.com/pr_news/66286758/brightoil-acquires-xinjiang-tarim-basin-dina-1-gas-field.

Elliott, Mark C. 2011. "National Minds and Imperial Frontiers: Inner Asia and China in the New Century." In *The People's Republic of China at 60: An International Assessment*, edited by W. C. Kirby, 401–12. Cambridge, MA: Harvard University Asia Center.

———. 2012. "Imperial Thinking" and the New Qing History. *Australian Centre on China in the World Seminar Series*. Australian National University.

Evans, Peter C., and Erica S. Downs. 2006. "Untangling China's Quest for Oil through State-Backed Financial Deals." *Policy Brief* 154 (May 2006).

Fabang.com. 2010. "Xinjiang shishi gongwuyuan gongzi gaige: 8 yue zhang gongzi [Xinjiang Implements Public Servants' Salary Reform: Raise Due in

August]." July 29. Retrieved November 18, 2011, http://www.fabang.com/a/20100729/172413.html.
Fan Deguang, Wu Xiaofeng, et al. 2001. "Bingtuan ying yi jiji de shichang jingji zhanlue tiaozhan da kaifa [Bingtuan Should Challenge the Western Development by Active Marketing Economical Strategy]." *Journal of Bingtuan Education Institute* 11 (3): 1–4.
Fan Renyuan and Zhou Gousheng. 2000. "Dui bingtuan shishi xibu da kaifa zhanlue zhong ji ge wenti de sikao [Thoughts on the Question of Bingtuan Carrying out 'Develop the West']." *Bingtuan Dangxiao Xuebao* 56 (2000:2): 7–10.
Fischer, Michael M. J. 1991. "The Uses of Life Histories." *Anthropology and Humanism Quarterly* 16 (1): 24–27.
Fong, Vanessa L. 2004. *Only Hope: Coming of Age under China's One Child Policy*. Stanford, CA: Stanford University Press.
Forbes, Andrew D. W. 1986. *Warlords and Muslims in Chinese Central Asia: A Political History of Republican Sinkiang, 1911–1949*. Cambridge: Cambridge University Press.
Foucault, Michel. 1977. *Discipline and Punish: The Birth of the Prison*. London: Allen Lane.
Frolic, B. Michael. 1980. *Mao's People: Sixteen Portraits of Life in Revolutionary China*. Cambridge, MA: Harvard University Press.
Fushita, Hironori. 2012. "Russia's Eastward Pivot: Circumstances in Russia Following Putin's Comeback and Japan's Reaction." *AJISS Commentary*, May 23, 149. Retrieved June 24, 2012, http://www.jiia.or.jp/en_commentary/201205/23-1.html.
Gaubatz, Piper Rae. 1996. *Beyond the Great Wall: Urban Form and Transformation on the Chinese Frontiers*. Stanford, CA: Stanford University Press.
Giersch, C. Pat. 2001. "'A Motley Throng': Social Change on Southwest China's Early Modern Frontier, 1700–1880." *Journal of Asian Studies* 60 (1): 67–94.
Gilley, Bruce. 2001. "China—'Uighurs Need Not Apply.'" *Far Eastern Economic Review*, August 23, 26.
Gladney, Dru. 1998a. "Clashed Civilizations? Muslim and Chinese Identities in the PRC." In *Making Majorities: Constituting the Nation in Japan, Korea, China, Malaysia, Fiji, Turkey, and the United States*, edited by D. Gladney, 106–31. Stanford, CA: Stanford University Press.
———. 1998b. "Internal Colonialism and the Uyghur Nationality: Chinese Nationalism and its Subaltern Subjects." *Cahiers d'Études sur la Méditerranée Orientale et le monde Turco-Iranien* [online edition] 25: 47–63.
Global Times. 2011a. "China's Xinjiang to Earn Five Bln Yuan in Resource Tax in 2011." *Global Times*, November 10. Retrieved November 18, 2011, http://www.globaltimes.cn/NEWS/tabid/99/ID/683296/Chinas-Xinjiang-to-earn-5-bln-yuan-in-resource-tax-in-2011.aspx.
———. 2011b. "Foreign Trade More Than Triples in China's Xinjiang." *Global Times*, February 14. Retrieved May 15, 2011, http://business.globaltimes.cn/china-economy/2011-02/622556.html.

———. 2011c. "Xinjiang's Future about More Than Resources." *Global Times*, September 15. Retrieved May 10, 2012, http://www.globaltimes.cn/NEWS/tabid/99/ID/675427/Xinjiangs-future-about-more-than-resources.aspx.

———. 2012. "Religious Freedom Doesn't Trump Protection of Minors." *Global Times*, June 12. Retrieved July 10, 2013, http://www.globaltimes.cn/content/714496.shtml.

———. 2014. "Southern Xinjiang Reforms Hukou in Effort to Draw Talent, Investment." *Global Times*, October 21. Retrieved March 30, 2015, http://www.globaltimes.cn/content/887353.shtml.

Gold, Thomas B., William Hurst, et al., eds. 2009. *Laid-Off Workers in a Workers' State: Unemployment with Chinese Characteristics*. New York: Palgrave Macmillan.

Gold, Thomas, Doug Guthrie, et al., eds. 2002. *Social Connections in China: Institutions, Culture, and the Changing Nature of Guanxi*. Cambridge: Cambridge University Press.

Grammaticas, Damian. 2010. "Trekking 1000 Km in China for E-Mail." February 11. Retrieved December 1, 2011, http://news.bbc.co.uk/2/hi/8506601.stm.

Gries, Peter Hays. 2004. *China's New Nationalism: Pride, Politics, and Diplomacy*. Berkeley: University of California Press.

Guardian. 2011. "China Puts Urumqi under 'Full Surveillance.'" January 25. Retrieved May 7, 2012, http://www.guardian.co.uk/world/2011/jan/25/china-urumqi-under-full-surveillance.

Haase, Wolfgang, and Hildegard Temporini, eds. 1992. *Rise and Decline of the Roman World: Principate, Part 2*. Berlin: de Gruyter.

Hansen, Mette Halskov. 2005. *Frontier People: Han Settlers in Minority Areas of China*. Vancouver: UBC Press.

Hardt, Michael, and Antonio Negri. 2000. *Empire*. Cambridge, MA: Harvard University Press.

Harrell, Stevan. 1995. "Introduction." In *Cultural Encounters on China's Ethnic Frontiers*, edited by S. Harrell, 3–36. Seattle: University of Washington Press.

Harris, Rachel. 2004. *Singing the Village: Music, Memory, and Ritual amongst the Sibe of Xinjiang*. Oxford: Oxford University Press.

———. 2009. "National Traditions and Illegal Religious Activities in Chinese Central Asia." In *Sounds of Power: Music, Politics and Ideology in the Middle East, North Africa and Central Asia*, edited by L. Nooshin, 165–85. Aldershot, UK: Ashgate.

Harris, Rachel, and Aziz Isa. 2011. "'Invitation to a Mourning Ceremony': Perspectives on the Uyghur Internet." *Inner Asia* 13 (1): 27–49.

He Zhanjun. 2011. "Zhang Chunxian zhili Xinjiang yi nian: pingjun budao 3 tian jiu you yi xiang huimin zhengce chutai [Zhang Chunxian's First Year of Governing Xinjiang: for Each Less Than Three-Day Period since He Took Office, an Average of One Policy to Benefit the People [of Xinjiang] Has Been Announced]." *Renmin Ribao*, April 24. Retrieved May 11, 2011, http://politics.people.com.cn/GB/14562/14467759.html.

Hess, Steve. 2009. "Dividing and Conquering the Shop Floor: Uyghur Labour Export and Labour Segmentation in China's Industrial East." *Central Asian Survey* 28 (4): 403–16.
Ho, Ping-ti. 1967. "The Significance of the Ch'ing Period in Chinese History." *Journal of Asian Studies* 26 (2): 189–95.
Hobson, J. A. 1902. Imperialism: A Study. London: James Nisbet.
Horner, Charles, and Eric Brown. 2011. "A Century after the Qing: Yesterday's Empire and Today's Republics." *China Heritage Quarterly* 27, http://www.chinaheritagequarterly.org/features.php?searchterm=027_century.inc&issue=027.
Hu Jintao. 2011. "Gaoceng Yanlun (Words from Above): Hu Jintao." *Lingdao Zhengce Xiaoxi (Leadership and Policy Information)* 37 (September): 2.
Hu Yue. 2010. "Hand in Hand: China Unveils a Partner Assistance Program to Propel Xinjiang toward Economic Prosperity and Social Stability." *Beijing Review* 23 (June 10). Retrieved May 15, 2011, http://www.bjreview.com.cn/business/txt/2010-06/07/content_277403.htm.
Hung, Eva, and Stephen Chiu. 2009. "Voices of Xiagang: Naming, Blaming, and Framing." In *Laid-Off Workers in a Workers' State: Unemployment with Chinese Characteristics*, edited by T. B. Gold, W. Hurst, J. Won, and L. Qiang, 95–114. New York: Palgrave Macmillan.
Hurst, William. 2008. "Mass Frames and Worker Protest." In *Popular Protest in China*, edited by K. J. O'Brien. Cambridge, MA: Harvard University Press.
International Oil Web. 2010. "Talimu youtian Tazhong 1 hao qitian jianshezhe su miao [The Constructors of Tazhong Number One Gas Field Work Quickly Without Compromise]." *Industry News*, October 29. Retrieved May 29, 2012, http://oil.in-en.com/html/oil-1114111490796221.html.
Jacka, Tamara. 2006. *Rural Women in Urban China: Gender, Migration, and Social Change*. Armonk, NY: M. E. Sharpe.
Jacobs, J. Bruce. 1979. "A Preliminary Model of Particularistic Ties in Chinese Political Alliances: Kan-ch'ing and Kuan-hsi in a Rural Taiwanese Township." *China Quarterly* 78: 237–73.
Jin Xianghong. 1994. *Bayinguoleng Menggu zizhizhou zhi (The Annals of Bayinguoleng Mongolian Autonomous Prefecture)*. Beijing: Dangdai Zhongguo chubanshe.
Jin Yonggang Huo Yuhua, et al. 2001. "Dui bingtuan shishi xibu da kaifa youhui zhengce wenti de sikao [Thoughts on the question of preferential policies for the bingtuan in carrying out 'Develop the West']." *Bingtuan Dangxiao Xuebao* 59 (2000:5): 13–15.
Kardos, Amy. 2010. "A Rock and a Hard Place: Chinese Soldiers in Xinjiang Caught between Centre and Periphery after 1949." In *China on the Margins*, edited by S. Cochran and P. G. Pickowicz, 135–57. Honolulu: University of Hawai'i Press.
Kennedy, Andrew B. 2010. "China's New Energy-Security Debate." *Survival: Global Politics and Strategy* 52 (3): 137–58.
Khalid, Adeeb. 2006. "Backwardness and the Quest for Civilization: Early Soviet Central Asia in Comparative Perspective." *Slavic Review* 65 (2): 231–51.

Kipnis, Andrew. 1997. *Producing Guanxi: Sentiment, Self, and Subculture in a North China Village*. Durham, NC: Duke University Press.

———. 2001. "The Disturbing Educational Discipline of 'Peasants.'" *China Journal* 46: 1–24.

———. 2011. *Governing Educational Desire: Culture, Politics, and Schooling in China*. Chicago: University of Chicago Press.

———. 2012. "Constructing Commonality: Standardization and Modernization in Chinese Nation-Building." *Journal of Asian Studies* 71 (03): 731–55.

Ko, Kilkon, and Cuifen Weng. 2011. "Critical Review of Conceptual Definitions of Chinese Corruption: a Formal Legal Perspective." *Journal of Contemporary China* 20 (70): 359–78.

Kopytoff, Igor, ed. 1987. *The African Frontier: The Reproduction of Traditional African Societies*. Bloomington: Indiana University Press.

Ku'erle Wanbao (Korla Evening News). 2009a. "9 yue Wulumuqi yidi gou fang jiaoyi liang hui wen [Housing Sales to Non-Urumchi Residents Stabilize in September]." Korla, Xinjiang Daily. 3784 (October 19): 2.

———. 2009b. "Quanli shenwa 'zhenci' anjian muhou zuzhizhe [All-Out Effort to Uncover the Organizers of the "Needlestick" Attacks]." Korla, Xinjiang Daily. 3750 (September 9): 6, 11.

———. 2009c. "Ru ci gan huo [Carrying Out Duties in This Manner]."Korla, Xinjiang Daily. 3714 (July 29): 4.

———. 2009d. "Shengchan huinuan wujia shuiping wen zhong you jiang [Indian Summer for Production: Commodity Prices Are Stable and Falling]." Korla, Xinjiang Daily. 3679 (June 18): 1.

———. 2009e. "Wulumuqi qian 7 ge yue shangpinfang chengjiaojia tongbi zengzhang jin er cheng [Commercial Housing in Urumchi Rises 20% in Previous Seven Months]." Korla, Xinjiang Daily. 3724 (August 10): 2.

———. 2009f. "Wulumuqi qian 8 ge yue shangpinfang chengjiaojia mei pingfangmi 3457 yuan [Urumchi Commercial Housing Averages 3457 RMB/m² in Previous 8 Months]." Korla, Xinjiang Daily. 3755 (September 15): 2.

———. 2009g. "Zizhiqu mianqu Li Zhi Wulumuqi shi wei shuji zhiwu: Zhu Hailun jieren [Autonomous Region Dismisses Li Zhi as Urumchi Party Secretary: Zhu Hailun Takes Over]." Korla, Xinjiang Daily. 3748 (September 7): 1, 11.

———. 2009h. "Zui Han sanbu yaoyan bei ju 10 tian [Drunk Man Gets 10 Days Jail for Spreading Rumors]." Korla, Xinjiang Daily. 3700 (July 13): 1.

Lary, Diana. 2007. "Introduction." In *The Chinese State at the Borders*, edited by D. Lary, 1–10. Vancouver: University of British Columbia Press.

Lattimore, Owen. 1962. "The Frontier in History." In *Studies in Frontier History: Collected Papers, 1928–1958*, 469–91. Paris: Mouton.

Leibold, James. 2011. "Searching for Han: Early Twentieth-Century Narratives of Chinese Origins and Development." In *Critical Han Studies: The History, Representation and Identity of China's Majority*, edited by T. Mullaney, J. Leibold, S. Gros, and E. V. Bussche, 346–87. Berkeley: University of California Press.

Lenin, Vladimir Il'ich. 1947 [1916]. *Imperialism, the Highest Stage of Capitalism (A Popular Outline)*. Moscow: Foreign Languages Publishing House.

Li, Ling. 2011. "Performing Bribery in China: Guanxi Practice, Corruption with a Human Face." *Journal of Contemporary China* 20 (68): 1–20.

Li, Qinggang. 2011. "The Force behind Leadership." *China Daily*, Opinion Online, July 1. Retrieved November 28, 2011, http://www.chinadaily.com.cn/china/cpc2011/2011-07/01/content_12814074.htm.

Li, Tseh. 1958. Big News in Oil. *China Reconstructs* 7 (11): 20–21. Beijing: China Welfare Institute.

Li Xing. 2009. "Zhongxuanbu lingdao zai wo qu weiwen diaoyan [Central Propaganda Ministry Leader in Xinjiang to Convey Sympathy and Conduct Investigation]." *Xinjiang Ribao (Xinjiang Daily)*. Urumchi: 1.

Liang Jingui. 2009. "Lun bingtuan wenhua de jingshen yu tezhi [Regarding the Spirit and Special Characteristics of Bingtuan Culture]." *Jiangnan Daxue Xuebao [Renwen Shehui Kexue Ban] (Journal of Jiangnan University [Humanities & Social Sciences Edition])* 8 (4).

Lieberthal, Kenneth, and Michel Oksenberg. 1988. *Policy Making in China: Leaders, Structures, and Processes*. Princeton, NJ: Princeton University Press.

Lim, Tai Wei. 2010. "Oil for the Center from the Margins." In *China on the Margins*, edited by S. Cochran and P. G. Pickowicz, 117–34. Honolulu: University of Hawai'i Press.

Lin, Nan, and Yanjie Bian. 1991. "Getting Ahead in Urban China." *American Journal of Sociology* 97 (3): 657–88.

Lin, Xin. 2014. "Police Crack Down on Thousands at Daqing Oilfield Jobs Protest." April 9. Retrieved June 4, 2014, http://www.rfa.org/english/news/china/protest-04092014114529.html.

Liu Xianghui. 2011. "Yuanjiang gongzuo shisi nian huigu yu zhanwang [Looking to the Past 14 Years and the Future of the Work to Assist Xinjiang]." *Xinjiang difang (Xinjiang)* 3: 34–38.

Liu, Xiaobo. 2011 [2006]. "Can It Be That the Chinese People Deserve Only 'Party-Led Democracy'?" *Journal of Democracy* 22 (1): 154–60.

Liu, Yong. 2010. "An Economic Band-Aid: Beijing's New Approach to Xinjiang." *China Security* 6 (2): 41–55.

Loomba, Ania. 1998. *Colonialism Postcolonialism*. London: Routledge.

Lu, Na. 2011. "S. Xinjiang's First National Economic Zone Established." *China.org.cn*, April 19. Retrieved May 15, 2011, http://www.china.org.cn/china/2011-04/19/content_22396350.htm.

Luo Guanzhong. 2000. *San guo yan yi (Three Kingdoms)*. Changsha: Hunan ren min chu ban she; Wai wen chu ban she.

Luo Xiaoli. 2011. "Zhang Chunxian shuji yaoqiu gonglu jianshezhe buji rong ru pinming kugan zaofu renmin [Secretary Zhang Chunxian Requests Highway Constructors Not to Think of Glory or Dishonour, to Work Hard and Bring Benefit to the People]." *Tianshannet*, April 12. Retrieved February 4,

2012, http://www.tianshannet.com.cn/gov/content/2011-04/12/content_5744513.htm.

Luo Yi. 1954. "Fucong guojia fenpei jiushi weile shehui zhuyi [Obeying National Job Distribution is in the Name of Socialism]." *Renmin Ribao* July 28, 3.

Manion, Melanie. 2004. *Corruption by Design: Building Clean Government in Mainland China and Hong Kong*. Cambridge, MA: Harvard University Press.

March, Andrew Lee. 1974. *The Idea of China: Myth and Theory in Geographic Thought*. Newton Abbot, Devon, UK: David & Charles.

McMillen, Donald H. 1981. "Xinjiang and the Production and Construction Corps: A Han Organisation in a Non-Han Region." *Australian Journal of Chinese Affairs* 6: 65–96.

Mertha, Andrew. 2008. *China's Water Warriors: Citizen Action and Policy Change*. Ithaca, NY: Cornell University Press.

———. 2009. "'Fragmented Authoritarianism 2.0': Political Pluralization in the Chinese Policy Process." *China Quarterly* 200: 995–1012.

Miller, Alice L. 2008. "Institutionalization and the Changing Dynamics of Chinese Leadership Politics." In *China's Changing Political Landscape: Prospects for Democracy*, edited by C. Li, 61–79. Washington, DC: Brookings Institution Press.

Mills, C. Wright. 1959 [1974]. *The Sociological Imagination*. London: Oxford University Press.

Millward, James. 1998. *Beyond the Pass: Economy, Ethnicity, and Empire in Qing Central Asia, 1759–1864*. Stanford, CA: Stanford University Press.

———. 2007. *Eurasian Crossroads: A History of Xinjiang*. London: C. Hurst and Company.

———. 2009. "Introduction: Does the 2009 Urumchi Violence Mark a Turning Point?" *Central Asian Survey* 28 (4): 347–60.

Milner, Lord Alfred. 1913. *The Nation and the Empire: Being a Collection of Speeches and Addresses*. London: Constable and Company.

Miyazaki, Hirokazu. 2004. *The Method of Hope: Anthropology, Philosophy, and Fijian Knowledge*. Stanford, CA: Stanford University Press.

———. 2006. "Economy of Dreams: Hope in Global Capitalism and Its Critiques." *Cultural Anthropology* 21 (2): 147–72.

MOFCOM. 2012. "Zizhiqu lingdao yu guoziwei ji bufen yangqi zeren zuotan gongshang qiye chanye yuanjiang daji [Autonomous Region Leaders, SASAC, and Enterprise Leaders Discuss Key Aspects of Industrial and Commercial Enterprises' Assistance to Xinjiang]." *Xinjiang Ribao*, March 2. Retrieved May 7 2012, http://www.mofcom.gov.cn/aarticle/difang/bingtuan/201203/20120307994055.html.

Mu Xin. 2008. *Wang Zhen de san ci changzheng [The Three Long Marches of Wang Zhen]*. Beijing: Renmin chubanshe (The People's Publishing House).

Mullaney, Thomas S. 2004a. "Introduction: 55 + 1 = 1 or The Strange Calculus of Chinese Nationhood." *China Information* 18 (2): 197–205.

———. 2004b. "Ethnic Classification Writ Large." *China Information* 18 (2): 207–41.

Myrdal, Gunnar. 1968. "Corruption—Its Causes and Effects." In *Asian Drama: An Inquiry into the Poverty of Nations*, 2: 937–58. London: Penguin Press.

Naughton, Barry. 1988. "The Third Front: Defence Industrialization in the Chinese Interior." *China Quarterly* 115: 351–86.

———. 2004. "Market Economy, Hierarchy, and Single Party Rule: How Does the Transition Path in China Shape the Emerging Market Economy?" International Economic Association, Hong Kong.

news.163.com. 2010. "Zhongyang jueding zai Xinjiang Kashi she jingji tequ [The Central Government Decides to Build a Special Economic Zone in Kashgar, Xinjiang]." *Renmin Wang (People's Daily Online)*, May 21. Retrieved May 14, 2011, http://news.163.com/10/0521/08/676ORIAO0001124J.html.

news.china.com.cn. 2010. "Xinjiang jinri qi quanmian huifu hulianwang yewu [Xinjiang's Internet Service Fully Restored]." May 14. Retrieved May 12, 2011, http://news.china.com.cn/txt/2010-05/14/content_20038848.htm.

Northrop, Douglas. 2004. *Veiled Empire: Gender and Power in Stalinist Central Asia*. Ithaca, NY: Cornell University Press.

O'Brien, Kevin J., and Lianjiang Li. 2006. *Rightful Resistance in Rural China*. New York: Cambridge University Press.

Osburg, John. 2013. *Anxious Wealth: Money and Morality among China's New Rich*. Stanford, CA: Stanford University Press.

Parker, Bradley J., and Lars Rodseth, eds. 2005. *Untaming the Frontier in Anthropology, Archaeology, and History*. Tucson: University of Arizona Press.

Pathway to China. 2012. "China's Tarim Oilfield: Gas Output to Increase by 40%." March. Retrieved May 28, 2012, http://www.pathwaytochina.com/blog.php?id=90&year=2012&month=3.

Pei, Minxin. 2006. *China's Trapped Transition: The Limits of Developmental Autocracy*. Cambridge, MA: Harvard University Press.

People's Daily. 2003. "Today in History." Retrieved February 20, 2011, http://www.people.com.cn/GB/historic/0205/5727.html.

———. 2011a. "China's Xinjiang Eases Rules for Foreign Investment to Boost Inbound Investment." March 22. Retrieved May 15, 2011, http://english.peopledaily.com.cn/90001/90778/90861/7326839.html.

———. 2011b. "Corps Keeps Development on Track in Xinjiang." March 9. Retrieved March 12, 2011, http://english.peopledaily.com.cn/90001/90776/90882/7313086.html.

———. 2011c. "Xinjiang Party Chief Opens Microblog to Better Hear Public Opinions." March 4. Retrieved May 11, 2011, http://english.peopledaily.com.cn/90001/90776/90882/7307711.html.

Perdue, Peter. 2005. "From Turfan to Taiwan: Trade and War on Two Chinese Frontiers." In *Untaming the Frontier in Anthropology, Archaeology, and History*, edited by B. J. Parker and L. Rodseth, 27–51. Tucson: University of Arizona Press.

Perry, Elizabeth J. 2008. "Chinese Conceptions of "Rights": From Mencius to Mao—and Now." *Perspectives on Politics* 6 (01): 37–50.

Perry, Elizabeth J., and Xiaobo Lu, eds. 1997. *Danwei: The Changing Chinese Workplace in Historical and Comparative Perspectives*. Armonk, NY: M. E. Sharpe.

Platts. 2011a. "Brightoil Appoints CNPC Unit as Contractor for China's Tuzi Gas Field." *Oilgram News*, March 31. Retrieved May 10, 2012, http://www.platts.com/RSSFeedDetailedNews/RSSFeed/Oil/7368831.

———. 2011b. "China's CNPC Says Central Asia Gas Pipeline Rate to Hit 30 Bcm/Year June 2012." *News and Analysis*, December 16. Retrieved September 4, 2012, http://www.platts.com/RSSFeedDetailedNews/RSSFeed/NaturalGas/7882712.

Qiushi Lilun. 2011. "Shenhua gaoxiao xuesheng de sixiang zhengzhi jiaoyu gongzuo: bu dongyao, bu xiedai, bu zheteng [Deepen College Students' Ideological and Political Education Work: Do Not Waver, Do Not Slacken, Do Not Procrastinate]." *Wenming Pinglun (Civilization Theory)*, July 18. http://xj.wenming.cn/wmpl/201107/t20110718_249257.shtml.

Radio Free Asia. 2009a. "A City Gripped by Fear." July 6. Retrieved June 10, 2011, http://www.rfa.org/english/multimedia/VideoXinjiangUnrest-07062009141835.html.

———. 2009b. "A Day of Violence in Urumqi." July 6. Retrieved June 10, 2011, http://www.rfa.org/english/multimedia/SlideshowUrumqiRiot-07062009121840.html.

———. 2011. "Farmers Sent to Reeducation Camp." August 15. Retrieved July 31, 2012, http://www.rfa.org/english/news/uyghur/herdsmen-02092012185043.html.

———. 2012. "Herdsmen Demand Answers, Compensation." February 9. Retrieved July 31, 2012, http://www.rfa.org/english/news/uyghur/herdsmen-02092012185043.html.

———. 2013a. "Farmers Complain of Land Grabbing, Corruption in Xinjiang Village." Retrieved July 10, 2013, http://www.rfa.org/english/news/uyghur/farm-06032013205126.html.

———. 2013b. "Four Uyghur Women Forced to Abort Their Babies in Xinjiang." December 30. Retrieved March 30, 2015, http://www.rfa.org/english/news/uyghur/abortion-12302013050902.html.

———. 2014. "Uyghur Petitioners Beaten, Detained over Land Grab." May 7. Retrieved March 30, 2015, http://www.rfa.org/english/news/uyghur/land-05072014144335.html.

———. 2015. "Authorities Put 25 Hotan Uyghurs on Public Trial for 'Endangering State Security.'" March 27. Retrieved March 30, 2015, http://www.rfa.org/english/news/uyghur/hotan-uyghurs-put-on-trial-03272015170151.html.

Rawski, Evelyn. 1996. "Reenvisioning the Qing: The Significance of the Qing Period in Chinese History." *Journal of Asian Studies* 55 (4): 829–50.

Raymo, James, and Yu Xie. 1997. "Income of the Urban Elderly in Postreform China: Political Capital, Human Capital, and the State." *PSC Research Report* 97 (404).

Renmin Ribao (People's Daily). 2009a. "Guanyu shixing Dang-Zheng lingdao ganbu wen ze de zanxing guiding [Regarding the Implementation of Provisional Measures to Hold High-Level Party and Government Cadres Accountable]." July 13. Retrieved December 7, 2010, http://renshi.people.com.cn/GB/9639591.html.

———. 2009b. "Zuguo da jiating [The Great Family of the Motherland]." Retrieved August 30, 2012, http://cpc.people.com.cn/GB/165240/166030/166031.

———. 2014a. "Daqing youtian jinnian yi qianyue 1075 ming biyesheng fei youtian zinv jin jiu cheng [Daqing Oilfield Has Employed 1,075 Graduates This Year; Nearly 90% Not Oil Workers' Children]." May 1. Retrieved June 4, 2014, http://hlj.people.com.cn/n/2014/0501/c220024-21116664.html.

———. 2014b. "Zhong Shiyou Daqing Youtian shu qian zhigong kangyi gaige zinv bao fenpei [1,000 Daqing Oilfield Employees Oppose the Reform of Children's Guaranteed Job Assignments]." April 30. Retrieved June 2, 2014, http://politics.people.com.cn/n/2014/0430/c1001-24959922.html.

Reuters. 2011. "China Slaps 10% Oil, Gas Resource Taxes Nationwide." November 3. Retrieved May 7, 2012, http://au.ibtimes.com/articles/242396/20111103/china-slaps-10-oil-gas-resource-taxes.htm.

———. 2011. "PetroChina to Raise Output in Tarim Oilfield 50 pct by 2015." *Energy & Oil*, May 17. Retrieved May 10, 2012, http://af.reuters.com/article/energyOilNews/idAFL4E7GH03320110517.

———. 2012a. "Amnesty Slams China for Uighur Crackdown Three Years after Riots." July 5. Retrieved July 31, 2012, http://www.reuters.com/article/2012/07/05/us-china-uighurs-idUSBRE86401Z20120705.

———. 2012b. "China's CNPC in Talks with Ecuador over $12.5 Billion Refinery." July 20. Retrieved September 4, 2012, http://www.reuters.com/article/2012/07/20/us-ecuador-refinery-cnpc-idUSBRE86J08C20120720.

———. 2012c. "Refining Losses Hit China's PetroChina, Sinopec." April 26. Retrieved May 28, 2012, http://www.reuters.com/article/2012/04/26/china-earnings-oil-idUSL3E8FP7S920120426?type=companyNews.

Rice, Prudence, and Don Rice. 2005. "The Final Frontier of the Maya: Central Peten, Guatemala, 1450–1700 CE." In *Untaming the Frontier in Anthropology, Archaeology, and History*, edited by B. J. Parker and L. Rodseth, 147–73. Tucson: University of Arizona Press.

Rodseth, Lars. 2005. "The Fragmentary Frontier: Expansion and Ethnogenesis in the Himalayas." In *Untaming the Frontier in Anthropology, Archaeology, and History*, edited by B. J. Parker and L. Rodseth, 83–109. Tucson: University of Arizona Press.

Rohlf, Greg. 2003. "Dreams of Oil and Fertile Fields: The Rush to Qinghai in the 1950s." *Modern China* 29: 455–88.

Rose, Nikolas. 1998. *Inventing Our Selves: Psychology, Power, and Personhood*. Cambridge: Cambridge University Press.

Rose, Steven Peter Russell. 2003 [1992]. *The Making of Memory*. London: Vintage.

Rudelson, Justin Jon. 1997. *Oasis Identities: Uyghur Nationalism along China's Silk Road*. New York: Columbia University Press.

Runia, Eelco. 2006. "Spots of Time." *History and Theory* 45 (Forum: On Presence): 305–16.

Rushdie, Salman. 2008. *Midnight's Children*. London: Vintage.

Sahadeo, Jeff. 2007. *Russian Colonial Society in Tashkent: 1865–1923*. Bloomington: Indiana University Press.

SASAC. 2011. "Zhongguo Qiye Bao: Wang Yong ding tiao 2012 qiye fazhan silu [China Enterprise: Wang Yong Sets the Development Track for Central Enterprises in 2012]." *12.19 zeren ren hui (December 19 Leaders' Meeting)*, 4496–03, December 20. Retrieved July 18, 2012, http://www.sasac.gov.cn/n1180/n12534878/n14167686/14167885.html.

Sautman, Barry. 2000. "Is Xinjiang an Internal Colony?" *Inner Asia* 2 (2).

SCMP. 1966. *Survey of People's Republic of China Press*. Hong Kong: American Consulate General.

Scott, James C. 1998. *Seeing Like a State: How Certain Schemes to Improve the Human Condition Have Failed*. New Haven, CT: Yale University Press.

Seeberg, Vilma. 1998. "Stratification Trends in Technical Professional Higher Education." In *Higher Education in Post-Mao China*, edited by M. Agelasto and B. Adamson, 211–35. Hong Kong: Hong Kong University Press.

SeekingAlpha. 2011. "PetroChina: Fueled for Future Growth." April 13. Retrieved May 28, 2012, http://seekingalpha.com/article/263237-petrochina-fueled-for-future-growth.

Seymour, James D. 2000. "Xinjiang's Production and Construction Corps, and the Sinification of Eastern Turkestan." *Inner Asia* 2 (2): 171–93.

Shao Wei and Mao Weihua. 2011. "Training Program to Boost Employment in Xinjiang." *China Daily*, March 26. Retrieved May 15, 2011, http://www.chinadaily.com.cn/bizchina/2011-03/26/content_12231521.htm.

Shapiro, Judith. 2001. *Mao's War against Nature: Politics and the Environment in Revolutionary China*. New York: Cambridge University Press.

Sharpe, Jenny. 1993. "The Unspeakable Limits of Rape: Colonial Violence and Counter-Insurgency." In *Colonial Discourse and Postcolonial Theory: A Reader*, edited by P. Williams and L. Chrisman, 221–43. New York: Harvester Wheatsheaf.

Shih, Victor. 2004. "Development, the Second Time Around: The Political Logic of Developing Western China." *Journal of East Asian Studies* (4): 427–51.

Sina.com. 2009. "Wulumuqi fasheng da-za-qiang-shao yanzhong baoli fanzui shijian [Violent Criminal Incident in Urumchi—Featuring Beating, Smashing, Looting and Burning]." July 6. Retrieved April 11, 2011, http://news.sina.com.cn/c/p/2009-07-06/042318160186.shtml.

Smith Finley, Joanne. 2011. "'No Rights without Duties': Minzu Pingdeng [Nationality Equality] in Xinjiang since the 1997 Ghulja Disturbances." *Inner Asia* 13 (1): 73–96.

———. 2013. *The Art of Symbolic Resistance: Uyghur Identities and Uyghur-Han Relations in Contemporary Xinjiang*. Leiden, Netherlands: Brill.

Social Development Research Group. 2010. "New Thinking on Stability Maintenance: Long-Term Social Stability via Institutionalised Expression of

Interests." March 26. Tsinghua University Department of Sociology. Retrieved May 16, 2011, http://chinaelectionsblog.net/?p=5220.

Starr, S. Frederick, ed. 2004. *Xinjiang: China's Muslim Borderland.* Armonk, NY: M. E. Sharpe.

Starr, S. Frederick, and Graham E. Fuller. 2004. *The Xinjiang Problem.* Washington, DC: Central Asia-Caucasus Institute, Johns Hopkins University.

State Council Information Office. 2009. "White Paper: Development and Progress in Xinjiang." *Xinhua: Window of China.* September 21. Retrieved May 4, 2011, http://news.xinhuanet.com/english/2009-09/21/content_12090477_8.htm.

Stern, Philip J. 2011. *The Company State: Corporate Sovereignty and the Early Modern Foundations of the British Empire in India.* New York: Oxford University Press.

Stoler, Ann Laura, and Carole McGranahan. 2007. "Refiguring Imperial Terrains." In *Imperial Formations*, edited by A. L. Stoler, C. McGranahan, and P. C. Perdue, 3–44. Santa Fe, AZ: School for Advanced Research Press.

Stoler, Ann Laura, Carole McGranahan, et al., eds. 2007. *Imperial Formations.* Santa Fe, AZ: School for Advanced Research Press.

Straits Times. 2000. "Revolutionary Flower Blooms in Desert." September 3. Retrieved December 10, 2004, http://newslink.asia1.com.sg.

Sun, Liping. 2010. "Sun Liping Discusses Social Stability in China." *Shanghaiist.* Retrieved December 4, 2010, http://shanghaiist.com/2007/11/09/sun_liping.php.

Sun Mingxu. 2007. Daqing jingshen tieren jingshen [The Spirit of Daqing: Iron Man Spirit]. CCP. Korla, Tarim Oilfield Company.

Tang, Beibei, Luigi Tomba, et al. 2011. "The Work-Unit Is Dead. Long Live the Work-Unit! Spatial Segregation and Privilege in a Work-Unit Housing Compound in Guangzhou." *Geographische Zeitschrift* 99 (1): 36–49.

Tang, Wenfang, and William L. Parish. 2000. *Chinese Urban Life under Reform: The Changing Social Contract.* Cambridge: Cambridge University Press.

Tewpiq. 2008. "Xinjiang People, I'm Sorry, Thank You." *New Dominion*, July 3. Retrieved May 14, 2011, http://www.thenewdominion.net/209/xinjiang-people-im-sorry-thank-you/—comment-2481.

Thomas, Nicholas. 1994. *Colonialism's Culture: Anthropology, Travel and Government.* Oxford: Polity Press.

Thompson, E. P. 1971. "The Moral Economy of the English Crowd in the Eighteenth Century." *Past & Present* (50): 76–136.

Tian Chengji. 1953. "Women nuli jianshe Xinjiang [We Make Great Efforts to Construct Xinjiang]." *Renmin Ribao*, April 19, 6.

Tianshannet. 2010. "Yongxin shouhu jiankang kaifang de wangluo huanjing [Diligently Protect a Healthy and Open Internet Environment]." May 14. Retrieved January 14, 2012, http://xjts.cn/news/content/2010-05/14/content_4972409.htm.

Tien, Chin-Chi. 1963. "Petroleum Output Shows Marked Rise." *China Reconstructs.* 12 (4): 6–7. Beijing: China Welfare Institute.

Tighe, Justin. 2009. "From Borderland to Heartland: The Discourse of the North-West in Early Republican China." *Twentieth-Century China* 35 (1): 54–74.

Tomba, Luigi. 2004. "Creating an Urban Middle Class." *China Journal* 51: 1–26.

———. 2008. "Making Neighbourhoods: The Government of Social Change in China's Cities." *China Perspectives* 4: 48–61.

Turdush, Rukiye. 2013. "Xinjiang Raids Point to Religious Controls." March 10. Retrieved March 12, 2013, http://www.eurasiareview.com/10032013-xinjiang-raids-point-to-religious-controls.

Turner, Jonathan. 1997. *The Institutional Order*. New York: Longman.

Turner, Victor. 1986. "Dewey, Dilthey, and Drama: An Essay in the Anthropology of Experience." In *The Anthropology of Experience*, edited by V. Turner and E. M. Bruner, 33–44. Urbana: University of Illinois Press.

Unger, Jonathan, and Anita Chan. 2008. "Associations in a Bind: The Emergence of Political Corporatism." In *Associations and the Chinese State: Contested Spaces*, edited by J. Unger, 48–68. New York: M. E. Sharpe.

van Roosmalen, Pauline K. M. 2011. "Designing Colonial Cities: The Making of Modern Town Planning in the Dutch East Indies and Indonesia (1905–1950)." *Newsletter* 57 (Summer): 7–9.

Walder, Andrew G. 1995. "Career Mobility and the Communist Political Order." *American Sociological Review* 60 (3): 309–28.

Walder, Andrew George. 1986. *Communist Neo-Traditionalism: Work and Authority in Chinese Industry*. Berkeley: University of California Press.

Waldron, Arthur. 1990. *The Great Wall of China: From History to Myth*. New York: Cambridge University Press.

Waley-Cohen, Joanna. 2003. "Changing Spaces of Empire in Eighteenth Century Qing China." In *Political Frontiers, Ethnic Boundaries, and Human Geographies in Chinese History*, edited by N. D. Cosmo and D. J. Wyatt. London: RoutledgeCurzon.

Wallerstein, Immanuel. 1983. *Historical Capitalism*. London: Verso.

Wang, Chin-Hsi. 1966. "The 'Man of Iron'—Wang Chin-Hsi." *China Reconstructs* 15 (5): 2–5. Beijing: China Welfare Institute.

Wang Enmao. 1985. "Xinjiang she kaituo jianshezhe da you zuowei de difang [Xinjiang Is a Place Where Constructors Engaged in Opening Up Can Make the Best of Themselves]." *Lilun Yuekan (The Theory Monthly)* 10: 2–4.

Wang Kun. 2008. "Xuexi chuancheng Daqing jingshen tieren jingshen [Study and Inherit the Spirit of Daqing—Iron Man Spirit]." *Beijing shiyou guanli ganbu xueyuan xuebao (The Journal of Beijing Petroleum Management Training Institute)* (Supplementary issue, 2008): 86–99.

Wang Lili. 2011. "Bingtuan jingshen de shijian shi dui Zhonghua minzu jingshen hongyang fazhan [The Practice of Bingtuan Spirit Carries Forward and Develops Chinese National Spirit]." *Tianshannet*, August 26. Retrieved February 4, 2012, http://www.tianshannet.com.cn/news/content/2011-08/26/content_6114540.htm.

Wang Lixiong. 2007a. *Wo de Xiyu, ni de Dong Tu [My West Land, Your East Country]*. Taibei Shi: Da kuai wen hua chu ban gu fen you xian gong si.

Wang, Ning. 2007b. "Border Banishment: Rightists in the Army Farms of Beidahuang." In *The Chinese State at the Borders*, edited by D. Lary, 352. Vancouver: University of British Columbia Press.

Wang Yong. 2010. "Wang Yong zai quanguo dangjian yanjiuhui guoyou qiye dangjian yanjiu zhuanye weiyuanhui chengli dahui ji diyi nianhui shang de zhici [Wang Yong, Inauguration Speech at the First Annual Meeting of the Party Building in State-Owned Enterprises Professional Committee, under the National Party Building Research Association]." Retrieved February 5, 2011, http://www.sasac.gov.cn/n1180/n1566/n259715/n263898/7529629.html.

———. 2011b. "Guoyou qiye yao zai tuijin shehui zhuyi hexin jiazhi tixi jianshe zhong fahui biaoshuai zuoyong [SOEs Must Draw on Their Role as Models in Order to Push Forward Construction of a Core Socialist Values System]." *Qiushi Lilun*, December 26. Retrieved May 8, 2012, http://www.qstheory.cn/tbzt/sqjlz/zgtsshzywh/gcls/201112/t20111226_131956.htm.

Wank, David L. 1999. *Commodifying Communism: Business, Trust, and Politics in a Chinese City*. Cambridge: Cambridge University Press.

Wenmingban. 2007, July. *Ku'erle shi jingshen wenming chuangjian zhidao shouce [Korla City Founding Spiritual Civilization Guidance Manual]*. Korla: Ku'erle shi chuangjian quanguo wenming chengshi bangongshi.

White, Lynn T. 1979. "The Road to Urumchi: Approved Institutions in Search of Attainable Goals during Pre-1968 Rustication from Shanghai." *China Quarterly* (79): 481–510.

White, Richard. 1991. *The Middle Ground: Indians, Empires, and Republics in the Great Lakes Region, 1650–1815*. Cambridge: Cambridge University Press.

Whyte, Martin King, and William L. Parish. 1984. *Urban Life in Contemporary China*. Chicago: University of Chicago Press.

Wiemer, Calla. 2004. "The Economy of Xinjiang." In *Xinjiang: China's Muslim Borderland*, edited by S. F. Starr, 163–89. Armonk, NY: M. E. Sharpe.

Wilson Center. 1949. "Cable, Filippov [Stalin] to Mao Zedong [via Kovalev]." June 18. *History and Public Policy Program Digital Archive*, APRF: F. 45, Op. 1, D. 331, Ll. 119. June 18. Retrieved April 26, 2015, http://digitalarchive.wilsoncenter.org/document/113379.

Wittfogel, Karl. 1957. *Oriental Despotism: A Comparative Study of Total Power*. New York: Random House.

Women of China. 2012. "Xinjiang Government Addresses Problems Facing Businesswomen." January 12. Retrieved January 17, 2012, http://www.womenofchina.com.cn/html/report/3784-1.htm.

Woodside, Alexander. 2007. "The Centre and the Borderlands in Chinese Political Theory." In *The Chinese State at the Borders*, edited by D. Lary, 11–28. Vancouver: University of British Columbia Press.

Workman, Mark E. 1993. "Tropes, Hopes, and Dopes." *Journal of American Folklore* 106 (420): 171–83.

Wright, Teresa. 2010. "Introduction." In *Accepting Authoritarianism: State Society Relations in China's Reform Era*, 1–36. Stanford, CA: Stanford University Press.

Wu Zhen. 2007. "Dali hongyang 'jianku fendou' de bingtuan jingshen; tuijin tunken shubian shiye xin fazhan [Energetically Carry Forward the Bingtuan Spirit of 'Working Hard in Spite of Difficulties'; Drive New Developments in Reclamation and Border Protection]." *Bingtuan Dangxiao Xuebao (Journal of the Bingtuan Party School)* 5: 10–12.

Xie, Liangbing. 2012. "The Party's Top Ranking Blogger." *Economic Observer*, January 10. Retrieved January 17, 2012, http://www.eeo.com.cn/ens/2012/0110/219390.shtml.

Xie, Yu, and Xiaogang Wu. 2008. "Danwei Profitability and Earnings Inequality in Urban China." *China Quarterly* 195: 558–81.

Xinhua. 2009a. "Civilians and Armed Police Officer Killed in Northwest China Violence." *Window of China*, July 6. Retrieved November 20, 2011, http://news.xinhuanet.com/english/2009-07/06/content_11658819.htm.

———. 2009b. "Travel Agencies Suspend Group Trips to Xinjiang." *TrueXinjiang*, July 11. Retrieved December 1, 2011, http://www.globaltimes.cn/www/english/truexinjiang/tourism/guide/2011-04/445484.html.

———. 2009c. "Wulumuqi tongbao 'zhenci shijian' song jian yangben jiance jieguo [Urumchi Releases Results of 'Hypodermic Needle Incident' Sample Examinations]." *Zhongguo xinwen*, September 13. Retrieved July 18, 2012, http://www.gov.cn/jrzg/2009-09/13/content_1416754.htm.

———. 2009d. "Zhou Yongkang qiangdiao: yange luoshi zeren quebao Xinjiang shehui daju wending [Zhou Yongkang Emphasizes: Resolutely Implement Responsibility; Guarantee Xinjiang's Overall Stability]." *Zhongguo xinwen*, July 13. Retrieved July 18, 2012, http://www.gov.cn/ldhd/2009-07/13/content_1364384.htm.

———. 2010. "Xinjiang Weiwu'er Zizhiqu dangwei zhuyao lingdao tongzhi zhiwu tiaozheng [Xinjiang Uyghur Autonomous Region Party Committee Adjusts Leaders' Duties]." April 24. Retrieved November 30, 2011, http://news.xinhuanet.com/politics/2010-04/24/c_1253737.htm.

———. 2010. "Chinese Central Government to Step up Support for Xinjiang: Senior Leaders." *Xinhua*, March 31. Retrieved May 11, 2011, http://news.xinhuanet.com/english2010/china/2010-03/31/c_13231387_2.htm.

———. 2011a. "Di er pi quanguo wenming chengshi (qu), wenming cun-zhen, wenming mingwei mingdan [List of the Second Round of All China Civilized Cities (Zones), Civilized Villages and Townships]." *People's Daily*, November 28. Retrieved July 31, 2012, http://expo.people.com.cn/GB/58536/16410101.html.

———. 2011b. "Di san pi quanguo wenming chengshi (qu), wenming cun-zhen, wenming mingwei mingdan [List of the Third Round of All China Civilized Cities (Zones), Civilized Villages and Townships]." *Wenming.cn*, December

21. Retrieved July 31, 2012, http://www.wenming.cn/wmcj_pd/wmcspx/yw/201112/t20111221_433400.shtml.
———. 2012a. "Core State Firms Aid Employment in W China." *China Daily*, June 13. Retrieved July 18, 2012, http://www.chinadaily.com.cn/business/2012-06/13/content_15499157.htm.
———. 2012b. "Guoziwei fuzhuren lai jiang ducha yuanjiang xiangmu jianshe [SASAC Vice Director in Xinjiang to Check on Assistance Projects]." April 20. Retrieved May 7, 2012, http://www.kelamayi.com.cn/news/2012-04/20/content_954631.htm.
———. 2014a. "CPC Branches Key to Xinjiang Stability: Xi." September 16. Retrieved March 30, 2015, http://news.xinhuanet.com/english/china/2014-09/16/c_133647795.htm.
———. 2014b. "Senior Official Stresses Enhancing Xinjiang Ethnic Cadres Training.", September 24. Retrieved March 30, 2015, http://news.xinhuanet.com/english/china/2014-09/23/c_133666620.htm.
———. 2015. "Xinjiang Promotes Over 2,000 Public Servants." February 27. Retrieved March 30, 2015, http://news.xinhuanet.com/english/2015-02/27/c_134023717.htm.
Xinjiang Bingtuan Jianchayuan. 2011. "Jiancha jiguan ruhe zai 'san ge weihu, yi ge quebao' fangmian genghao de fahui zhineng zuoyong [How to Best Give Full Play to the Functions of the Prosecutors Office in Terms of 'Three Safeguards' and 'One Guarantee']." December 30. Retrieved February 4, 2012, http://www.xjbtjcy.gov.cn/newsShow.asp?id=1092.
Xinjiang Ribao. 2010. "Xinjiang zhengfu jigou gaige chuji chengxiao: jianquan zhengfu zeren tizhi [Xinjiang Government Structural Reforms Sees Early Results: Strengthen Government Responsibility System]." May 27. Retrieved May 7, 2012, http://politics.people.com.cn/GB/14562/11708653.html.
———. 2012. "Zhang Chunxian: bawo xiandai wenhua fazhan dashi, jianchi xiandai wenhua yinling [Zhang Chunxian: Firmly Grasp the Developmental Trend of Modern Culture, Insist on the Leading Role of Modern Culture]." *Zhongguo Gongchandang Xinwen*. May 22. Retrieved August 28, 2012, http://cpc.people.com.cn/GB/64093/64102/17950782.html.
Xinjiang Wenhua Bu. 2011. "Qiantan xin shiqi xuyao Xinjiang jingshen [A Brief Discussion of the New Era's Need for Xinjiang Spirit]." October 25. Retrieved November 27, 2011, http://www.qzgw.org/templet/dangwei/ShowArticle.jsp?id=122703.
Xiyu Wang. 2010. "Xinjiang bingtuan nong qi shi 1950 nian dashiji [Xinjiang Bingtuan Seventh Agricultural Division Chronicle of Events 1950]." October 20. Retrieved February 4, 2012, http://www.xyscnet.cn/a/shenmibingtuan/zhongdashijian/2010/1020/155.html.
XJ50N. 2005. *Xinjiang 50 Years 1955–2005*. Beijing: China Statistical Press.
XJASS. 2012. "Qiye chanye yuanjiang tisu xinjiang kuayueshi fazhan [Central SOEs' Industrial Assistance Speed up Xinjiang's Leapfrog Development]." *Quyu Jingji* Xinjiang shehui kexue yuan (Xinjiang Academy of Social Science),

April 22. Retrieved May 7, 2012, http://www.xjass.com/jj/content/2012-04/22/content_229462.htm.

XJSYB 1955–2005. 2005. *Xinjiang Statistical Yearbook 1955–2005.* Xinjiang Statistical Bureau. Urumchi: Xinjiang University Publishing House.

XJTJNJ. 2010. *Xinjiang tongji nianjian (Xinjiang Statistical Yearbook).* Urumchi: Xinjiang University Publishing House.

Yang, Mayfair Mei-hui. 1994. *Gifts, Favors, and Banquets: The Art of Social Relationships in China.* Ithaca, NY: Cornell University Press.

———. 1989. "The Gift Economy and State Power in China." *Comparative Studies in Society and History* 31 (1): 25–54.

———. 2002. "The Resilience of Guanxi and Its New Deployments: A Critique of Some New Guanxi Scholarship." *China Quarterly* 170: 459–76.

Yao Yong and Zhang Ning. 2005. "Qian xi jianguo chuqi Shandong nvxing jin Jiang de lishi beijing [A Review of the Women Who Migrated into Xinjiang from Shandong Province at the Founding of the PRC]." *Nanfang Renkou (South China Population)* 20 (3): 24–30.

Yaxin. 2011. "Xinjiang Bazhou 10 ming chengxin nashui dahu huo 160 wan jianggu [The 10 Honest and Sincere the Taxpayers of Bazhou, Xinjiang, Receive Prizes of 1.6 Million Renminbi]." *Yaxin Net,* April 26. Retrieved May 28, 2012, http://news.iyaxin.com/content/2011-04/26/content_2687808.htm.

Yen, Erh-Wen. 1966. "Oil to Dominate Old China." *China Reconstructs.* 15 (4): 15–17. Beijing: China Welfare Institute.

Yili Govt. 1999. "Xibu da kaifa—Xinjiang kaifa guihua silu [Great Western Development—a Roadmap for Xinjiang's Development]." *Touzi Zhinan (Investment Guide).* Retrieved April 19, 2012, http://www.xjyl.gov.cn/Article/ShowArticle.aspx?ArticleID=8393.

Yili SASAC. 2011. "Yili zhou guoziwei kaizhan 'Xinjiang jingshen' da taolun huodong shishi fang' an [Yili Autonomous Region SASAC Launches 'Xinjiang Spirit' Grand Discussion Campaign Implementation Scheme]." *Dangjian Gongzuo (Party Building Work),* June 20. Retrieved April 19, 2012, http://www.xjyl.gov.cn/Article/ShowArticle.aspx?ArticleID=8393.

YouTube. 2009. "Uygur Mobs Killing Chinese Clip 2 of 3. July 5, 2009 Urumqi, Xinjiang, China." August 22. Retrieved March 27, 2012, http://www.youtube.com/watch?v=aQZVY7wDxYE.

Yuan, Qing-li. 1990. "Population Changes in the Xinjiang Uighur Autonomous Region (1949–1984)." *Central Asian Survey* 9 (1): 49–73.

Zang, Xiaowei. 2011. "Uyghur Han Earnings Differentials in Urumchi." *China Journal* 65: 141–55.

ZGJYTJNJ. 2009. *Zhongguo jiaoyu tongji nianjian (China Education Statistical Yearbook).* Beijing: China Statistical Publishing House.

ZGLDTJNJ. 1990. *Zhongguo laodong tongji nianjian (China Labor Statistical Yearbook).* Beijing: China Statistical Press.

———. 2009. *Zhongguo laodong tongji nianjian (China Labor Statistical Yearbook).* Beijing: China Statistical Press.

ZGNYTJNJ. 2010. *Zhongguo nengyuan tongji nianjian (China Energy Statistical Yearbook)*. Beijing: China Statistical Publishing House.

ZGTJNJ. 2010. *Zhongguo tongji nianjian (China Statistical Yearbook)*. Beijing: China Statistical Publishing House.

Zhang Chunxian. 2014. "Fenli puxie Xinjiang shehui wending he changzhijiu'an xin pianzhang: shenru xuexi guanche di'erci Zhongyang Xinjiang Gongzuo Zuotanhui jingshen [Spare No Effort to Compose a New Chapter of Social Stability in Xinjiang and Long-Term Rule: Deeply Study and Implement the Spirit of the Second Xinjiang Work Meeting]." *Qiushi* 15 (July 31).

Zhang Xue. 2011. "Xinjiang shixing jiceng ganbu gangwei butie deng 4 xiang zhengce [Xinjiang Implements Four Policies to Support Grassroots Cadres]." September 30. Retrieved November 18, 2011, http://www.shache.gov.cn/ReadNews.asp?NewsId=4149.

Zhang Zhenhua. 2009a. "Lun Zhonghua minzu jingshen zai Xinjiang de peiyu yu hongyang [Regarding Nurturing and Carrying Forward Chinese National Spirit in Xinjiang]." *Shihezi Daxue Xuebao [Zhexue Shehui Kexue Ban] (Journal of Shihezi University [Philosophy and Social Sciences])* 23 (2): 1–5.

Zhang Zongtang. 2009b. "Nuli chengwei shixian Zhonghua minzu weida fuxing de jianshezhe [Make a Great Effort to Become Constructors Bringing about the Great Resurgence of the Chinese Nation]." *Minzu yu Fazhi (Democracy and Legal System)* 19: 10–11.

Zhou, Xueguang. 2004. *The State and Life Chances in Urban China: Redistribution and Stratification, 1949–1994*. New York: Cambridge University Press.

Zhou Yubin and Chen Ke. 2012. "Xinjiang shengchan jianshe bingtuan xinxing chengzhenhua daolu jiexi yiqi cheng-xiang guihua tixi goujian tansuo [A Study of XPCC's New Urbanization and Planning System Construction]." *Chengshi fazhan yanjiu (Urban Studies)* 19 (5): 34–43.

Index

advertisements, 35, 39, 41, 118–20, 136–37, 165
aesthetics: *bingtuan*, 51, 57–60, 70; of Korla, 20, 34–49; metropolitan, 6, 28, 49, 206; oil company, 62–70; political, 28, 36, 206, 209; suburban, 62–64
agency: of constructors, 32, 35, 44–48; role of in social mobility, 25, 102, 124, 148, 177; stoicism as, 125; and structure or chance, 5, 25, 26, 102, 124–27
argument of images, 18–19
aspiration, 3, 25, 50, 64, 73, 75, 125, 127–29; institutional, 9, 25, 51, 101, 127–29; as prospective orientation, 44, 100, 116; social or institutional reproduction, 99, 111, 121–24; status, 44, 97, 100, 125. *See also* stability (socioeconomic, political) as object of aspiration
Assist Xinjiang Plan (*yuanjiang*), 198, 202
asynchronicity, 26, 212

Becquelin, Nicolas, 5, 70, 173, 217
behindness (*luohou* as state discourse), 156, 159–60, 174, 178, 209, 212; imperialism and, 6, 12, 212, 216; of periphery, peripheral populations, xi, 2, 5, 43, 65, 106, 149, 208, 213, 216; structural problem of, 159, 172
bendiren (Korla "locals"), 24–27, 131, 155

Benjamin, Walter, 43
bingtuan, 1, 4, 217; aesthetics, 37, 51, 57–60, 70; antipathy toward, 52, 54, 139, 144, 149; construction, 12, 27–32, 51, 68, 155, 212; economy, 54, 57, 67, 139, 150, 187, 203, 213; history, 28–32, 104; oil company vs., 12–13, 24, 50, 55, 68–72, 116, 144; pioneer experiences, 5, 27, 29, 32, 45, 51, 71, 86, 92, 102–6, 121, 139, 149, 156, 160; spirit, 32, 155
biographies: Director Jia, 51; Section Chief Jing, 56, 102; Boss Kang, 139; Mary, 73–75, 87, 92, 97; Director Ren, 57, 102; Rhys, 161; Director Wei, 171–79; Mr. Wu, 109, 172; Director Xie, 79, 91–95; Yanyan, 27, 148; Zhang Yonglei, 1–2, 44–48; Zhou Yu, 166; Party Secretary Zhang, 96. *See also names of individuals*
biography: as coordinate point, 17; and photography, 18
Bloch, Ernst, 179
Bovingdon, Gardner, x, 6, 14, 18, 184, 191, 217
Braudel, Fernand, 18, 100, 159, 173
bureaucratic rank, 62, 69, 78, 83, 97, 169

capitalism, 7, 8, 46, 174
capital types: economic, 57, 66, 102, 125, 182, 197, 201–6; political, 12, 77, 191; social/cultural, 57, 121, 128, 125, 143; youth as, 162

247

INDEX

central government–controlled SOEs (*zhongyang qiye*), 4, 26, 50, 73, 99, 185, 202, 214
certainty: as constraint, 93–94; as a privilege, 94, 99. *See also* chapters 3, 4, 6
Chan, Anita, 71, 78, 91, 134
chance: as prospective possibility, 127–28; retrospective occurrences, 57, 127–28; and structure, agency, influence on life course, 5, 102, 124–28
Chinese Civil War, 31, 112
Chinese Communist Party (CCP), 4, 7, 32, 97, 111, 112, 145–47, 174–78, 184, 188–90, 200, 203, 206, 209, 215
civilization (*wenming*): civilized city construction, 27, 34–39; spiritual, material, 6, 24, 28, 34, 136, 156; as verb (*wenminghua*), 11, 12, 44, 209
civilizing project, 6, 9, 24, 28, 43, 48
Coetzee, J. M., 180
cohort, 5, 53, 56–57, 88, 92–93, 102, 121–24
colonial endeavor, 4, 6, 9, 138, 179, 208
colonialism, 6–13; and culture, 8, 32, 203–8, 214; internal colony, 6. *See also* imperialism
compensation for land, 40, 41, 61
connections, 25, 102, 107, 125, 130–33, 142, 152, 156, 159, 171, 196. See also *guanxi*
consciousness: Chinese national, 32; of constructor, 27–28, 44–46, 49, 154–55. See also *bingtuan*: spirit; Daqing spirit
conscription, 51, 81, 102–4
construction: agents or objects of, 28, 34, 48–49; as state project, 27–44
constructor (*jianshezhe*), 6, 27–28, 34, 48–49; discourse, 27–34, 71, 118, 154–55
co-ordinate points (for study of human lives), 17
core area. *See* metropole
core-periphery relationship, 5, 11–12, 23–26, 70, 117, 174, 205, 207, 209, 215. *See also* empire theme; normalization
corruption, 142, 145, 146, 174; effect on social or political stability, 89, 176, 189
Cultural Revolution, 25, 52, 101, 105, 110, 113–15, 124, 149
culture, 29, 39, 145; colonialism and, 5, 8–13, 33, 48–49, 147, 156, 176, 203, 206–7, 215; Han and, 32, 48–49, 183, 199; Uyghurs and, 28, 118, 203

cyclical phenomenon: economy, 70, 160; frontier, 11; morality, 143, 147; nation/empire unity, 8, 11; stability/instability, 143–44, 187–88, 194, 207

danwei (work unit), 25, 62, 68, 73, 77, 97; neo-*danwei*, 77, 138, 157; system, 50, 67, 86
Daqing spirit, 110, 114, 115, 117, 121
demography. *See* population
difang ren (people administered by local government), 24, 156
Dilthey, Wilhelm, 17
Dirks, Nicholas, 8, 9
discourses of the state, Xinjiang: need to develop (*see* behindness); need to normalize (*see* peripherality); need to securitize (*see* instability)
discursive space, 49, 124, 190
Duara, Prasenjit, 7, 147
dui kou (counterpart assistance) scheme, 198–99, 205

economy: of *bingtuan*, 30, 105; of Korla, 30, 50, 65, 67, 161, 169; market, 91–92, 98, 140, 160, 171; planned, 134, 140, 206; production and consumption, 34, 39, 43, 65, 71, 188; tax, 65, 133, 153, 169, 200–202; of uncertainty, 25; of Xinjiang, 34, 36, 66, 191, 198, 213–14
education: facilities, policies, 9, 77, 82, 85–86, 92–93, 122–23, 169, 203; as object of aspiration, regret, 52–55, 85, 88, 101, 121–22, 139, 148; university intakes, 52, 57, 82, 88, 106, 122–23, 133, 139, 150
educational level, as factor in social mobility, 77, 85, 88, 93–94, 101–2, 108, 121–24, 128
Elliott, Mark, x, 209, 215, 221
embeddedness, social, 18, 26, 131, 160, 174
empire theme, the core-periphery relationship, 4–13, 36, 51, 99, 208, 215
employment relations, 4, 40, 46, 48, 55–56, 64–99, 106–11, 121–29, 151–56, 159, 169–73, 185, 189–90
energy resources, politics, 69, 112, 117, 202
entitlement, 27, 33, 75, 82–84, 87–91, 98, 107, 111, 155, 172, 185, 218
entrepreneurship, 66, 130, 134–38, 147, 152, 160, 172, 198
era-defining institutions, 50

248

INDEX

ethnic minorities, 6, 10, 23, 32, 48, 103, 117, 147, 148, 154–57, 160, 178, 180, 188, 199, 203–7, 209, 215, 218
expectation, 75, 83, 93, 97, 98, 101, 164, 173, 186
experience: anthropological theories of, 16–19, 100, 109, 111, 143, 156, 173, 177; shared, 13, 24, 121, 140, 142, 152, 158, 183, 208–12

fieldwork, 19, 22–23
formal structure, 24, 73, 76, 98, 146, 168, 172, 207
Foucault, Michel, 5
frontier: of control or settlement, 10–13, 184, 204, 213; as culturally distinct, 9–16, 99, 204–9, 212–16; cyclical nature of, 10–11; as place of exile, 1, 109 (*see also* behindness); as place of innovation, 10, 12, 117; as place of opportunity, 1, 33, 44–46, 116, 121; temporal status of, 4, 26, 117, 209
future-focus. *See* prospective orientation
FutureZone, 44, plate 5

Gaubatz, Piper, 10–11, 49
gender: *guanxi*-practice, 148, 157; social mobility, 75, 86, 164
Gold, Thomas, x, 130, 141, 145
governance, 8, 36, 97, 130, 160, 174–76, 198–99, 207
Great Leap Forward, 51, 103–5, 124
Great Western Development Plan (*xibu da kaifa*), 174, 221
guanxi (connections), chapters 5, 6; corruption and, 142–46, 156; as game, 133, 140–42; status and, 131, 141, 157
guoyou qiye. *See* state-owned enterprises, SOEs

habits, reshaping of, 34, 43–44, 48, 162
habitus, 34
Han social groups in Xinjiang: Han elite, 71, 78, 100, 134, 159, 174, 185; Han mainstream, 154, 183–87, 193, 204, 206; Han subaltern, 31, 49, 69, 185–86. See also *bendiren*; *bingtuan*: pioneer experiences; *difang ren*; recent settlers
harmony, social, 87, 118, 137; and Tazhi hierarchy, 24, 88
hierarchy, social: within oil company, 24–25, 81, 83, 84, 88, 98; in Xinjiang, 5, 45–46, 52, 55–56, 133, 154, 169, 215

hierarchy, spatial, 45, 56, 65, 92, 117, 127, 171
hope, 101, 116, 127, 176–79, 209; realization of, 178; uncertainty and, 160, 177
housing, 1–2, 39, 56, 62–64, 77, 84–85, 132, 162, 197–98, 204, 218
Hui, 23
Hu Jintao, 33, 176, 196
hukou (household registration), 14, 71, 132, 186, 205, 217

identity, 10, 14, 48, 74, 99, 146, 206, 216
ideology, 31, 34, 36, 89, 173, 176, 207
imperialism, 6–13; imperial center, 8, 212; imperial formations, 8–9; imperial thinking, 26, 209, 214; imperial tradition, 203
industrial structure of Xinjiang, 65–72, 159, 168–74, 202
inevitability: as imperial ideology, 34, 43–44; as individual fear, 167–68, 171–74
infidelity, 164, 166–68
informal institutions or structures, 73, 76, 98, 130, 146–47, 160, 168–76, 207. See also marriage economy; social networks
inscriptions, 28, 51, 125
inside the system (*tizhi nei*), 67, 75, 159, 168, 186
instability (*bu wending* as state discourse), 16, 25, 144, 164, 187–88, 194, 197, 205–11, 216
institutional cities, Xinjiang, 68
institutional complementarity, 70
institutions, social, 5, 76, 146–47, 173, 176
institutions, state: aspirations of, 25, 99, 100–101, 127–29; era defining, 50, 72, 101; frontier, 10–13, 50, 68, 72, 173, 176, 213; individual and, 50–51, 100–101, 116, 127–29, 144
integration of periphery: conditions of, 10–12, 200; impossibility of, 12, 215–16; undesirability of, 215
interest group, 26, 28, 111–12, 135, 185–87, 189, 218
inter-ethnic relations, 16; conflict, 22–23, 26, 180, 205, 211; merging, fragmentation, 10–12
intra-ethnic, 16, 28, 49, 205–6, 216
iron rice bowl mentality, 78, 160, 172–73, 179, 214; *danwei* mentality, 75
irrigation, 12, 30–31, 40, 47, 51, 201, 213
Islam, 9, 15–16, 23, 48, 146, 203–4, 206

249

INDEX

Jia (biography), 51
Jing (biography), 56, 102

Kang (biography), 139
Kipnis, Andrew, ix, x, 48, 123, 134, 218
Korla: economy, 30, 50, 65, 67, 161, 169; urban space of, 37–49
Korla Economic Technology Development Zone, 47, 201, plate 5

large-scale stories, 111, 116, 121, 128
Lary, Diana, 11, 14, 215
Lattimore, Owen, 10, 11
legends: of potential, hardship, 25, 100–101, 109, 111, 128, 209; visual expression of, 116–21
Lenin, Vladimir, 7, 8
life chances, 14, 25, 50, 101–2, 130, 159, 171. *See also* social mobility, factors
life histories, as methodology, ix, 4–5, 17, 19, 101–2, 123, 125, 127, 130, 208. *See also* biographies
loyalty: emotional, 163–66, 178; to the party or nation, 8, 23, 26, 34, 97, 137–38, 173, 179, 186–87

Mao era, 5, 8, 29, 51, 89, 110
marriage economy, 74, 78, 87–88, 161–68, 178
Mary (biography), 73–75, 87, 92, 97
mass frames, 182–84
McGranahan, Carole, 8, 209
memory, 19, 25
metropole, 1, 4, 6, 8, 11–12, 28, 49, 128, 209, 215. *See also* imperialism: imperial center; *neidi*
migrant workers, 9, 24, 34, 47, 70–71, 186, 217, plate 7; status hierarchies of, 45; Uyghurs as, 9, 34, 43, 203
migration reasons: conscription, 51, 81, 102–4; famine, poverty, 51, 103–5, 139; fortune seeking, 1, 44, 74, 92; marriage, 86, 103–4, 139, 219; social conditions, 104, 109; state order, 46, 51, 109, 148
migration theme, how people got to where they are, 5; Han in-migration to Xinjiang, 4–6, 29–31, 71, 86, 172, 204, 217, 219; social mobility, out-migration from Xinjiang, 197. *See also* social mobility, factors
Mills, C. W., 17–18

Millward, James, 5, 12, 29, 173, 211, 221
Miyazaki, Hirokazu, 173, 177
mobility. *See* social mobility, factors
modernism, modernity, 2, 8, 24, 36–39, 44, 48–51, 117, 124, 179, 213, 215
morals, morality, 12, 45, 76, 143, 146, 166, 175, 192, 199

narrative, 17–19, 23, 39, 101, 111, 116, 124, 144, 188, 196
nation, 6, 8, 34, 49, 69, 117, 199, 211–12, 215
nationalism, 9, 32, 112, 187
Nationalist (*Guomindang*), 51, 102–4, 139, 149
nation building, 4, 34, 86, 110, 118, 121, 156
neidi (central, eastern China), 1, 6, 65, 143, 149, 160, 172, 198, 203
normalization, 5, 11, 25, 90, 131, 144, 199, 200, 203–4, 213
nostalgia, 89, 160, 168, 172–73, 179, 206

oil: and imperialism, 12–13, 113; and national strength, 25, 111
old home (*laojia*), 14, 155
old Xinjiang people, 14, 28, 30, 56, 179, 186, 193, 206; photo essay, plates 9–16
Olympics: Beijing, 22, 178, plate 6; Los Angeles, 54
organized dependence, 160, 171–74, 179, 182–83, 206, 214
outside the system (*tizhi wai*), 159, 168, 171, 186

People's Liberation Army (PLA), 33, 51, 54, 102, 109, 139
peripherality, geographic/cultural (*pianyuan* as state discourse), 6, 11–12, 48–49, 67, 145, 148, 155–56, 192, 208–9, 216
periphery, 11–12, 48, 70, 99, 117, 174, 205, 207, 209, 215
petroleum faction (elite Chinese politics), 112, 114–15
photography, use of in book, 18–19
political economy, 25, 50, 160–61, 191, 213
popular protest, 89, 180–83, 192, 197
population (demographics), 4, 10, 14, 24, 26, 30, 32, 48, 56, 67, 69, 154, 217
possibility: certainty vs., 5, 25, 144; as enabling hope, 160, 177–79

250

postponement, 9, 161, 179
pragmatism: *guanxi* networks and, 142; hope and, 168, 176–77; in marriage, 88, 163, 165, 168, 177
privilege, stability as, 44, 78, 97, 99
problems with Xinjiang (as perceived by Han). *See* behindness; industrial structure of Xinjiang; instability; peripherality, geographic/cultural
progress, 6, 8, 34
prospective orientation, 6, 25, 39, 41, 209. *See also* aspiration; hope; legends: of potential, hardship; postponement; waiting
psychological structures, 12, 93, 98, 160, 172, 173, 183, 206

quotas: birth control, 98, 203; educational, 57; employment, 106–7; fines, 133

recent settlers (*wailai renkou*), 14, 24, 28, 46, 186
reform, structural, 73, 75, 79, 85, 89, 140, 160, 168, 172–76, 179, 202
reform era, 7, 14, 76, 89, 98, 122
relative deprivation, 148–50, 189
Ren (biography), 57, 102
resources, natural: land, 30, 213; oil, 12–13, 70, 117, 201; water, 12–13, 30
resources, political: *guanxi* as, 157; Han settlers as, 69; instability perception as, 187; vested interests as, 173–75
resources tax law (2010), 200–202
Rhys (biography), 161
rumor, 23, 167, 183, 193–96, 210
rural conditions, 56, 104, 110, 149
rural space, 30–31, 57–60
Rushdie, Salman, ix

sacrifice as entitlement/status claim, 70, 101, 109, 121, 155
Sahadeo, Jeff, 7, 12
salary, examples of: on *bingtuan*, 54, 55, 139, 150; in Korla city, 83; in oil company, 75, 82–84, 92, 173
Scott, James, 36, 37, 40, 51, 90, 117
Second Agricultural Division of *bingtuan*, 30, 69
sent-down, 149, 150, 156
September 25, 1949, "mutiny," 102, 139
settlement, Han, 4, 11, 13, 14, 31, 132, 184

social contract, 76
social control, mechanisms of, 69, 90, 95–97, 168–74, 206
social engineering, 33. *See also* civilization
social mobility, factors: age cohort, 92–93, 110, 121–22, 149; economic capital, 51, 54–55, 85. *See also* educational level; gender; *guanxi*
social networks (*guanxi wang*): as informal institution, 81, 96, 130–38, 168, 172, 186, 191–93; role in normalization, 25, 131, 144, 156, 193
social order. *See* social control, mechanisms of
social status, 5, 24, 26, 68, 71, 73, 75, 87, 127, 131, 220. *See also* social mobility, factors
social structure, 17–18, 25–26, 56, 76, 79, 98, 102, 124–27, 132, 146, 159, 168, 178, 202, 204
South Xinjiang Oil Exploration Company, 55, 60
sovereignty, 29, 176, 211
space: hierarchies of, 56, 65, 92, 117, 125; personal, 58, 82
spatial mobility. *See* migration theme
stability (socioeconomic, political) as object of aspiration: individual, 4, 94, 99, 123, 125, 128–29, 143–44, 169, 177, 194; institutional, 74, 75, 96–97, 128–29; national/Xinjiang, 16, 25, 29, 36, 95–97, 105, 144, 176, 179, 180, 184–88, 198–99, 205, 207, 211, 213
stability and development, 31, 156, 189–92
standard of living, 57, 82, 122
state corporatism, 134
state discourses, 6, 34, 46, 160, 198. *See also* large-scale stories
state-owned enterprises, SOEs (*guoyou qiye*): employment relations, 64, *see also* chapter 3; political role in Xinjiang, 26, 29, 50, 67, 77, 108, 111, 159, 169, 171–74, 202, 214
status: individual, 5, 25, 45, 68, 73–75, 80, 87, 91, 101, 127, 141, 161, 169; institutional, 62, 66, 69, 71, 77, 99, 118, 128, 213, 215. *See also* social status
status symbols: *danwei*, 77, 169; residential location, 39, 84–85; sexual infidelity, 167. *See also* educational level
Stoler, Ann Laura, 8, 209

251

INDEX

structure : as analytical concept vs. agency, chance, 5, 17–18, 24–26, 56, 102, 124–27, 159, 171, 177–79; as problem (*tizhi wenti*), 26, 159–60, 171–74, 200. *See also* formal structure; industrial structure of Xinjiang; informal institutions or structures; psychological structures; social structure
structure of experience, 17–18, 109, 143, 156, 177
suburbia, 62–64

Tarim model, 62, 69, 76, 79, 91, 97, 128, 202
Tarim Oilfield Company. *See* Tazhi
Tazhi (Tarim Oilfield Company), 4, 70–72, 138, 144, 157, 166–67, 202, 219. *See also* chapter 2; *bingtuan*; era-defining institutions
Third Front, 4, 46, 67, 113, 133, 189, 195
Thomas, Nicholas, 8, 9
time theme, patterns of past, present, and future, 6; asynchronicity, 212; of frontier, 209–16; temporal context, 23, 56, 102, 124, 156, 178, 179, 209
Tomba, Luigi, ix, 73, 77, 85, 97
trust, ix, 19–22, 126, 140, 142, 145–47, 157–58, 163, 179, 193
Turner, Victor, 17, 111
29th Regiment, 30, 51–53, 57–59, 148, 213

uncertainty: as condition for possibility, 5, 94, 144, 177–79; economy of, 25; as fear, 25, 99
Unger, Jonathan, 78, 91, 134
unity: of China, 8, 34, 49, 156, 194, 215; of Han, 9
urban space, 4, 34, 43, 70
Urumchi riots (July 2009), 22–23, 62, 153, 178, 216. *See also* chapter 7
Uyghurs, Han imagination of, 4, 9, 14–16, 30, 39, 103, 117–18, 132, 146, 180–84, 186, 190, 194, 197, 203–6, 211, 216

voluntarism, 32, 49, 70

waiting, 170, 210, 213, plates 9–16
Walder, Andrew, 77, 78, 94, 98, 138, 160
Wang Enmao, 33, 105, 118
Wang Jinxi, 54, 114
Wang Lequan, 182, 188, 190–98, 200, 203
Wang Zhen, 51, 102, 190, 211, 212 (fig.)
water: as essential resource, 12–13, 69, 213; imperialism and, 12–13; infrastructure, 30–31, 201; as status symbol, 39, 64, 68
Wei (biography), 171–79
Woodside, Alexander, 12, 212
work unit. *See danwei*
Wu (biography), 109, 172

xiagang (laid off), 141, 172
Xie (biography), 79, 91–95
Xi Jinping, 115, 178, 207
Xinjiang, Han views of: as exceptional, 16, 34, 183, 187–88, 197, 198, 216; "peaceful liberation" of, 30, 102. *See also* problems with Xinjiang
Xinjiang Han: diversity of, 13–17, 19, 23–24, 28, 45, 49, 179, 185–86, 208; sense of belonging, 155, 208; worldviews of, 70, 179, 182, 188–93, 205, 208–16
Xinjiang Oil Management Bureau, 55, 107, 125–26
Xinjiang Production and Construction Corps. *See bingtuan*
Xinjiang Wilderness Reclamation Army, 29

Yang, Mayfair, 134, 145
Yanyan (biography), 27, 148

Zhang, party secretary (biography), 96
Zhang Chunxian, 33, 182, 198–200, 203–4, 206
Zhang Yonglei (biography), 1–2, 44–48
Zhonghua minzu, 32, 49, 206, 217, 218
zhongyang qiye. *See* central government–controlled SOEs
Zhou Yongkang, 33–34, 115, 116, 118, 182, 188, 211

252